THE MOST

FAMOUS WOMAN
IN CHINA

INTERNATIONAL PRESS PRAISES YUE-SAI KAN

"Her programs have an inescapable innocent charm, and to the Chinese people, they're nothing less than a revelation."

CBS-TV, USA

"By Peking broadcast standards, (One World) is prime-time hot. And that goes double for the show's new Chinese-American host, Yue-Sai Kan."

Newsweek, International

"There's no age limit for ONE WORLD fans...ONE WORLD audience is aware that they are gaining a global consciousness indispensable for the country's modernization."

China Daily, International

"This woman making world of difference on Chinese TV... in the world of television, (Yue-Sai Kan) is bigger in terms of ratings and share than Barbara Walters, Phil Donahue, Johnny Carson and Oprah Winfrey put together."

Chicago Tribune, USA

The Most Famous Woman in China is published under
Aspire, a sectionalized division under Di Angelo
Publications, Inc.

Aspire is an imprint of Di Angelo Publications.
Copyright 2024.
All rights reserved.
Printed in the United States of America.

Di Angelo Publications
Los Angeles, California

Library of Congress
The Most Famous Woman in China
ISBN: 978-1-955690-79-9
Hardback

Words: Yue-Sai Kan
Cover Design: Savina Mayeur
Interior Design: Kimberly James
Editors: Hollie S. McKay, Willy Rowberry

Downloadable via www.dapbooks.shop and other e-book
retailers.

For educational, business, and bulk orders, contact
distribution@diangelopublications.com.

1. Biography & Autobiography --- Cultural, Ethnic &
Regional --- Asian & Asian American
2. Business & Economics --- Women in Business
3. Biography & Autobiography --- Business

THE MOST

FAMOUS WOMAN IN CHINA

AND HOW SHE DID IT

YUE-SAI KAN

AUTHOR'S NOTE

If your name or picture graces these pages, it signifies your impact on my life. If it's absent, it could just be that I couldn't find a good photo of you! All jokes aside, I view life as a vibrant canvas, and I'm grateful for your presence and contribution to this ongoing creative odyssey.

Alongside my cherished family, a select few have been unwavering pillars of support. I extend heartfelt thanks to my long-standing accountant, John Muskus, and financial manager, Andrew Summers, both of whom have stood by me for over thirty years. My trusted lawyer of a decade, David Hryck, playfully credited with keeping me out of jail! I owe a debt of gratitude to my former assistant, Min Fan, for her dedicated fifteen-plus years of service. Monica Xu and Jackie Du are my capable and caring assistants, with me for seventeen and thirteen years, respectively. Although Echo Gu is new to the team, she is making significant contributions. Moreover, Allan Pollack's presence has added a special charm to my everyday.

As I write this English rendition of my autobiography, I must express profound gratitude to my cowriter, Hollie McKay, whose brilliant prose has brought my life to vivid detail. Working with my highly astute publisher, Sequoia, who is not just a pretty face; her team at DAP has been an absolute pleasure. I sincerely appreciate your commitment and collaboration.

From the bottom of my heart, thank you!

—Yue-Sai Kan

靳羽西

FOREWORD

Tian Jiyun

序

1987年夏，我第一次在北戴河会见了靳羽西女士。她的《世界各地》节目为中国人打开了第一扇窗。它像清风一样吹进中国大地，让我们第一次了解了多姿多彩的世界。当时正巧我要去巴西工作访问，出访前我专门请中央电视台工作人员录下《世界各地》节目里关于巴西的内容，以供我做参考。

1990年，外商纷纷撤离中国，刚刚改革开放的局面遇到困难。我时任国务院副总理并负责外商投资和深圳经济特区发展等事宜。正逢靳羽西女士和丈夫来中国度蜜月，在钓鱼台宴请他们夫妇时，我建议他们到中国投资。令人惊讶的是他们欣然同意，并说想以"羽西"命名做一个化妆品品牌，我非常赞同也希望她能成功！靳羽西女士仅用几年时间就将羽西化妆品牌做到家喻户晓，成为中国制造和创新品牌的楷模。

靳羽西女士不仅是中国改革开放所取成就的见证人，更是参与者和先驱者。这本书通过讲述靳羽西女士传奇精彩的人生经历和鲜为人知的励志奋斗故事，不仅可以让新一代年轻人更了解我们中国改革开放的时代背景，同时也可以激励他们为梦想努力拼搏。

靳羽西女士虽远在太平洋彼岸但我们的心是联在一起的，因为我们同是炎黄子孙，中华儿女。在她的新书面世之际，我借此文向她表示衷心的祝贺，并祝她今后能在为人类文明而奋斗的伟大事业中取得更大，更辉煌的成就！继续用美的力量改变世界！

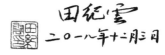

田纪云
二〇一八年十二月三日

田纪云

前国务院副总理

In the summer of 1987, I met Ms. Yue-Sai Kan for the first time in the Chinese coastal resort town of Beidaihe. Her "One World" TV programs opened a window on the outside world for the Chinese. Like a cool breeze blowing over our land, the series gave us a much coveted first look at the colorful lives being lived in other parts of the world. That same year, I was scheduled to go to Brazil for an official visit. Before I went, I specifically asked the "One World" episode about Brazil be taped for my reference.

In 1990, foreign investors withdrew from China en masse. China's new Reform and Opening Up Initiative met with great difficulties. At the time, I was Vice Premier and was responsible for foreign investment and development of the Shenzhen Special Economic Zone. It so happened that Yue-Sai and her husband came to China on their honeymoon. During a dinner I hosted for them in our leaders' compound in Zhongnanhai, I suggested they invest in China. Without hesitation, they agreed! Later, Yue-Sai told me that they wanted to set up a cosmetics brand called "Yue-Sai." I offered my support and wished her success. Within just a few years, Yue-Sai made Yue-Sai Cosmetics a household name and became a model for creating and innovating brands in China.

The year 2018 marked the 40th Anniversary of the Reform and Opening Up of the People's Republic of China. Yue-Sai is not only a witness to the reform in the past 40 years but also a participant and a pioneer. This book retells the legendary and wonderful life experience of Yue-Sai and some little-known inspirational struggles. It will not only help a new generation of young people better understand the background of China's Reform and Opening up but also will inspire them to work hard for their dreams.

As a Chinese American, Yue-Sai never forgets her roots in China. Our hearts are linked because we are all descendants of the Yan and Huang Emperors, and we are the children of China. On the occasion of the publication of her autobiography, I express my heartfelt congratulations to her and wish her greater achievements in advancing human civilization in the future. May she continue to change the world with the power of beauty!

Tian Jiyun
Vice Premier of the People's Republic of China,
1983–1993

CONTENTS

AUTHOR'S NOTE   6
FOREWORD   8

THE MOST WATCHED PERSON IN THE WORLD
Starting Very Small   29
Right Place, Right Time   40
Becoming a Household Name   46
Producing One World, Making History   64
TV as an Instrument of Peace   68
For the Record   73
Exceptional Kindness   76

HOW I BECAME ME
Migration to Hong Kong   97
Mother   107
Father   112
Sisters   116
In the Words of Vickie Kan   118
In the Words of Yu-San Kan   120
Two Young Men Who Changed My Life   123
Life at Brigham Young University Hawaii   131
In the Words of Helen Goo   136
I Was Crowned a Princess!   138
In the Words of Angela Conley   144
Returning to Hong Kong   146
New York, the Capital of the World   151
Learning Immigrant Wisdom   158
My Greek Mother   160
Looking to the Stars   167

CHANGING THE FACE OF CHINA, ONE LIPSTICK AT A TIME
In the Words of Sam   195
In the Words of Sherry   201
In the Words of Holly Yao Duncan (姚红)   209
In the Words of Donna Fumoso   212
Teaching the Influencers   219
In the Words of Stephanie Jacobs   227
In the Words of Jackie Du (杜谭明) and Monica Xu (徐吉英)   239

IT AIN'T ALL ABOUT THE MONEY: FINDING MEANING IN
EVERYTHING I DO
Why I Created a China Doll   254
In the Words of Jenny Chen (陈涓玲)   259
I Adore Quincy Jones, My Brother from Another Mother   269
An International TV Festival When We Barely Had TV   276
In the Words of Stephanie Jacobs   280
Ambassador to the Shanghai International Film Festival   280
God's Gift of Beauty Must Be Used for Good   286
Charity as a Driving Force   306
Paying It Forward   313
The China Institute: Promoting   322
Cultural Exchange for 97 Years   322

NAVIGATING TOUGH TIMES
Marriage, Love and Business Are All Based on Trust   333
Doing Business in China Ain't Easy   355
China's Media Maze   361
Education in a Changing China   365
What Else You Might Not Know   374

MY RETURN TO PARADISE
It's Easy to Feel at Home in Hawaii   402
Blessing the Land   404
In the Words of Cecilia He   406
In the Words of Allan Pollock   409
In the Words of Yuan Dan   411
A New Leaf, More Learning   413
Learning Conservation from the   415
Youngest in My Family   415
Home Again   416

EPILOGUE: ON BEING AMERICAN AND CHINESE   424
Appendix: American Chinese Contributors   433

FRIENDS FROM ALL OVER THE WORLD   437
ABOUT THE PUBLISHER   449

1

THE MOST

WATCHED PERSON
IN THE WORLD

I stood amongst the swelling crowds of smiling faces at the annual Lantern Festival (元宵节) held on February 24, 1986, marking the end of the New Year holiday. It should have been the most magical night imaginable as soft, glowing rose-colored embers of all shapes and sizes lit up the dark sky, and the thrilling sounds of young laughter chorused through the cool air. Family, friends and the long-lost united to celebrate the cherished event to enjoy a bountiful dinner and indulge in tang yuan (汤圆), sweet dumplings filled with candied, aromatic, lava-like black sesame.

Beijing was abuzz with life and momentum. Children giddily skipped through the bustling streets holding red paper lanterns, and the more daring ones shrieked wildly as they lit firecrackers toward the stars while revelers from all walks of life strolled through the vibrant city. The year's first full moon shone large and vibrant, radiating a kind of white light that seemed to dull the steadily dipping temperature.

However, I hardly took any of this in, as if watching a foreign movie unfurl from behind a frosted glass window with sweaty palms and glazed eyes. I was a nervous wreck trying to comprehend that this life was mine. Two years ago, I received the long-awaited green light from China Central Television (CCTV) (中央电视台) to air "One World (世界各地)," a show that was to introduce Chinese viewers to the world. My television production team and I worked endlessly navigating scripts, shot lists, travel, and coordination to arrive at this moment: the much-anticipated premiere. The first episode was slated to be broadcast at 9 p.m. that evening on CCTV, potentially reaching 400 million people. I did not know what this meant, nobody did, other than every bone in my body screamed that it would be something big, something life changing. China was a self-contained, mysterious place. Yet there I was, walking into the void alongside television cameras. I may as well have been walking on Mars.

The chapters of my life cloaked in anonymity and innocence were closing. Although I did not know it then, I was on the precipice – about to leap from the ledge onto an untrodden path from which I would never return.

I invited some of the advertisers I had managed to hustle to support the first episode to dinner at the Chinese restaurant in the Jian Guo Hotel (建国饭店), the first "western style" hotel in Beijing. The place was just a few stories high, comprised of musty, dimly lit rooms – not a sliver of today's opulent standards. But for many Chinese, the Jian Guo Hotel was a structure of deep intrigue, earning its "Western" moniker because one could order a cheeseburger at night or eggs and toast for breakfast; just the way it is done in the far-removed American-dominated world.

After our meal, we all shuffled up to my suite. My heart thumped so heavily I thought it might burst out of my chest. The lights faded, and everything else seemed to fall into the fog of slow motion. I heard our opening theme music – a suspenseful, monotone rift on repeat – played against a computerized loop of country shapes gliding across a black screen before settling on the show's logo: China illuminated from the map with the words "One World" in Chinese, glowing in bright tangerine.

Then, when I saw myself smile into the camera, sporting

a classic 1980s bob haircut with bangs, a high-collared pink-and-black blouse and oversized pearl earrings. This was all on Chinese national TV, and I instantly sunk into a state of total disbelief. That could not be me. Could it? In my passable Mandarin, I spoke softly yet confidently as I introduced the first episode, "New York City," and there was no escaping that the young woman before me was the same young woman right now holding an anxious breath in a Beijing Hotel room. I had endeavored with fearless abandon to bring the sprawling planet into every Chinese living room. But this was no longer a pipedream. I was doing it.

I chose New York as the subject of our inaugural episode because it was the city I had called home for several years, the illustrious metropolis that had clutched my heart and never let go. I longed to share with Chinese viewers how many nationalities worldwide lived together on this bustling island, a vastly different concept from the then very homogeneous China.

Immediately after the thirty-second intro, I started to sob uncontrollably, releasing the years of built-up stress and hardship I had endured to reach this point – the point where millions would experience my work, and I could no longer control, nor tinker, nor change the final product. My child, as the show was in many aspects, was now in the hands of the world. The show's airing on CCTV was the realization of a dream. No show like mine had ever been on Chinese television before, and I knew I had sprung into unchartered waters.

A survey of CCTV's offerings at the time showed that, on any given day, viewers might be exposed to eclectic snippets from around both China and the globe showcasing the Shandong Opera, marionettes, Japanese cartoons, cycling races, or the artistic masterpieces of Pablo Picasso. Sometimes CCTV may broadcast lessons on making Korean pickles, a documentary on the Shenzhen Special Economic Zone, or highlighted Chinese women dressed like flamenco dancers clacking away with castanets. However, nothing on the air in China in early 1986 featured a host with a Chinese face like mine touring the planet with a Chinese viewership in mind, speaking to people from seemingly mystical and far-flung cultures – in Mandarin. Just in crafting such a concept, I felt as though I was walking to the moon, and I was walking alone.

The first episode of "One World" revealed America as a country of immigrants and the boroughs of New York as a city comprised of many ethnic villages, a sharp contrast to the very inward China of the time. I escorted the viewers on an expedition through the graffiti-strewn subways and past the sea of blinding lights and yellow cabs and into its wildly diverse communities, from the Hasidic Jewish people to conservative Muslims to the run-of-the-mill men selling pretzels on a crowded street corner. The episode concluded with a segment in my parents' simple but homely Manhattan apartment, with its beige walls and carpets accentuated by apricot lampshades, wedged into the city's Midtown East. My dad dutifully worked on a delicate brush painting in ink as my sisters and niece, speaking English but eating Chinese food, sat giggling around the family table, providing the Chinese audience with an unprecedented glimpse into expat life. I wanted viewers to see how traditional family life can be preserved even inside a cosmos bubbling with diversity.

I glanced at the sponsors, who all seemed rather pleased and enthralled, their eyes fixated on the small glaring boxed television. I had done it. I had landed on the moon.

After the guests left my hotel suite, I collapsed into the soft pearl white sheets, allowing exhaustion to unleash through every bone in my body for the first time in many months. Despite the ongoing crackle and boom of fireworks into the wee hours as the Lantern Festival celebrations churned on, I slept soundly and dreamlessly for the first time in two years. But then, I rose the following day in an almost confused stupor, riddled with anxiety. What had happened? Was it all a figment of a delirious imagination? Had I really graced Chinese national television, reaching hundreds of millions? A pit dropped in my stomach, and I curled my body into a fetal position, my mind knotted with critiques and questions I could not answer. What if the show was poorly received? What if nobody liked it? What if I'd been misunderstood and somehow had offended the audience? What if the Chinese Communist Party leadership demanded it canceled right away?

I still had much to learn about China. My only real exposure to the country was the kind and supportive individuals who worked for CCTV. While my audience was the Chinese, I wasn't shooting inside the country as the content we captured focused on lands far and wide. Nobody at the time discussed politics. Instead, the burning questions on all our minds were how to wrench open this land and help people inside and out understand a much wider world.

As the first streaks of daylight cracked through the blinds

in the early hours, I heard a loud rapping on the door. I pulled on a robe, drew a deep breath and hurried to the door, barely able to put one foot in front of the other. A uniformed hotel staff member nodded politely, handed me a package, and disappeared down the hallway without a word. I closed the door and turned to place the long shape wrapped in brown paper down on my unmade bed, hands shaking. Was the show going to be over before it had even really begun? I pulled back the thin paper, and a scroll rolled out onto the bed sheets. I opened it to see a beautiful ink brush painting. Out dropped a handwritten letter:

Dear Yue-Sai,

I would like to congratulate you on the premiere of the TV show "One World," produced and hosted by you. I genuinely believe it will be a huge success, highly praised and appreciated by the audience all over China.

Since you were born into an intellectual family and your father is a great traditional Chinese painter, I would like to gift you with a painting by He Xiangning (何香凝), entitled "Plum Blossom" as a memento to celebrate the launch of "One World."

May you make even greater contributions to the development of friendship between the Chinese and the American people.

Hu Qili (胡启立)
Feb 25, 1986

靳小姐：

热烈祝贺您拍摄的《世界各地》节目首次播出。我相信它会受到中国广大群众的喜爱。

从电视屏幕上看到您有一个幸福的诗玉之家。您的父亲喜爱国画。谨以何香凝老人创作《红梅》一卷相赠，作为"看世界"首映成功的记念。

祝您为发展中美两国人民的友谊作出更大的贡献。

胡启立

1986.2.25

Hu was a very influential figure, one of the few high-ranking decision-makers shaping state television at the behest of the Chinese government. I could not quite comprehend that I had just received a handwritten letter from one of just seventeen men who led the Party and the nation, lauding what he had seen of my work the night before.

Later in the day, electrified with excitement but still unsure what it all meant, I showed the letter to my friend and guide, Mr. Xu Chuangcheng (徐创成), CCTV's Foreign Affairs director, who looked at it and smiled broadly, reassuring me that all that was happening was real, important, and positive.

"Ms. Kan, nobody gets a handwritten letter of congratulations from a member of the Politburo," Xu said enthusiastically. "This is something for us to celebrate."

I sensed that he, too, was relieved that the country's top brass viewed the partnership favorably. This signaled that we could continue making and airing episodes – at least for now.

"One World" helped pave the way for the opening of

China's airwaves, and nothing for a long time would come anywhere close to matching it in its efforts to educate Chinese viewers about the world in true documentary style. My show found a home on Sunday evenings in prime time, twice, once in Mandarin and once in English. It would be another year, as a part of the government policy of opening up, before viewers in China would be treated to imported shows such as the detective serial "Columbo," or the soap opera "Falcon Crest," or American Football from the NFL, or Mickey Mouse and Donald Duck cartoons.

Deep down, I knew that from that chilly February night in Beijing, my purpose and existence were forever changed. No matter where I stepped from this point forward, my legacy would always be beautifully entwined with the Chinese people. I had forged a crack in the symbolic doorway for fresh air to waft into the country, a door that could never be closed again.

Almost overnight, I became a household name across China. My bobbed hairstyle and bright red lipstick were subjects of great curiosity and adoration from footstep-seeking fans. There was a sense of wit and spontaneity about each episode that set them apart from most Chinese TV programming of the day.

Shelley Lim (林向芸), a friend of many years from Shanghai, recently reminisced about watching "One World" with her family as a young woman, with everyone sitting around the small box-style television, wide-eyed and waiting to slip into the next adventure.

"My grandparents on both sides left China for Southeast Asia and Vienna, but as a kid, my idea of the outside world was in the buildings of the French Concession in Shanghai," Shelly recalled. "I saw those French homes growing up, but they represented an imaginary world. We didn't know how things were in France until we saw Yue-Sai's 'One World' program on England and France."

Moreover, Lisa Wang (王丽莎), a close friend since around 2015, remembers watching my show on a 12-inch, black-and-white television with her whole family in Beijing.

"We thought, 'She's not really Chinese,'" noted Lisa, who had a lengthy career with the terminal operator Ports America Group and now lives in Los Angeles. "But we couldn't look away, either. That face! That lipstick! You showed us that the U.S. was a land filled with people from all over the world."

By offering Chinese viewers a window to the soul of other cultures, customs, and styles, I was suddenly the TV host with the world's largest audience. This all happened years prior to international networks such as CNN broadcasting via satellite and decades before hundreds of cable television, streaming and social media channels were staples in the social fabric.

At the time, China was a nation gripped by economic hardship, a newly implemented "one child" policy and immense uncertainty for what future years would bring. And yet, neighbors still gathered around the village TV set to catch my show, and teachers pulled together scores of students to watch it in both Chinese and English. The lasting effect of those early shows on CCTV continues to reveal itself to me decades later, often in the most surprising places. A few years ago, I attended a lecture in English by a Chinese official at the United Nations. I tried to congratulate him afterward, but he spoke first.

"Miss Kan, I know who you are," he said. "I learned English through your program."

No matter where I am in the world, irrespective of which street corner, elevator restaurant or dinner party, this sort of appreciation still emanates in the most random of situations. Chinese people who saw me on "One World" in the 1980s treat me like an old friend and feel encouraged to come up and offer a thank you, even though Mandarin was my third language and far from perfect on the program, influenced by a mixture of the English and Cantonese accents I heard growing up in Hong Kong.

Admittedly, how this would be perceived in China worried me, and long before "One World" hit the air, several CCTV executives expressed vehement concern.

"Yue-Sai's Chinese is so poor," one executive protested in an internal meeting. "We are the government station. Our hosts should speak impeccably."

However, after the show started its fiercely popular run, Ai Zhisheng (艾知生), Director of the State Administration of Radio, Film and Television (SARFT), China's Ministry-level media regulator, informed the tense CCTV executives, "Yue-Sai has become such a superstar! I told you not to worry about her poor Mandarin. It was never the problem. People watch her not to learn Chinese but to learn about the world through her."

It even turned out that my mish-mash Chinese came to be considered chic and was widely copied. CCTV Deputy Director Chen Hanyuan (陈汉元), the official responsible for my series seeing the light of day, concurred that I was "a breath of fresh air in every way."

"Her looks, style, the content, and the way the programs are produced are totally different from what we have seen," he told associates. "We have a lot to learn from her."

Much to my surprise, "One World" also generated a great deal of excitement back in the United States. Some Americans called me a Citizen Ambassador, the metaphorical bridge connecting the U.S. with China. TIME Magazine declared me "Queen of the Middle Kingdom" and Newsday "The Most Watched Woman in the World." The popular TV hosts Charlie Rose and David Letterman could not get over the notion that I reached some 400 million viewers each week and invited me to appear on their programs.

Their inquisitive questions about China continued: "What do you eat in China?" "What did you see there?" "What did they tell you?" "Were you told what not to film?" "What restrictions do they impose on you?" These highly influential, middle-aged, white American television sensations were curious about China because it was an unknown territory, a seemingly recluse nation on the edge of the earth. Thus, I was critical in teaching Chinese people about the wider world and soon, equally pivotal in improving American's understanding of this distant nation.

While "One World" changed my life and the lives of many others in a myriad of ways, it didn't generate enough revenue to cover production. My original agreement with CCTV called for producing 104 weekly shows, but because we ran out of money, we completed 96. CCTV did not provide funds for our production costs, and we did not have to give them a dime for the airtime. The onus was on me to sell all the advertising slots and make up the balance from the money we acquired from my sister television show, "Looking East," a series on American channels designed to educate Americans about Asia that I launched a little while later.

Despite the shortfall, "One World" continued to shatter ground in its content and format. Sun Xiaohong (孙晓红), a well-known Chinese TV announcer and producer, told me that my program introduced a whole new way for hosts to speak.

"In 'One World,' Yue-Sai Kan didn't just sit in a studio and talk; she walked out and used her camera to introduce the world to Chinese audiences," he observed. "It brought new ideas and impacted a generation of TV producers and hosts."

Furthermore, the State media's reaction to the series was unanimously optimistic.

"Though she is not an architect, she is building a cultural bridge across the Pacific Ocean; though she is not a weaver, she is busy weaving a ribbon of friendship between the Chinese people and people all over the world." - The Guangzhou Evening News (广州晚报).

"With the broadcast of "One World," Yue-Sai Kan has entered into millions of Chinese homes. Her graceful and natural style, distinctive hairstyle and even her foreign-accented Mandarin have become everyone's favorite subject of discussion."

Shanghai's top newspaper, the Wenhuibao (文汇报).

I sincerely appreciated the praise but never let it go to my head or hamper my work ethic. I was only getting started and had a long way to go before I could ever even contemplate settling into a lull of self-gratification and accomplishment.

STARTING VERY SMALL

Long before my advance to the small screen, I was already in the throes of entrepreneurship. But to my work hard-wired mind, it wasn't about building an empire — it was simply about executing one's due diligence to make ends meet. Starting in 1971 from our tiny apartment on Manhattan's Upper East Side, my younger sister Vickie and I ran our own trading company. We bought and sold fabrics and home furnishings from China, the mysterious country I left at age three, in the post-War era of 1949.

Our major clients were Walmart and Sears, for whom we made pillows and throws. However, it was hardly a deluge of revenue, and I did what I needed to do to survive, with no idea that a television career lingered in my not-to-distant future.

Cable television was just beginning in the 1970s, and when my friend Luo Zhonglang (罗中郎) announced that he was starting a show catering to New York's Chinese viewers and wanted me to host it. I wasn't necessarily excited as much as I was intrigued to experience a medium I had never given much thought to before. Having an artistic mindset, I wasn't concerned about earning no money, but was enthralled by the concept of creating and giving back.

It was an internship of sorts, and I was young and eager to learn the ropes. Every weekend, I trekked downtown to Mr.

Luo's tiny Chinatown studio – the headquarters of a station that only broadcast on Sundays. Everything was rudimentary and far from the illustrious glamour most of us believed television to be. The studio was stuffed inside a second-floor walk-up of an old, creaking building with crooked steps and chipped walls. On rainy days, the roof leaked. I didn't mind. I was just playing around, never taking it too seriously. That was, until one day at a dinner party, I met a professor from Stanford University who asked me what I did in my spare time.

"Oh, every Sunday, I do a little TV for fun for a friend," I said with a nonchalant shrug.

He looked at me harshly for a moment and shook his head.

"Anytime you do something that can influence the perceptions of people, their beliefs and their ideas, it's not a frivolous thing and should never be treated as such," the professor cautioned.

With that, my outlook on the power of television began to change.

President Richard Nixon visited China in 1972, breaking the ice with Beijing and helping China come out of three decades of isolation, famine, and internal political turmoil. Even Americans paying attention had no idea what to make of this giant swath of humanity. The professor was right, I conceded. Being Chinese on television in America carried with it specific opportunities and responsibilities to be the ultimate communicator between these two significantly divergent countries.

From then on, I took every show seriously and tried to make it worthwhile for the viewers. I became intensely involved despite the lack of pay. I insisted not only on hosting the show but also doing the preparation and undertaking the interviews and news reports every week, even though the show in those days probably had an audience of two — my mother and father, who, their health failing, had moved to New York from Hong Kong in 1979 to be close to my sisters and me.

I taped the TV show in Cantonese, in the dominant dialect spoken in Hong Kong, where I spent most of my childhood. I also performed simultaneous interpretation when I interviewed people who didn't speak Cantonese. On one occasion, I gave Ed Koch, the Mayor of New York City, a chance to talk directly to his growing number of Cantonese-speaking constituents, my parents included. Like the rest of the world, New York was waking up to the Chinese, a people whose influence in the city today is remarkable. These days, for instance, the iconic Rockefeller Center – which once was owned by Japanese investors – has China's sovereign wealth fund, the China Investment Corporation, as its largest shareholder.

It wasn't until the late 1970s that I learned to do everything related to television – beyond the in-front-of-camera role. I once interviewed Joan Fontaine, winner of an Oscar for her role in Alfred Hitchcock's 1941 thriller "Suspicion." She immediately became a close girlfriend and generously passed on tips learned from decades working in the Golden Age of Hollywood. For one, Joan cautioned that I should never sit on a swivel chair because it moves too much and is distracting on camera, adding that the camera should always be slightly higher than my head to make my face look smaller.

While working on the show, which was fundamentally Sunday community television centered around interviews, I noticed that every time we did a segment about China's vast culinary traditions, our little studio's phone rang off the hook with people asking where they could find the foods we featured. We once aired a segment about the Chinese wellness exercise discipline called qigong – developed thousands of years ago using exercises to optimize energy within the body, mind, and spirit – and, again, we couldn't keep up with the volume of calls. Even viewers who couldn't understand what they were hearing wanted to know more about what they saw. Americans were becoming interested in Asia, particularly China, and we were in an excellent position to start showcasing that part of the world to the audience.

Around this time, I attended a dinner party and met Dr. Arthur Sackler, the brilliant art collector, entrepreneur, and publisher of the weekly Medical Tribune for physicians. He possessed soft gray hair and rectangle glasses that slipped to his nose and was overall incredibly charming. Dr. Sackler wasn't just a run-of-the-mill doctor; he was a fascinating individual with a specialty in psychiatry and a passion for disseminating medical information and breakthroughs and helping as many people as possible. I was also captivated by the fact that he owned the most extensive collection of Chinese art in private hands at the time.

I'm deeply saddened that, in recent years, Dr. Sackler's name has been dragged through the mud as a purveyor of the opioid crisis with some vicious intent to ignite a nation of addicts. This could not have been further from the truth.

Dr. Sackler died in 1987, long before the opioid mayhem. He was a kind man who longed to alleviate people's suffering by successfully developing and marketing drugs such as Valium and Librium. I do not believe he should be held accountable for the over-prescribing malpractice of physicians in later years. As long as I knew him, Dr. Sackler donated tirelessly to numerous foundations, from the Smithsonian to the Metropolitan Museum of Art. He founded and contributed to scores of scientific institutions and helped racially integrate New York City's first blood banks. It pains me that these acts of giving have been erased today, tarnished by a cloud of controversy regarding the Sackler family name.

Nevertheless, after our first lengthy chat over dinner, Dr. Sackler asked me to help him produce and host a series of medical TV programs. I was flattered that he thought I would make a good host. Although Sackler's idea for a medical TV show never materialized, his encouragement expanded how I viewed my budding career in television.

I thought America's growing interest in Asia meant something. It amplified my interest in the part of the world I'd left behind, and I felt very strongly in my gut that this was only the beginning and that there was so much to come.

Then, one day, I abruptly informed my sister Vickie that I would quit our trading company and sell her my shares so I could turn all my attention to making television about Asia. If she was surprised, she didn't show it. Vickie shrugged and agreed. My family sensed at this point that something unknown, something revolutionary, sat somewhere on my horizon. Still, some people, including my mother, thought

I was nuts. With the sting of defeat in Vietnam still fresh and an initial unease surrounding the arrival of Japanese automobiles on America's roads and these odd rice and fish rectangles called sushi on its menus, a large contingency of 1970s America bestowed few positive associations with Asia – but I wanted to be the vessel for change.

Furthermore, the competition to succeed on the small screen was intense, given the broad variety of TV programming available in the U.S. Even then, viewers could channel surf, pushing the then-new-fangled battery-operated remote control twenty times a minute, coming up with a different program for their pleasure each time. Yet I was determined not to talk myself down before I had even begun. I put a lot of pressure on myself to produce a show that would not only make a splash but also make a difference in how American audiences perceived China.

At the time, most Americans viewed China as a distant, dismal land with strange foods and even stranger people and political policies that were far from the capitalism and freedom boasted by the U.S. leadership. But on a very human level, I was convinced that despite our disparate ways of life, there was so much more that unifies the two populations than divides, and that there was an abundance of wisdom we could each extract from the other's point of view.

I mentioned to CBS News anchor and "60 Minutes" star Mike Wallace, whom I'd met through a socialite friend while visiting Martha's Vineyard, that I was also in television and mentioned my idea. Of course, I couldn't have imagined he would be interested in what I was doing. I was small potatoes compared to his reach and influence. Yet immediately, Mike seemed to place a very personal importance on my endeavor and listened to my spiel very carefully.

"I don't think anyone will watch a show about Asia," he concluded regretfully.

I remained undeterred, sensing he didn't have his finger on the pulse this time. From my lens, all kinds of Americans were beginning to get curious about Asia, fed, in part, by the arrival of Bruce Lee's "Kung Fu" films in American movie theaters and on television, which seemed to pique curiosity about Chinese wisdom and philosophical traditions.

Premiering on public access television in the fall of 1977, my half-hour weekly show in English, called "Looking East (看东方)," was the only program about Asia broadcast in the United States at the time. The show was initially intended to be about all of Asia but tended to concentrate on China because it's the continent's biggest country and because I wanted to learn more about the land from which my forebears hailed.

In the beginning, it was just an interview show. We booked guests who had visited China or were experts on Chinese culture and others who came to us fresh from visits to other Asian countries, and I probed them about their thoughts and experiences. We focused on culture, art, people, personalities and, rarely, political figures.

Not long after its debut, Mike Wallace called to say that by accident, he saw a segment I did on Netsuke, the intricate miniatures first carved in 17th Century Japan. In a somewhat sexist compliment not atypical of the time, Mike remarked that I looked beautiful on screen and that he was surprised by my intelligent questions. Not one to waste an opportunity, I asked him to write me a testimonial. Mike did, referring to me as an "unsung glory on cable TV." He then proceeded to introduce me to his agent. However, the agent wasn't interested because he thought I lacked proper training and was concerned that no TV station would take me on.

I was disappointed, but if no one would take me, I figured I would have to do the show independently, with or without representation. I was learning on the job that I should not let others' doubts drown my self-confidence. If I was going to do this, I had to rely chiefly on myself and not on the opinions of others. There was no time for self-pity, and I think if I had gone down the conventional route of representation and started in a small town, working my way up to bigger and bigger markets, I would never have gone on to create and build the big-bang programs that I did. I understood from early on that for a fresh-faced ethnic woman to succeed, I had to be a pioneer – not merely follow in already well-entrenched footsteps. There was something about the individual drive and bustle that became my oxygen and kept me hungry for more, never to rest on my laurels.

When I started "Looking East," it was broadcast only on the New York Community TV channel. At the time, every city in the U.S. had such public access stations. New York's teeming, pent-up gay community found a home there that it could not find on mainstream television, as did new-age healers and eccentrics. Production quality was low simply because content creators did not have much money. In those days, you needed money to produce decent quality. Nobody had cheap handheld home video cameras, and the iPhone was still a quarter century away. Only we never failed to generate creative solutions.

In the first year, I rented a time slot in a studio specializing in inexpensive productions. The shoebox room had simple lighting, two cameras and three chairs flanked by artificial trees. I would go into the studio, record an interview with my guests, pay for the time, and they would give me a tape. This was the perfect training ground to learn to make cheap TV shows.

As there were no cable TV networks and the likes of CNN were not yet born, I picked up the landline and called all the community stations around the country, offering station managers "Looking East" for free. In a time when there were no national networks, I created my own. The way I saw it was that my show wasn't time sensitive. Every week, we mailed video cassette tapes to a dozen stations nationwide. When you're poor, there is no shortage of pushing to develop innovative solutions to continue doing what you love. This business model of airing the program without charge, with the hopes of gaining enough traction to sign on serious sponsors someday soon, certainly paid dividends.

In that first year, I paid and covered all the expenses myself. Once I had taped a handful of guests with recognizable names, including designer Mary McFadden, Chinese actress Joan Chen (陈冲), and writer Gore Vidal, just back from a trip to Mongolia, I put together a showreel with testimonials from the likes of Mike Wallace and started to shop it around. Fear was never in my vocabulary. Even when I don't know what to do next, I take the reins of a situation and go forth without any doubt.

Soon, "Looking East" attracted some big-time sponsors, and we started location-shooting in various Asian countries, particularly those whose businesses backed us. We journeyed to Borneo and filmed the primitive Iban people. We traveled upriver, and I slept in their longhouses with all my crew members, and we brought our cook because we were told the food would be terrible. As much as I wanted to integrate into the local community, I figured we would all be miserable and unenthusiastic without some sound sustenance in our stomachs.

The whole experience fascinated me — the crew and the concept of an American television audience, who had never seen anything like it. After the show aired, many people wrote to ask us to explain the line in our script about the Iban discontinuing their tradition of head-hunting — except during the Japanese occupation in World War II. The Iban, it turns out, had revived the tradition to counter Japanese wartime atrocities.

Despite my profound zest for the work, the series was arduous work, and the budget was tight, but the real riches stemmed from the fact it led me to breathtaking places and into human experiences no money could buy. However, I could not help but worry that our last day of filming was only a breath or two away. On several occasions, I announced to the crew that if we didn't get additional advertising right away, we would have to cancel the show. Miraculously, each time we faced the end, help arrived from somewhere.

I was an independent TV producer, and no TV station was paying the tab. Imagine me, an unknown Chinese girl in New York, trying to win over advertisers and sponsors for a public access TV show about Asia. Again, I laid out the information and assembled a plan born from logic and hope. I deciphered which brands and organizations might be interested in viewers who were themselves interested in Asia, made a list, and then contacted them one by one – from Kikkoman Soy Sauce and the tourist associations of Hong Kong, Singapore, Malaysia and Japan to United Airlines and Royal Viking Cruises. I visited each of these companies and their advertising agencies. I was thrilled if I made a hundred phone calls and received one or two in return.

In the early 1980s, as China shook off the decade-long trauma of the Cultural Revolution and felt an air of openness and optimism, "Looking East" focused on introducing Americans to basic Chinese culture, from its vast agricultural society to its tradition of ink brush painting. My first English-language show on American television coincided with a shift in China's landscape. China's state-controlled broadcasts began at Beijing Television in 1958, when there were only 20 TV sets in all of China and expanded to Shanghai in 1959. By the 1970s, China CCTV — whose stated purpose was spreading government propaganda — pushed out from the capital to all the provinces. The government paid for all programming, so there was no need for advertising — never mind that there were next to no products on China's shelves to advertise. It wasn't until January of 1979 that residents of Shanghai, China's most cosmopolitan city, saw China's first television commercial, a ninety-second spot for Shen Gui Tonic Wine.

While the source of revenue and support for programming commercialized, authorities' control over what got to air remained as strict as it was from the start, especially in news programming. For instance, important news, first disseminated via broadcast on China National Radio each night at 8 p.m., was moved back to 7 p.m. and put out on CCTV, a practice still in place today.

A key element to understanding long-lasting misunderstandings between China and the United States lies in each country's approach to the media. Simply put, modern China's mass media focuses on good news and America's on bad. While China's state media promotes the nation's, and the Party's successes, America's commercially funded media companies compete for viewers and learned early that scandal, tragedy, and hardship sell, perhaps a side-effect of Democracy, where parties compete for control and must have an opponent to blame for societal ills. Otherwise, why would all the advertised products to make life easier hold any appeal?

I longed to find the middle ground, that fragile balance that could bring both sides together.

RIGHT PLACE, RIGHT TIME

Among the fast-expanding audience for "Looking East" was Joan Konner, head of the Public Broadcasting System (PBS), a network of local not-for-profit stations across the United

States. On September 28, 1984, Konner called to ask if I would provide off-camera, voice-over commentary on a broadcast scheduled for October 1, marking the 35th anniversary of the founding of the People's Republic of China.

Televising China's National Day Parade in America would mark the first cooperation between a U.S. broadcaster and state-run China Central Television. Joan explained that she had just found out CCTV's live feed from Tiananmen Square (天安门广场) in central Beijing would have no narration but would feature a prepared speech by China's top leader Deng Xiaoping (邓小平), the reformer who opened the country to foreign investment and visited President Jimmy Carter at the White House in 1979.

Without the addition of an English narration, no PBS station across the U.S. would pick up the broadcast, rendering the cooperation a failure and a major loss of face for both sides. Thus, Konner asked me to do a live narration, but off-camera, a concept I instinctively felt wasn't right. This was when a voice beyond me, the fabled figure from upstairs, told me sharply, "This is a big moment – dare to ask for what's right."

"Would you ask Walter Cronkite to be off camera?" I asked with more confidence than I felt, referring to the iconic CBS News anchor. "I'm just as much of an expert on China as he is in his area."

This was not really true. Despite my Chinese face, I knew extraordinarily little about China. I couldn't even speak Mandarin, China's national language, but I sensed this was a spotlight that would bring about much greater possibilities to expand my scope and audience. Most people might shy away from such an enormous challenge. Instead, I sought it out. To this day, I don't quite know where this surge of boldness sprung from – but I wasn't backing down.

"PBS is a union operation," Joan replied matter-of-factly. "If we turned on the camera to feature you on-screen, we would have to pay staff the union rate of $5,000."

That was an exorbitant amount of money at the time, and Joan explained that she could not find a sponsor to cover such costs in just two days.

"Give me two hours," I said, the weight of responsibility bearing down on my shoulders.

I hung up and immediately called a gentleman I had sat next to at a dinner party a few nights before. Michel Fribourg owned Continental Grain and oozed with enthusiasm about the growing agricultural trade volume in his business with China. After exchanging a few niceties, I cut to the chase and asked Michel if he wanted his company to exclusively sponsor a historic broadcast. To my surprise, without skipping a beat, he sent a check to PBS for $5,000 within the hour.

This was actually happening.

I began conducting frantic research the moment PBS agreed to put me on camera. I had less than 48 hours to prepare, and all CCTV issued us was a rundown of the live feed from Beijing.

First, there was to be a military parade of the People's Liberation Army, the Air Force, and the Navy, followed by civilian floats with names such as "Model Beijing Family" and "Number 1 Document." There were no further details. This was pre-Internet and at a time when the U.S. was not the repository of reference material on China that it is today. I drew a deep breath, willing myself to focus and not consume myself with panic that would not serve the project.

With guidance from Mr. Xu Liugen (徐留根), a Chinese official with the Mission to the United Nations and my two assistants helping me at the National Committee on U.S.-China Relations library in Manhattan, I pored over books on the Chinese military. We crammed an entire country and its 5,000-year history and culture onto a stack of notecards. I studied vigorously into the early hours of the morning as if my life depended on it.

Just a few hours before the broadcast, CCTV released the transcript of the speech to be given by Deng Xiaoping. It was customary that speeches delivered by Chinese leaders are never released until last minute. We scrambled to translate it, grateful to have an advance copy because Deng's strong accent from Sichuan, in southwest China, would have been hard for me to follow at the moment. Just imagine – it was the night of September 30 in New York, and there I was with my notecards at the PBS studio in Manhattan, watching the footage coming to us from the future, from the morning of October 1 in Beijing. My job was to explain what we, in the West, were all seeing for the first time live: the new China.

The air over Tiananmen, the largest public square in the world, glowed bright and a sea of tens of thousands of Chinese troops and workers, students and model families, all color coordinated according to their work units, panned across the screen.

As he passes by an assembled militia or battalion, the soldiers will salute, and he will greet the soldiers by saying:

"Tongzhimen hao!" ("同志们好!")

"Tongzhimen xinkule!" ("同志们辛苦了!")

"How do you do, comrades!"

"Thank you for your hard work, comrades!" I translated with all the stately calm I could muster.

The soldiers respond saying "Shouzhang hao!" ("首长好!")

"Wei ren min fu wu!" ("为人民服务!")

I had to translate it to

"How do you do, commander!"

"We serve the people!"

Following the inspection, Deng returned to the Tiananmen Gate for the Military parade proper.

It was during that parade that a group of young students from Peking University unfurled a banner: "Xiaoping, ni hao!" ("小平, 你好!")

"Xiaoping, hello!" I explained it and deeply moved by the students enthusiasm for the man they viewed as a paragon of hope, a leader who would lead their families and nation out of a dark and grim time.

After Chairman Mao Zedong died in 1976, Xiaoping Deng steadily rose through the political ranks to lead China from 1978 to 1989, implementing extensive global reforms and introducing the population to an international market, elevating a billion people from the bowels of poverty.

The two-hour parade featured many floats. There was one float filled with farmers displaying a banner emblazoned with the words "No. 1 Document" ("1号文件") about the state's major reform guaranteeing that Chinese farmers now had the right to use their land any way they saw fit for 50 years.

Another float showed off the "Model Beijing Family" ("北京模范家庭") with two pairs of grandparents, a husband and wife and one and only one child, emphasizing China's policy of one child per family. On another stood China's first Olympians since 1952, including Li Ning (李宁), the star gymnast who had wowed the Summer Games in Los Angeles a few months earlier, winning three gold medals, two silver, and one bronze. With teary eyes, I saw Li Ning as a symbol of hope, of a can-do attitude that seemed new to the Chinese.

Nevertheless, narrating the CCTV feed was impossibly stressful, not only physically but emotionally, too. Whether I liked it or not, I was the barge bringing the most important voices in China to America that day, a position I took very seriously. One challenging feat leads to another, and when we do something well, with all our effort, doors open. Yet what happened next ventured beyond my wildest imagination and changed the course of my life.

Soon after the broadcast, a famous TV journalist working for CCTV visited me in New York to gift me a beautiful ceramic horse as an expression of gratitude from CCTV. The State-run network was so immensely proud of the broadcast cooperation that they showed a group of high-level Chinese leaders the version with my English commentary translated back into Chinese. It was incredibly gratifying to envision the leaders' curiosity about me; this New York girl was of Chinese lineage.

Reaction to the broadcast in the U.S. was also affirmative overall, even if PBS took flak from some quarters for giving China a platform for what American conservatives labeled propaganda. But among Chinese Americans, the reaction was unanimously positive. It was the first time many people of Chinese descent living in America saw images of the country many of them or their parents fled during the Revolution. It was a very emotional experience for them. The show was featured on the front page or near the top of the broadcast in most Chinese language media in the U.S., which made CCTV even happier. It was all a significant step in opening up the relationship between China and the Western world, and I found myself riddled with a kind of excited emotion at the wheels I had helped set in motion.

Xu Chuangcheng (徐创成), CCTV's head of foreign affairs, whose job it was to research the medium and how to improve it to help China's development, later visited my apartment in New York. And in his flawless English, extended a formal invitation to Beijing. The overture felt surreal, but I immediately accepted – eager to connect with the people of my heritage.

BECOMING A HOUSEHOLD NAME

Two months later, on December 18, 1984 – heeding CCTV's invitation – I flew alone from New York to Beijing. In retrospect, it was extraordinary that I had no fear about jetting by myself into a country that, at the time, was very much like the Hermit Kingdom North Korea is today – overstuffed with dreary, Soviet-style buildings under the pall that ignorance about what was happening can cast over any scene. China was still plunged in so much of the unknown.

Nevertheless, I was only enraptured by excitement and curiosity. I never worried that the Chinese were evil as portrayed by much of the media at the time, as those I had dealt with, and continued to deal with from that point, were among the sweetest and most polite people I had ever encountered. Of course, CCTV was thrilled to embark on the first-ever joint venture between Chinese and American television, and I felt tremendous pride and responsibility as the person to make it possible.

I touched down in the eponymous capital late at night and into the small, ailing, dingy mess of the Beijing Capital Airport, bereft of even basic lighting.

I was so relieved to see the sweet face of Mr. Xu, the soft-spoken gentleman who greeted me as I disembarked. He smiled warmly and explained that he would be my guide during my stay. It was the beginning of a lifelong friendship with Mr. Xu, who guided me through the next few years as my life dramatically transformed.

I felt an instant connection to this tender-hearted gentleman, the only person I knew who could speak fluent English, as my Mandarin skills did not then exist. Mr. Xu hailed from an Indonesian-Chinese family that had migrated to Indonesia as China grappled with immense struggle and starvation. But when Chairman Mao called for the reunification and revitalization of the country in 1956, Mr. Xu returned as a young man with a zeal to help build a new China, to breathe fresh life into a nation burned and devastated by decades of humiliation. The Chinese returnees were especially determined to make something of the country after being treated so poorly and with such disdain even in other Asian countries, even though that meant enduring decades of hardship. Mr. Xu, given his remarkable language skills acquired abroad, was later recruited by CCTV to handle the foreign office, and he took me graciously under his wing and cared for me the way one would care for a baby sister.

From the airport to downtown, we drove along a narrow road lined with naked trees, and past endless wintery fields. There were no highways back then, only small roads, farmland, donkey carts and bicycles. I had no preconceived ideas about what to expect; I just knew that China would be quite the contrast from the grand bridges and highways and dynamic and wealth-saturated world epicenter that is New York. I took everything in like a little girl peering into a toy store window for the very first time.

Along the dusty patches of road, I observed farmers selling tipping mounds of cabbage, one of the few perishable staples that could be stored through winter, absorbed the sweet aroma of roasted chestnuts, and marveled at the weather-creased faces of the farmers cooking sweet potatoes over coals glowing in old oil drums. Hungry after the long flight, I could smell their syrupy, delicious aroma and asked our driver if we could stop so that I could buy everyone a treat.

Mr. Xu's face balked.

"I ate nothing but sweet potatoes for the last decade," he said with a shudder. "I cannot stand to taste them again."

During the long struggle that was the Cultural Revolution, Xu's family, like so many, suffered immense poverty. Sweet potatoes were now a bitter memory. I nodded, absorbing these small but significant details like a sponge as we spluttered on through the throngs of gentle faces, wizened by lives spent working hard beneath the harsh elements. It seemed to me that people's lives were banal, beautiful, basic, and baffling all at once. It hit me how little I knew about the real China and how much more I needed to learn, wanted to learn, and was desperate to learn.

I can't help but marvel at how far China has come in such a short time. Today, Chinese people can eat anything from anywhere in the world, with the finest quality. But that right there, the many men with their backs bent over underneath the diminishing sunshine peddling vegetables, lucky if they made sixty dollars a year, marked the beginning of the country's turn toward entrepreneurship.

As insignificant as it might have then appeared, the man who was selling sweet potatoes or cabbage on the side of the road was the start of capitalism in China.

We soon arrived at the Beijing Hotel, the most prestigious in China's capital at that time. However, you can tell when a country is poor by the lighting. The streets outside languished in darkness, and there was barely enough flickering amber luminescence inside the supposedly top-notch hotel to maneuver through the grim lobby and into my large but bleak room.

I placed my bag on the bed and noticed that the white sheets were worn gray. The nightstand featured nothing more than a thermos of hot water with a few tea bags and a cup in the side, and the curtains were dirty and frayed, reeking of age and mold. The bathroom was also very primitive, and the door to the room didn't even have a lock and key. I pushed a chair against the entrance and tepidly slipped into the bed, trying to ignore the rat that had scampered through a hole in the corner. I folded myself into the decaying sheets, slowly drifting into slumber as my mind spun with many thoughts and questions.

However, early the next morning, upon awakening, I was rendered speechless.

There, out my smudged window, were the yellow ceramic tiled roofs of the Forbidden City, home to China's emperors, their peaks covered in swirls of snow as dainty as lace. The stunning visual feast momentarily took my breath away. This was an entirely different world for me, a world I knew nothing about, and I could not wait to embark on this adventure, pinching myself that this was really happening.

Later that morning, I met with leading officials of CCTV and Mr. Ai Zhisheng (艾知生) of the Broadcast Ministry, a wing controlled by the Central Propaganda Department of the CCP. The government authorities were highly cordial, congratulating me on the success of the PBS broadcast and sharing their determination to use television to educate the Chinese public about the outside world.

"How can we open China if the Chinese do not know one thing about the outside world and the outside world knows nothing about us?" Mr. Ai declared.

Ai, the broadcast minister, informed me that the Central Government wanted to produce a TV series to speed up the Chinese people's adjustment to the late 20th century after 35 years of isolation. The idea struck me as necessary, but only if the matter was handled the right way. It took all my courage to be honest with these men.

"How can you possibly do this with television producers who all were indoctrinated inside China Central Television?" I asked.

The men's eyebrows arched briefly, but they did not protest, motioning me to proceed.

"You need an outsider," I pressed on. "A neutral outsider like me."

Ai agreed immediately. And, just like that, "One World" – the first TV documentary television series produced in the West and shown in China – was conceived. I couldn't believe this was real, that my role as a cultural cavalcade was about to expand exponentially, and I knew that nobody in New York would either unless I had this all down on paper.

I requested a contract to seal the deal. Ai and his CCTV colleagues glanced at each other with slight perplexity. Ai shrugged and told me to prepare one myself. So that night, my heart pounding with excitement, I drafted out one page with eight clauses – one of the shortest contracts in CCTV history. To my surprise, the executives hurriedly signed and stamped the contract.

It was in such moments that I cherished the fact I had pushed myself as a budding reporter to learn all facets of the industry, to understand more than just what it took to be a formidable force in front of the camera.

Many years later, I asked Liu Jinru (刘瑾如), the lady who was then in charge of what little advertising CCTV carried, about the speed of signing initial contracts.

"Why didn't CCTV draft the contract themselves?" I asked, triggering uproarious laughter from Ms. Liu.

"Because we didn't know how to write a contract!" she confessed.

Nevertheless, there I was, with a sudden mandate to produce a series of TV shows to educate the Chinese public about the world. I promised 104 episodes of 15 minutes each to be recorded in both Mandarin and English even though I couldn't, at that point, even speak any Mandarin. The truth was I could not even say my own name in Mandarin. Reality dawned. Feelings of intense vertigo rushed through me. I felt nauseous and exalted as if I were hanging out a ninety-story window and didn't know if I would fly or fall. But I was steadfast in my mission to grow some wings – and grow them fast.

In those days, there were very few Mandarin teachers in New York. But through word of mouth, I hunted down three different tutors, paying them whatever I could, which, at the time, wasn't much. For the following six months, every weekday evening, I studied from 6 p.m. to 9 p.m., and on weekends from 9 a.m. to 9 p.m. I worked with each of the teachers separately and exhausted them all, immersing myself in the learning process to the brink of insanity. Everywhere I went, my Walkman drilled Mandarin into my eardrums.

Moreover, I asked my Chinese friends to help me by recording ancient Chinese poems and novels, including Ba Jin (巴金)'s The Family (家). I listened to them over and over. I followed the accent and spoke out the words while vigorously listening.

For six months, I declined all dinner invitations and all gatherings with friends. I was determined to be fluent enough in Mandarin to present "One World" myself, and tackling this faraway language became my obsession in every waking moment. At night, I willed myself to dream in Mandarin – believing that is when my life of genuine connection to the Chinese people would begin.

Of course, I never stopped learning, and it would take years to reach the point of immaculate Mandarin. But half a year in, I at least felt comfortable enough to begin taping the "One World" shows, starting in New York before spanning the planet.

We filmed the first three pilot shows for the CCTV leaders to review, and I spent three hours taping the first thirty seconds of the first Mandarin show over and over again. It needed to be good, not just good enough. I accepted I might never shed my accent, but as long as a Chinese audience could understand me, I had a fighting chance.

The three pilot shows needed to be approved by Ai, the broadcast minister, and also by Chen Hanyuan, Deputy Director of CCTV before I could produce more. I was cautious with every aspect of the production. I filmed each pilot dressed in a simple black-and-white jacket and I wore no makeup on my face, careful not to appear egregious at a time when many were still clawing their way out of destitution.

I flew to Beijing to present the shows directly to Ai. It felt vital to be there in person as if I were carrying the world outside on a fragile platter for my Chinese cohorts to witness for the first time. We watched them together, and I held my breath, waiting for a reaction.

"Yue-Sai, the content of the programs is excellent," Ai said, turning to me with a smile. "But is this how you look in your productions in America?"

"Well, no," I replied.

"I want you to produce the show as you would in America," Ai stressed.

Such a sentiment shocked me because no television hosts in China at that time wore any makeup, and they all had the same unremarkable haircut. With his approval, I was to wear colorful clothes with earrings and makeup from that point on. I almost sighed with relief. This signaled that the higher-ups believed China was ready for change, and the most fantastic part of all was that a small group of the country's most powerful men allowed an American passport holder to speak directly to China's vast audience.

This was 1985, and even they knew little about the world. The CCTV decision-makers needed my help. They wouldn't have known how to direct me if they tried, so the duty was on me to show them the power of television and what it could do.

Then came the hard part. How to pay for it? CCTV executives admitted they had no money because there was no advertising in those days. Remember, there was next to nothing to buy and no broad selection market in China anyhow, hence nothing to advertise. CCTV was the poorest large broadcaster in the world. Thus, in keeping with all I had learned from my days in American television, I suggested they carve out advertising time. I would sell this to advertisers to raise funds for the production, a groundbreaking arrangement for Chinese television.

I departed Beijing with the contract in hand, knowing it would change my life forever. Without the contract, no sponsor would believe what I told them about such a radical change in Chinese state television. With it, I could instinctively feel just how big it would be – so big that I couldn't bring myself to mention it to the two American businessmen friends I bumped into on the flight home. I needed to keep it close to my heart for a little longer. We stayed in Tokyo for several hours and shared a meal, yet I kept my secret. It is incredible to think how far China has flourished since just a few decades ago when the concept of a contract was akin to flying to the stars on an alien spaceship.

And then, back in New York, I couldn't bring myself to mention this remarkable development to anyone except my parents for a whole week. It just seemed too big, too monumental, and I needed to digest the conception that I was the one tasked with unlocking the gates inside this nation of more than a billion.

Finally, over dinner, I summoned the courage. My parents were dumbfounded. They couldn't believe it either. China had changed so much in such a fleeting time, and I think they experienced a wide range of emotions and a bout of cultural whiplash. They didn't know what to make of it. Meanwhile, many of my friends spanning America to Hong Kong to China really feared me working for CCTV when they found out the news. The unknown felt gloomy and unnerving to them, and their immediate reaction was that I would end up in some kind of trouble or entangled in a trap that would be impossible to escape.

Armed with my contract from CCTV, I set about seeking advertisers. I traveled thousands of miles from the USA to England, Japan, and Hong Kong to call on potential sponsors. It would be much harder for them to refuse if I were there in person with a big smile and oozing with passion, unwilling to take no for an answer.

Pretty soon, I secured our first major sponsor. Irwin Shane, then Director of International General Foods, sensed the significance of our series in China. Subsequently, his popular Maxwell House Coffee was the first sponsor to buy advertising on "One World." One of their big products, of course, was instant coffee. Coffee? They wanted to sell coffee in a land of tea drinkers? How would we convince the Chinese to drink coffee? I was skeptical but pleasantly surprised by how wrong I could be about what the new Chinese consumer wanted. He, too, believed the Chinese were open to change in many more ways than one. I believe one of the greatest attributes of the Chinese people is their willingness, and readiness, to accept and embrace new ways of life. It is this curiosity and openness that has enabled China to prosper so vastly over the past three decades.

Aspiration and relaxation, that's what they were selling as much as freeze-dried coffee grounds. All the Maxwell House coffee they prepared for China sold out in the first three months.

I then secured another sponsor – Procter & Gamble, the largest advertiser in the world and the owner of some of the biggest consumer brands, including Tide laundry detergent and Wella and Head & Shoulders shampoo. I telexed CCTV of P&G's interest and asked for permission, but they immediately declined. Why? Because they thought P&G was a gambling company, and China did not allow gambling. I patiently explained to them that the "G" in P&G stood for the name of one of the company's founders, James Gamble. Mr. Ed Arzst, then head of International, subsequently became chairman of Procter and Gamble and wanted to visit China. I arranged for him to meet with the head of CCTV to introduce his company. He mentioned to the leaders that advertising is essential because, through such visual marketing, the consumer knows what is available to them – the concept, albeit very new to the Chinese, seemed to resonate with the CCTV team.

Nevertheless, the responsibility of the world I had embarked upon weighed heavily. I felt a tremendous sense of mission to help educate a billion people who had been cut off from the outside world for thirty-five years. The universe had given me the means to inform them about the world in a way they had never seen before. Out of all the thousands of TV journalists across the globe, I thought God chose me for this task. It was a rare opportunity, and I needed to produce each program the best I could. I was constantly and painfully aware that this rare window of opportunity would close if I did something wrong.

For years, I learned to survive – and thrive – under the immense cloak of pressure. I had to take responsibility for every tiny production element, from the finances and wardrobe to the visas, travel timetables, scheduling, and storylines. Once a country and location were confirmed, I would send a producer a week in advance to assist with the organization, often juggling multiple crews in various places at once. However, even when an episode was complete, there was no guarantee it would see the light of day as the approval process through CCTV and Chinese officials was far from an understood science.

Yet somehow, it all just seemed to click. The success of "One World" opened greater access to China for my production team back in the U.S. In 1988, almost two years after the show launch, I was invited to lunch at Zhongnanhai (中南海), the heavily guarded headquarters of the Chinese Communist Party, just West of Tiananmen. The compound's crimson exterior walls rise like swords high into the sky behind stern-faced armed guards who man the gates at all times. Nevertheless, inside, every building and garden has a peaked tile roof in the charming traditional style, and I felt the thrill of being transported back into lifetimes ago.

My host in what is a part of the former Imperial Palace, home to Chinese emperors for centuries, was Hu Qili, the member of the Politburo who had sent me a congratulatory note after the "One World" premiere.

During the multicourse banquet, I asked Hu what places had never been filmed in China.

"Chairman Mao's home," Hu said without hesitation.

Hu suggested we shoot a segment in the former residence of Mao Zedong (毛泽东), right there in Zhongnanhai, the true inner sanctum for the leader who led China from its founding in 1949 until his death there in 1976. To say I was excited to show this place to my audience would be an understatement. It had never been done before, not by anybody – not for

Chinese viewers and certainly not for foreigners.

When CCTV heard I was going to shoot at the fabled home of Chairman Mao Zedong – the fabled writer, the theorist, the revolutionary and the founder of the People's Republic of China – they wanted to piggyback and shoot a separate segment. Still, Hu said no, this shoot was mine alone.

Mao's home rests in a lush garden in the middle of modern China's seat of power. It's called the Library of Chrysanthemum Fragrance (菊香书屋), and while its bookshelves were jam-packed, the rooms are otherwise spartan: a wooden bed, four chairs around a simple square dining table, on which are set simple bowls and chopsticks. On a desk stood the objects of a scholar: a calendar, writing brushes, ink tablets, and paper. Books were piled up on the table beside the bed. They covered a wide range of topics and included many translated foreign-language volumes.

From a reasonably wealthy peasant family, Mao was well-educated and supplemented his learning from an early age with voracious reading and individualized study. He was very curious about the world. He wrote poetry, and his calligraphy, hung there in the residence, is powerful to behold. As I moved slowly through the cottage-like home, poised in the middle of lush greenery overlooking a pond, I couldn't help but wonder how I had come to deserve such a privilege, my soul brimming with gratitude to experience so many "firsts" I could share with many, many more millions who would never have a chance to experience this themselves.

Out of all of "Looking East," a show that aired on as many as 120 channels in the U.S. from 1977-1989, my visit to Mao's home is the episode of which I am most proud. In the decade-plus that I made the show, I would pass through the gates of Zhongnanhai several times to meet Hu or Vice Premier Mr. Tian Jiyun (田纪云). Even my professor's father and homemaker's mother were invited to lunch there with the head of CCTV, the Minister of Propaganda, and the Minister of Radio, Film and Television. For an aging couple that had fled with their small child from Guangxi (广西) in the south at the time of the victory of the Communist revolution, my parents were impressed with how their little American transplant was navigating the northern capital of their much-changed homeland. We all gleefully talked about art and culture and society, although nothing political was ever discussed.

CCTV executives told me that when Hu, one of the seventeen most powerful men in China, invited me and my parents to lunch, the government did not allocate a budget in those days, thus Hu did not have the funds to cover the food expenses, so CCTV paid for it.

"Mr. Kan," Hu asked my father, "Aren't you proud that millions love your daughter?"

"Oh yes!" my father replied. "But she only needs one!"

Everyone laughed. My being single was a hot topic. In Chinese culture, this is known as the "sheng-nv stigma," 剩女 aka "leftover women" whereby single women over 27 are too often caricatured and pressured into marriage to escape the social stain. Thankfully, life in the United States opened up many more possibilities for who and what an untied woman could be. Too many women barter too much to avoid loneliness, or the perceived social stigma. I never allowed myself to be trapped in the pressure vortex of having to get married. My life at that point felt very hectic yet very complete at the same time. I was overwhelmed with work and wasn't on the hunt for love, but I wasn't closed off to it.

One person wanted to set me up with the son of a provincial party secretary. On other occasions, I was introduced to the most attractive son of a military general and to a man from a powerful political family who had graduated from a Japanese university. There was never a dull moment, but none of these would-be suitors appealed to me.

On the odd occasion, I would meet a terrific guy, but then a week later, be off to the other side of the planet for a month or so. Over that time, any chemistry would fizzle out. My work was not a focus of my life; it was the focus.

Many Chinese leaders I met during the late 1980s were humble family men who genuinely wanted to improve people's lives, a notion that pulled at my heartstrings and never let go. Hu Qili whimsically told me of plans to increase workers' wages so they could afford their own apartments.

"Right," I thought to myself in great disbelief. "Why, after decades of telling people where they could live, why are they going to believe that you want them to have their own apartments?"

At the time, urban workers lived in apartments or rooms allocated to them by their government-designated work groups, or danwei (单位). One evening, I was at one such place for dinner, the home of the Vice Premier of China's State Council, Tian Jiyun, another one of the nation's most powerful leaders at the time. I was shocked to see how simply he lived. Beyond the television he used as a part of his job to keep an eye on the work of the Xinhua News Agency (新华社) and CCTV, Tian, and his wife and four children lived without a single luxury. His wife, Li Yinghua (李英华), explained she was excited because they were moving to a bigger apartment.

"How much bigger?" I asked.

"Oh, one more bedroom," Li replied.

I thought to myself, "Only one more?!"

Even today, there is no freehold property ownership in China, but an early 1990s policy that gave people the right to lease and use property for up to seventy years triggered a building boom. Like a vast ocean liner, China began to shift course slowly when the men I met in the optimistic current of the late 1980s tapped the nation's rudder in the right direction. The change they set their sights on, establishing a property market, created a middle class that has not stopped growing since.

But at this juncture of growth and change, when television in China began to include shows such as mine – shows that ended with question marks instead of the exclamation points that characterized programming during the Cultural Revolution – Chinese of all ages, but especially the young, became eager to exercise their newfound knowledge of the outside world.

I needed to establish basic information for each audience and then add nuance. As the producer and host, I was the decision-maker for interviews and editing. I needed to be familiar with the limitations of each country's television landscape and make sure every program's flow was lively and exciting. My commentary always worked best when it was simple. Mixing simple words with real images is a complex and comprehensive art that results in a magical and powerful form of storytelling. I loved every minute.

Someone once asked me about the difference between producing programs about China for the U.S. and programs about the U.S. for China.

"There is no difference," I answered, "because each country is equally ignorant about the other."

Unfortunately, this is still the case today, even though I think, generally speaking, that the Chinese know a little more about Americans than most Americans know about China, and even less since the pandemic, which drastically restricted travel. I'm not referring to the government but to the ordinary, everyday people. To many of my American brethren, China remains an opaque cosmos in and of itself. But the reality is that ordinary Chinese citizens are remarkably interesting and very innovative places with fantastic food and incredibly kind demeanors. Of course, I am a celebrity and have never had a bad experience dealing with Chinese people.

Yet, Chinese people are some of the most generous and accepting human beings. After all these years and all this work, it pains me to think that the exaggerated hate and discourse that permeates U.S. media has led to such anti-Asian sentiment even inside a nation as multicultural and diverse as the United States of America.

PRODUCING ONE WORLD, MAKING HISTORY __

Since I was the boss, ensuring I was always on time was pivotal. I was responsible for paying for the cameraman, the sound man and all the other crew members, thus if I was late, I was wasting my own money – and I certainly could not afford to allow a single penny to slide. Nevertheless, no matter how I tried to remain frugal, there is nothing like a TV production burning through money rapidly.

Many countries where we wished to shoot required a filming fee up-front payment. In Egypt, for example, the cost was $300 per minute, although we negotiated a slightly better price with the assistance of the Chinese Embassy in Cairo. Wherever we traveled, Chinese Embassy staff understood what I was trying to accomplish and were happy to help me coach my Mandarin. Furthermore, some countries restricted the use of copyrighted video and music clips. In Sweden, we wanted to feature a thirty-second clip of atomic bomb tests for which the usage fee was supposed to be $1,500. Swedish officials finally agreed to allow us to use the clips for a smaller price in return for Chinese television audience data.

Ours was a small production company with a tiny staff and tight funding, and no matter where I went, I endeavored to achieve the best bang for the buck. I aimed to spend the least money for the most significant return possible. With no money to rent a professional television studio, I started using my modest apartment in New York as our office. At that time, my place in midtown Manhattan was so small that I had to do much of the work in the bedroom, including video editing, music production and dubbing. The dining table was the desk for our research, scriptwriting, and producer groups. As for lengthy or uninterrupted sleep, that quickly became a rare extravagance. Most of the time, I only got to lie on the bed for a while after the other team members left, and even then, my brain was still running through all the things not yet done.

In short, I took charge of doing everything: I hired people, I was the host, I was the advertising sales manager, and I did all the voice-overs. Occasionally, I became too busy to manage the amount of to-dos on the agenda, and there were not enough hours in the day, so I had to find another narrator. This proved a challenge because there were fewer Chinese people in the United States then, and only a few I encountered had voice-over experience. However, my post-production manager, Anne Yan Zhengan (颜正安), devised a clever idea: hiring Chinese students studying in the United States. Among the people we used for voice-overs were the then-unknown artist Ai Weiwei (艾未未) and the musician and composer Tan Dun (谭盾), both now world-famous. I paid them each $40 per session, quite a lot of money then. And when I saw the stellar performances, it all felt worth it.

We also needed to be ultra-creative and tenacious to succeed at the tasks we set ourselves. While half of our team was shooting on location, the other half, back in my New York apartment, planned out storyboards and concepts, conducted research and drafted the scripts for upcoming shows, and undertook the grueling video editing and post-production work to condense all the material we'd just captured into

15-minute segments ready for broadcast. It always felt like there was never enough time to produce two shows, one in Mandarin and the other in English, every week, yet somehow we got it done. There was no other option than to do.

Television is a complex art form, and I was constantly thinking: "Maybe the music needs to come in two seconds earlier," or "Maybe this sentence needs to be rephrased," or "The camera angle needs to be moved to the left a little bit, doesn't it?" As someone who strives to do her best in everything, I was often riddled with anxiety.

But slowly, I was learning that perfection does not exist. My program was limited by time and budget, and there was no way to explore to my complete satisfaction a complex theme, let alone a whole national culture, in fifteen minutes. I had little choice but to come to terms with the reality of time and instead strive to make it the most insightful quarter of an hour possible.

I was producing the shows for an audience that knew little about the world beyond their immediate bubble, so I needed to choose subject matters to which they could relate, providing an emotional and intellectual foundation to the experience.

In our shows about Egypt, for instance, we highlighted the pyramids at Giza, illuminating the culture's pride in its longevity, which many Chinese could understand on a very visceral level.

I also chronicled how the ancient Egyptians made paper with the papyrus plant, something the Chinese could relate to as paper, known today, was invented in China. In addition, we included a segment about farmers in the Nile Delta, people whose lives might resonate with hundreds of millions of Chinese viewers tuning in from the village television set, and I slept a night on an Egyptian farm to shoot the cotton harvest at dawn. After the episode aired, the Egyptian ambassador in China contacted me to say he had never seen such television about his country and even asked if he could buy the rights to air the show on Egyptian TV stations.

In Denmark, we talked with a husband who cared for his children at home while his wife worked a job outside, an idea unheard of in China then. In Singapore, I filmed an entire segment on that tiny nation-state's creative solutions for housing the poor, which included assistance with job seeking and treating any underlying addictions and illnesses.

In Greece, we stayed on a small island and shadowed fishermen at 3 a.m. to haul in the day's catch. And when we went to Italy, we filmed a part of "Turandot," the only classic Western opera with a Chinese theme – it is set in China and follows the Prince Calaf, who falls in love with the cold and hard-to-reach Princess Turandot – which was performed al fresco at the Baths of Caracalla.

Once my exhausted crew had shot enough footage, I cut them loose to return to the hotel while I stayed on to watch the performance to the end. I will never forget that warm summer night in Rome, watching a Chinese-themed opera under the stars, the magical notes revitalizing every bone in my tired but deeply contented body.

TV AS AN INSTRUMENT OF PEACE _____

It was on that Rome shoot, after much coordination and with the help of many people, including the former mayor of New York, Robert Wagner and Archbishop John Foley putting in a good word on my behalf, that I was invited to film a general audience of Pope John Paul in the open square in front of St. Peter's inside The Vatican. It was July 24, 1985.

My TV crew set up at the center of the square, facing the Pope's podium, and Archbishop Foley came to me in advance to say that the Pope planned to say something significant. I took my seat in the VIP area, brimming with anticipation. As was customary, Pope John Paul spoke in several languages, but all of a sudden, he delivered a long message in English:

"I am happy to welcome a TV crew in Rome to prepare a program for China. And it gives me great joy to be able to, through them, send my warm greetings to the noble Chinese nation. The Catholic Church looks upon China as one great family," he said. "The birthplace of lofty traditions and vital energies rooted in the antiquity of her history and culture. The church is sympathetic to the commitment to modernization and progress in which the Chinese people are engaged. This was the attitude of the famous Father Matteo Ricci when he came into contact with China. I am sure the Chinese who are followers of Jesus Christ, as was Matteo Ricci, will contribute to the common good of their people. With these thoughts, I pray that Almighty God may abundantly bless the Chinese people and their worthy aspiration for progress and peace."

For the first few moments, I could not fully process what I was hearing. Then, as His Holiness continued, I burst into tears, thinking how fortunate I was to do what I believed to be my higher calling: using television as a vessel to bring about peace. Let me be an instrument of peace, I prayed, my head bowed, but my mind raised toward the heavens.

His Holiness finished his sermon and came down to where I sat. He held my hands and said, "Thank you for what you are doing for the Chinese people. Bless you, and the Chinese people. Bless everyone involved in your program."

I was overcome with emotion, nearly breathless. While not technically Catholic, I attended Catholic School growing up and felt deeply connected to Christianity and the institution. All I managed to stutter in reply: "Your Holiness, I am very happy to be here!" To this day, I wish I'd come up with something more meaningful to say. But as tears streamed down my cheeks, I understood – really understood – the power the media possesses as a peacemaker, a force for reckoning, a vessel for healing and positivity.

I often think of this moment when I hear horror stories about the nasty rhetoric that has become synonymous with social media today. Some, especially in the West, bemoan the Chinese government's restrictions and timing controls on the likes of Instagram and YouTube. But from their shoes, I concur that over-exposure to such platforms harms children and adults alike.

The day after the Pope's engagement, all of the Italian newspapers covered the story and published the poignant message from the Pope. It was a big deal, a milestone in the long-term back-and-forth between Beijing and The Vatican about the status of the Roman Catholic Church in China, where it has been banned for decades. It is said that the only organization with a larger membership than that of the Chinese Communist Party (CCP) is the Roman Catholic Church.

I knew the Communist Party would watch me closely as I always contacted the Chinese embassies wherever I planned to shoot an episode. Admittedly, I was apprehensive when the Chinese Embassy in Rome called me the day after the Pope's speech. However, as soon as I heard the gentle tone of voice of the Chinese Ambassador to Rome, I rested easy. He told me he was delighted with the Pope's statement. His Holiness had not made mention of Taiwan, and he said China was one great family – not two, mainland China and Taiwan – a very controversial and sensitive subject even today.

A Ministry of Foreign Affairs representative asked me for the footage, and I agreed to hand it over. What I shot in the Vatican did not air as a part of "One World" on CCTV, but at least my show was not canceled. I was disappointed, but I understood the nature of these decisions was far from my control. Although I was not able to share the Pope's message about China with anybody inside China except the leaders of the CCP, I incorporated the segment into an episode of "Looking East," showing the rest of the world that the head of the Roman Catholic Church was ready to engage China.

In an exercise in flexible thinking, I also managed to air my interview with another influential Catholic on CCTV as a part of "One World." Subsequently, my interview with Mother Teresa of Calcutta remains one of the most profound experiences of my life.

Albanian by birth, this extraordinary woman devoted most of her life to helping the poorest of the poor in Kolkata (Calcutta), India and Italy. I met Mother Teresa in Rome the day before we filmed the Pope, on July 23, 1985. We had the honor of spending the entire day with her. She held my hand throughout the day while visiting orphanages, homes for unwed mothers and hospitals. I remember Mother Teresa's firm touch; her parched, calloused hands and staring into the maze of sun-drenched creases across her face. Vanity or self-care did not grace the to-do list of Mother Teresa. She drew me close and illuminated that the singular devotion of her life was to bring glory to God. You could feel her authenticity, forbearance, and fervor pulsating from her pores, sending chills down my spine.

I asked Mother Teresa where she lived, and she suggested with a gentle smile that we visit her home. It was a nunnery, a sprawling place composed of several large pearl-white buildings and a chapel in one of the corners. As our vans drove up the ramp into the manicured courtyard, many nuns rushed out to welcome her and broke into the most joyous song. It was so moving that we all started crying, including my burly 6-foot-5 American cameraman. Mother Teresa guided us into one of the buildings, and we all sat cross-legged on the floor of one of the rooms while the sisters sat around us. That's where we conducted our interview, seated on the hard wooden floor.

I asked Mother Teresa how she raised the money she used to run so many projects in Calcutta and Rome, and she replied that she never thought of money. She explained that whenever she started a project, somehow, the finances just surfaced. Mother Teresa was so pure and so singular in her life's mission, to help the unfortunate and the deeply downtrodden, and I believe that, in turn, the universe provided whatever she needed whenever she needed it.

I departed that day with the most uplifted mind. Mother Teresa's influence and kind touch stayed with me for a long time. She inspired me to give more in this world because to do so makes life worth living.

We had to be ten episodes ahead of schedule, with one episode sent to CCTV weekly. They then had to complete extensive reviews and approvals, and we had to make corresponding amendments according to their requirements. We were lucky that CCTV did not interfere with the content or format as we explored each country and city, always trying to show something different, featuring topics that would resonate with Chinese viewers. The Western press often asked me if my show was censored, and the honest answer is hardly at all. I believe that I was left alone by CCTV because by not actively interfering, CCTV protected itself from censure from higher-ups in the government. Giving us freedom was CCTV's way of not taking responsibility for the show if something went wrong.

During the whole series, only twice did we make some changes. Once, we were asked to cut footage of topless bathers on a beach in Denmark. We had been cautious to film only their backs, but that much-exposed skin was still too much for China's censors, and we had to take them out. The second time was due to concern over my interview with Mother Teresa. I pre-anticipated that this would raise red flags, yet some of me still hoped that her shining message would be enough to let worries slide.

However, since the Chinese government does not recognize the Roman Catholic Church, it would have been asking for trouble to highlight Mother Teresa's connection to the religious institution. Understanding Beijing's thinking but still devastated at losing the chance to introduce Chinese viewers to this remarkable woman, I pivoted and included the interview with Mother Teresa in an episode I shot in Sweden at the Karolinska Institute. This medical university awards the Nobel Peace Prize each year. I convinced CCTV that it was more important to illuminate that Mother Teresa was a Nobel Laureate who so happened to be a Roman Catholic nun.

The ability to think quickly and creatively is the ingredient that will make or break a television career. While I don't always know where my power in this area came from, it has functioned like a guiding light time and time again in my professional life.

FOR THE RECORD

In 1988, after wrapping the last episode of "One World," I co-produced a one-hour documentary entitled "Journey Through A Changing China (变化中的中国)" with Alvin Perlmutter, an executive who left NBC to become one of the all-time great American public television producers, known for shows such as "Adam Smith's Money World," and "The Great American

Dream Machine."

I set out with Alvin, one of the most brilliant television visionaries I have ever encountered to this day, to record China's unfolding, a society embarking on the monumental economic and social revolution whose results we see in evidence in the powerhouse economy of today. We shot all over China, starting in my birthplace, Guilin (桂林), in the Southwest.

We then went north to Shanghai (上海), Xi'an (西安), and up to Heilongjiang Province (黑龙江省), on the border with Russia. We shot there twice, once in the summer and once in the dead of winter when temperatures can drop to -38C. We were the first foreigners to film the now-famous Ice Festival of Harbin (哈尔滨), whose miles of giant ice sculptures of castles and dragons and sections of the Great Wall gleam under brilliant, colored lights. I remember trying to utter words to the camera, yet in less than a minute, my lips would freeze, and it felt like frost would seep and cement into my bones. We had to work incredibly fast against the elements.

We also were the first to film in a region called Yanji (延吉), home to a large population of ethnic Koreans. We stayed with a Chinese Korean family in their modest and tidy house. We had a blast filming the community elders competing in various events at the Old People Festival.

In another breakthrough act, we were the pioneering foreign film crew to sail the Amur River, dividing China from what was then the Soviet Union. The roads of Heihe (黑河), the old and primitive city on the Chinese bank of the river, were little more than dust and rubble, and our primeval hotel lacked hot water.

Instead, two hulking Chinese men brought boiled water in pails for my bath. Remember, this was at the height of the Cold War, in one of the coldest spots imaginable. Nonetheless, the Russians on the side of the river from which we were barred from crossing seemed equally warm. They waved enthusiastically at us as if delighted by the idea of human contact in the frosted air that felt so close – and yet so far.

Although clad in a thick coat, hat and gloves, my face remained exposed, and my lips gradually froze, generating the strangest feeling of losing my cognition. I tried to finish my standup in front of the camera, describing the ice fishermen at work and people young and old diving into the freezing river for exercise in ordinary swimwear. However, it took many takes to utter something legible enough to make the cut. Eventually, the documentary, sponsored by American Express, aired to great acclaim in the United States.

Senator Daniel Inouye of Hawaii, President Pro Temps of The Senate and third in the presidential line of succession watched the episode, went to the trouble to track me down, and called to say that he was so impressed with the show that he had to call me with his congratulations. As I had with Mike Wallace, I asked the Senator to put his appreciation in writing. These were mementos I wanted to hold close. The highest-ranking Asian American politician of the day went further, entering his accolades into the U.S. Congressional Record on July 27, 1988.

Heilongjiang's governor, Hou Jie (侯捷), later awarded me Honorary Citizenship in a ceremony to which my parents and three sisters, plus a niece and nephew, were invited. We were treated as guests of the state, filling my parents with pride and making it the most marvelous family trip we ever took.

EXCEPTIONAL KINDNESS _____

After the trip, my parents flew back to New York. But soon afterward, my mom complained of severe pain in her spine. We took her to a New York hospital where doctors performed a spinal tap. The following day, her doctor confirmed that she was okay.

"Yes! The test was good," he assured me. "She is cleared to go!"

We went home, relieved, and I decided to spend a weekend in Connecticut. But on Sunday, my sister frantically called to tell me that our mother had collapsed in the bathroom and was rushed to the emergency room. I learned she was in a terrible state, and her leg had turned green as a blood clot in her groin blocked the blood flow. I hurried home, praying I could hold my mother's hand again and reiterate how much she was loved and appreciated.

Doctors performed surgery and undertook endless scans that indicated more clots, including one in the brain that had caused a stroke. We discovered that Mom had been taking the blood thinner Coumadin, however, the doctor had taken her off it and forgot to tell her to start again when he checked her out from the last visit. Her blood thickened into clots that nearly killed her in just a few days. I was so upset and blamed myself for not being more assertive and for being too trusting of strangers. I vowed never again to let a doctor practice without asking many questions. I should have done better.

While Mom was still in emergency, I received a long-distance call from China from the Secretary of the Office of the Politburo.

"We heard your mother had a stroke," Secretary Yang said, his voice cracking with emotion. "Acupuncture is really good for strokes, and we will send a doctor to help your mother. His name is Dr. Jin. He is a famous acupuncturist in China who cares for the Chinese leaders. He will fly in from Beijing in two days."

My jaw dropped. I was floored. I offered to buy the doctor a plane ticket, arrange accommodations and pay for his services, grateful that the best of the best would be coming to treat my mother. Nothing meant more to me than her health.

"No, we have taken care of all that," Secretary Yang quickly responded. "He will stay at the Consulate's guest room. You may want to take him out to dinner once in a while."

The thoughtfulness and generosity deeply touched me. I hung up the phone and started to sob out of gratitude. Dr. Jin treated my mom every day for two months, sneaking into her hospital room to administer acupuncture without the Western medical staff knowing, as it was likely to have caused a clash. Once at home, treating my mom was much easier.

After the stroke, my beloved mother could no longer talk, but she communicated with her expressive and gentle eyes. We credited Dr. Jin with her recovery and were sad to see him go. The only other person I know of for whom the Chinese government dispatched a doctor was the American journalist

Edgar Snow, whose book "Red Star Over China," published in 1937, changed perceptions of the Chinese Communist Party. Then, still, a guerrilla army obscure to the world, his book sympathetically painted the picture of a force with much more to offer.

The People's Republic of China, under the leadership of the Chinese Communist Party, had come a long way since Beijing and Washington established formal diplomatic ties on January 1, 1979. Beijing put to the side the fact that the U.S. – a few weeks later – passed the Taiwan Relations Act, which requires the United States government to help defend Taiwan against attack. Instead, the CCP attempted to continue restoring relations. Deng Xiaoping visited America and donned a cowboy hat at a rodeo in Texas, and the government loaned Pandas, which are only owned by China, to zoos across America. In the mid-1980s, President Ronald Reagan walked hand-in-hand in the rain with Premier Zhao Ziyang (赵紫阳). That picture, to me, was the height of the love fest between my adoptive home and the home of my birth, a diplomatic merger of the two places I revered most in the world.

Relations froze for several years. Such a freeze profoundly and ironically impacted China's future and my future.

From that suspension in diplomatic progress came the rapid growth of private enterprise in China, the development of a property market, and the birth of a consumer market, followed by the emergence of a middle class. This is how China changed by turning the downside of 1989 into a string of upsides.

That year, before the crackdown in Beijing, I hosted a

television documentary for the ABC TV network called "China Walls and Bridges" (中国的墙与桥). We examined China's opening up of religious freedoms after the shutdown of the Cultural Revolution. The country, raised under the tenets of atheism, was beginning to print Bibles – an immense step forward that was not lost on us or our American viewership. In 1989, the show earned us a Daytime Emmy in the Outstanding Special Class Program Area category.

Moreover, a four-part series called "Doing Business In Asia" (如何在亚洲经商), produced for PBS and broadcast in October and November 1990, was one of the most financially successful series I ever did. The governors of Minnesota and Washington proclaimed "Doing Business in Asia Week" when the show premiered, an honor at a time when there was so little television programming about Asia on the U.S. airwaves. For years afterward, the series was sold to business schools and libraries worldwide. One day, years later, a young man approached me in a cafe in Paris to say he had learned a lot in a graduate business school course that showed my episode on how to do business in South Korea.

In those early years of my television career, I traveled endlessly between China and the United States. The work to help teach each country about the other was gratifying yet tiring. Stopping was not an option; my work was still in its dawn. But by the end of the series, my weight had dwindled from a mere 90 lbs. I lived a life of perpetual jetlag. Still, I did not feel it was time to take a break. I won many awards and was recognized by influential members of both governments and supported by audiences on both sides of the Pacific.

With such success, I went on to make more television in China. In 2011, my attempt to bring the "Miss Universe" franchise to Chinese television was met with last-minute resistance from the satellite TV authorities in my parents' province of Guangxi. Unfortunately, the beauty pageant was relegated to an Internet-only audience, which, given its size in China at the time, was easy to consider a win. Sometimes, I'm optimistic to a fault and am reminded that quality does not always mean I will overcome the challenges I face in the way I wish to face them. It is always important to pivot and find the silver linings to be grateful for what we can achieve.

My friend Shelley refers to this as my "glass-half-full optimism," born from a life of constant pivoting and overcoming but refusing the notion of failure. Meeting obstacles is no reason to give up. Today, I have projects in the world that barely resemble the one in which my career started. I don't think anybody today can do what I did in the mid-1980s, which was to break through to a closed, relatively uneducated audience and connect them to the broader world. Maybe this could happen in impoverished markets across Africa, but not in hyper-networked China and certainly not in the media-jaded United States.

The Internet and social media have entirely cannibalized the television audience in the developed world. Even I, who watched "60 Minutes" every Sunday evening because it was so well done, now turn to Google for the hottest segments and skip the rest.

"Looking East" ended its run on the U.S. airwaves on the Discovery Channel in 1989. "One World" stopped on CCTV the same year. It was a beautiful run, but I was ready and relieved to open a new chapter in my life. I am somebody who understands when enough is enough, and I am always excited to dive into new and fresh projects.

With my bare hands and innate tenacity, I pushed through the hardships and tears to reach as many people as possible, pioneering programs that would stand the test of time and impact several generations to come. Nothing was easy, and nothing was handed to me. Every step involved immense stress, sacrifice, ingenuity, and a willingness not to cower and back down. I had no mentors and no path to follow. I was the first carving the way that I could only hope other Chinese and American producers would someday use as a guide to follow, if only to believe what is possible.

In 2018, I visited Chen Hanyuan, the man responsible for greenlighting "One World" at CCTV back in 1986, in an assisted living facility in Beijing. He repeated to me what he'd always said about "One World" reaching China's people when it did, as they were coming out of the Cultural Revolution.

"It was like a fresh wind blowing over a stale land," Chen told me.

While some leaders I met and worked with had already given me and China's people an invaluable gift. This small group of men supported me in creating the conditions that taught me how to make television for China and, in turn, helped to open China's audience to the world from which it had been shut off for decades. They aided me in forming connections with the Chinese people who led me through many adventures, straight to the next ample career opportunity.

In my early TV days, my bedroom was also an editing studio.

Travelling around in Sarawak

With Princess Mahachakri of Thailand in Grand Palace

With an elephant trainer in Thailand

In Padang, I interviewed the then-Prince and future King Abdullah of Malaysia

Interview with Malaysian Prime Minister Mahathir Mohamad

In Malaysia with the mother and wife of the village patriarch

In Malaysia Bornio headhunter village, this was only place for a morning wash

In Singapore with Ah Meng, the famous
Orangutan in Singapore zoo

Filming in Korean DMZ

October 1, 1984, hosted the 35th anniversary parade

In St. Peter's Square, Rome, honored to
meet His Holiness, Pope John Paul

Spent a whole day in Rome with the
divine Mother Teresa

At the Acropolis, Athens, with First Lady
Margaret Papandreou

In Denmark with Queen Margrethe and
Consort Henrik

Interviewed Jacques Chirac in Paris, and
President José Sarney in Brazil

In Tonga, we interviewed the King of
Tonga, Tāufa' āhau Tupou IV

Filming near the pyramids of Egypt

Production team snacking on sugar cane
while travelling

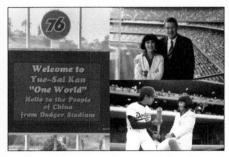

One World episode of baseball in America

One World filming in Hollywood

So happy with Kermit the Frog and the
late Jim Henson

Filming gold diggers in Heilongjiang
Province

Filming in Taiwan

Filming in the countryside of Guangxi Province.

Old Korean folks are feted in an annual festival in northern China

Sheep herders in Beijing countryside

Shopping for my favorite hairy crab in Shanghai

So rare to see foreigners in Hubei, China, those days

Vendor of rabbits, so cute!

With the Imam at the Great Mosque in Xian, built in 742 AD

I was a dash of red in a country without bright colors

HOW I
BECAME ME

In 1989, superstar late-night American television talk show host David Letterman, accompanied by his trademark ear-to-ear smile, asked me on air, "How did you become the most watched person in the world?" My words failed me for a moment. As I considered this profound question, I was inspired to explore the example of close relatives who came before me.

I know only a little about my family's background because my parents never talked too much about their early lives and histories. I do know that my paternal grandfather, Kan Ling-De (靳棱德), was born in the town of Panyu (番禺) near Guangzhou (广州), the capital of Guangdong Province (广东省), in southern China. He was only sixteen when he fled the nest to live in San Francisco with his uncle. So many men from Canton, as Guangzhou was then known to the English colonizers, traveled across the Pacific in the 19th Century to escape poverty. Many went to work in the California gold fields – an outgrowth of the American Dream – and to build the Transcontinental Railroad, whose tunnels through the Sierra Nevada mountains enabled Westward expansion. Without the influx of immigrants, such enormous projects would never have been finished.

From what I could unearth, my grandfather traveled to the "Old Gold Mountain," which the Chinese called San Francisco, at some point in the 1890s as an incredibly young man, barely out of his teens. San Francisco, in those years, served as the base for Chinese people on the West Coast of the United States. Although they risked their lives and limbs to build much of the crucial infrastructure, the United States treated them as though they were second-class citizens for a long time.

It would have taken extreme guts for my grandfather to leave his home to venture off to an alien land far from the familiar. Imagine a young man at 16 who could not speak English, embarking on a journey where he would have only had second-hand knowledge and knew no one on the other side. I am sure he must have been an extraordinarily courageous and interesting person. One relative told me that he dealt in antiques in San Francisco; another said he ran a pawnshop. The pawnshop story is probably true, or a combination of both.

I don't think I was as inspired by my grandfather as much as I found him a source of immense interest. Like me, he picked up his life and surged into the mysterious United States, flushed with curiosity about the possibilities of other places and other lives. It must have been quite an adjustment. He didn't allow the language barrier to hold him back, trailblazing the foundations of a life most of his peers could never have imagined. My grandfather was certainly a pioneer in my family, and a source of my great admiration.

Then, in 1906, a 7.9 earthquake struck San Francisco. It killed 3,000 people and wiped-out 80 percent of the city's buildings. My grandfather's pawn shop held precious items that nobody returned to claim after the devastating quake. In eventually selling them, he made a small fortune. A few years later, my grandfather returned to China, married a young lady with beautiful porcelain white skin, bought land along three streets in Guangzhou, and erected buildings. He named the streets after himself: Lingde New Street (棱德新街), Lingde First

Street (棱德1号街) and Lingde Second Street (棱德2号街). We can still see one of them today. My grandfather subsequently had ten children and gifted each of them a building, including a building on a corner, as a wedding present for my mom. He died in 1938.

Then, in the late 1980s, after I had become famous in China, the government gave us back the building my mother received as a family wedding gift. According to my mother's will, the structure gifted to her by her father-in-law, Kan Ling-De, my paternal grandfather, was to be divided into five parts: one for each of the daughters and a portion for my dad. I asked my sisters if they wanted to own the house, but they were pessimistic about China's future and declined. Thus, I bought all their shares since they were inexpensive then. Several years later, to the envy of my siblings, I sold the whole building for a pretty impressive portion of money, forecasting today a real estate boom that continues all across China. I am not entirely sure where this eye for success came from, but when my intuition knocks, I listen.

Meanwhile, my grandfather's wife – my paternal grandmother – owned expansive farmland in Panyu and my father, the eighth of ten children, was her favorite son. My dad, Kan Wing-Lin, grew up in a wealthy family, and was also handsome, a top-performing student, and a champion swimmer. He played the two-stringed Chinese instrument, the erhu (二胡), and learned to intricately paint in the (LingNan style of ink and color).

My grandmother asked my father to study agriculture so he could one day take over the family farms, sending him off to Guilin (桂林), the capital of neighboring Guangxi Province (广西省), to Guangxi University (广西大学), the most famous in China for its Agriculture and Horticulture department at that time. After graduation, as a result of his good grades, the faculty requested my father remain at the university to teach. This was a great honor in a culture that revered scholars and it was a job that would exalt him in the eyes of his peers and, most importantly, in the eyes of the woman who would become my mother.

My mother, Li Hui-Gen (李惠根), was born in Foshan (佛山), close to Guangzhou and known today as the epicenter for Cantonese opera and lion dancing. But when the Communists came to the city in 1949, they confiscated her family home and converted it into the city government headquarters. My mother's father was an acclaimed physician who loved collecting art and calligraphy. Under orders from the new government to document personal wealth, it took my maternal grandfather four days and nights to make a record of his massive collection.

My mother and father first locked eyes while at a hospital in the city. My mom was studying, and dad was already a professor at Guangxi University. My mother's uncle was being treated at the hospital while daddy was there for a minor operation. As fate would have it, my mother's uncle and my father's beds were placed next to one another. While visiting, my mother noticed daddy's popularity as a ceaseless stream of professors and students came to see him. As a thoughtful and understanding intellectual, he always had admirers. Scholars were highly esteemed in China, and my father would have appeared quite appealing to a young student such as my mother.

After learning that his family resided far away, my mom brought him some homemade soup. That's how their romance began, straight to his heart through his stomach.

I was born at the strike of noon on October 6, 1947, in the middle of China's civil war and the year of the Fire Pig, according to the Chinese zodiac. Pigs, in general, are honest, sincere, and genuine, with hearts of gold. They are called upon when advice is needed and will always lend a helping hand. Fire pigs possess the additional qualities of bravery, quick-wittedness, and great ambition. I don't blush at this description as it matches my character.

My place of birth is Guilin, a city of limestone karst hills on the west bank of the Li River, which borders Hunan to the north. I always felt lucky that I was born there because, for centuries, scholars, writers, and philosophers referred to the Guilin as "the most beautiful place between heaven and earth." And with a name that means "forest of sweet osmanthus," given the extensive mass of fragrant sweet osmanthus trees that adorn the picturesque, there is no more enchanting terrain of which one can enter the world. Guilin's karst topography has long been the favorite subject of poets and photographers. You might have seen it featured as the backdrop of the Hollywood movie "Star Wars: Episode 3 – Revenge of the Sith," set against tendrils of morning mist swirling around the emerald forest and ponds of azure.

My parents named me Yu-Xi 羽西 (Yue-Sai, in Cantonese). Yu means "new feather," like that of a newborn bird, and

"Xi" means "West." All Chinese names have meanings and names which we very much take to heart. My parents wanted me to remember my homeland, to cherish that I was born – the eldest – in the Western part of China, in the spellbinding Guangxi Province.

"She weighed nine pounds," my father wrote in a short memoir he completed for a journalist who asked him to write something about my early years in 1987. "Her hair was dark and thick. She was extremely healthy and cried lustily when she was born. Minutes after her birth, her uncle brought to the hospital two gold bars earned from the sale of some land in the countryside. Her mother was overjoyed to receive the gold, thinking it was a good omen and that her daughter would lead a blessed life."

I only have a couple of such precious letters in my possession today, composed by father's delicate hand, and I treasure them more than anything else.

However, since I was so young, I possess no direct memory of those early years of my life in Guilin. All that remains from that time are a handful of lovely pictures of myself with my parents in exquisite garden settings, where we smiled in front of streams and a bridge as round as a full moon. I returned to Guilin many years ago to seek out my childhood home. A man informed me it had been torn down, and I felt a tiny part of me break. Nevertheless, I packed a little bottle of Guilin soil to bring back with me to the United States as a relic of my beginnings.

I went again sometime later after a dear friend, Fei Fei, told me about an extraordinary, lush garden I had to see. It turned out to be a very calculated lure – one of the most wonderful tricks of my life. The garden's director greeted and led me to a lovely Chinese Dynasty house they called the "prince pavilion," built in the Qing Dynasty, which reined from 1644 to 1911. The home was worn by the passage of time, yet I could immediately tell it was incredibly elegant. The director urged me to walk over to a large stone plague erected in front of the home. The inscription read: "The Prince Pavilion, Once the Home of Yue-Sai Kan."

Imagine the goose pimples that prickled down my spine. I wanted to take a close look inside, but it was locked. The house had been left dormant for a long time. As I glanced around at the cobblestone path and pond overlooking the misty mountains in the distance, I could finally understand the fuzzy black-and-white childhood pictures of myself in the yard with my mother and alongside my parents in front of a moon-shaped bridge. Those pictures were taken in this gorgeous garden, the famous and succulent oasis of green and life famously known as "yan shan yuan," which refers to the first garden in Guangxi Province that surrounded me. The garden is considered one of the finest landmarks in Guilin, and many scholars and celebrities have visited or resided there over recent decades.

"Yue-Sai was our first daughter," my father wrote in his letters to a journalist about me before he died. "She was bright, healthy, lovable, and lively. Naturally, we cherished her as the apple of our eye. There is an old saying, ' You can see a person's whole life when they are three years old. ' 三岁定八十。Yue-Sai was small, cute, charming and everyone loved her."

As the armed struggle heated up between China's Nationalists and Communists, both trying to regain control of the country after the defeat of the occupying Japanese in the Second World War, my parents moved us from Guilin to Guangzhou to the safety of my paternal grandfather's house. We stayed nearly one year in that house, in the home of a man who'd been to America and back and was rich with the experience of survival against steep odds. Whether or not those stories were told openly, the knowledge of his courage to take a risk, and the possibility of reward from such risk, would have instilled my parent's courage. Surrounded by that bravery, I flourished.

"We lived on the second floor," my father wrote. "Yue-Sai wouldn't stay at home alone and sneaked out to the streets all day long. Every morning when I woke up, she'd already be tiptoeing down the stairs."

My father always knew I would never follow the well-worn path into a conventional life, and that I was destined to live life counter to the societal grain.

"She talked about many topics, and it was rare that a kid so young was so funny, mature, and eloquent. The couple next door doted on her and said she would be a special girl when she grew up, thanks to her white, chubby face and excellent talker. She had a unique personality, curious and proud. She was outgoing and loved to play with the boys."

The Communist Army took Canton from Chiang Kai Shek (蒋介石)'s Nationalists in April. On October 1, 1949, days before my second birthday, Mao Zedong (毛泽东) proclaimed the establishment of the People's Republic of China in Beijing, in the north. My parents, uncles and aunties became overwhelmed with fear over the civil war. They thought that Canton was a ticking time bomb, and they needed to escape before it was too late.

MIGRATION TO HONG KONG

There were only two options to migrate from China in those days: Taiwan or Hong Kong. My parents set their sights on Hong Kong, believing that living under British rule would be better than living under the authority of CCP adversary Chiang Kai Shek in Taiwan.

Hong Kong was then a backward colonial port town. However, my parents and thousands of other refugees still sought refuge there, perhaps whimsically, or intuitively, hoping it would metastasize into a land of opportunity.

My parents left everything they had worked for and loved behind, taking only what they could carry – a few clothes and family keepsakes – plus my almost four-year-old self onto a rickety boat bound for an unknown land. Many Chinese swam to Hong Kong or paid smugglers to sneak them in. We were among the last ones to leave China for Hong Kong. After that, the CCP ordered the borders closed.

I don't remember much about those early days, except that everyone in Hong Kong seemed thin and hardworking and in hindsight, desperately impoverished. My parents were, too, forced to start over with almost nothing, spending days and nights working for whatever meager income they could garner. Only I never understood what poor meant back then. This was all I knew, the immigrant existence, and I had no comprehension of what a life filled with riches could be.

It is hard to envisage how difficult it must have been for my parents to make that trip. The boat, crammed with nervous refugees, could not have been comfortable in the searing Southeast Asian heat. Going through Hong Kong customs must have been as nerve-wracking as it was terrifying. After lining up for hours that for many stretched into days, the officers could have turned them away for any reason, leaving them nowhere to call home except the open seas.

But my parents picked up their lives and left with little more than hopes and dreams and pushed through every obstacle. This experience of starting anew must be akin to those encountered by those who went through Ellis Island in New York, holding on to an absolution that something better existed. The most incredible part of my parents' journey of hardship and rebuilding, at least to me, is that they never once complained about it to us children. I learned this unique attitude of acceptance from them. If something is unpleasant or life throws you a wicked curveball, don't talk about it; instead, look for solutions and a better future ahead

Sometimes, people accuse me of forgetting or glossing over unpleasant events in my life. It's not that I forget. It is that I have learned to push the misfortunes through a filter in my mind that softens sharp edges, freeing me of the burden of developing a grudge. In the end, harboring hard feelings only hurts the bearer.

The first Hong Kong home I remember was on the ground floor of a non-descript government-subsidized apartment building on Po On Road (保安道) in Kowloon (九龙). We lived there until I was fourteen. The home was decent, with a small backyard for which we could play, and offered us a slight sense of dignity despite our low status as immigrants in a British-colonized society.

At the same time, we operated a working farm in the New Territories, a rural area to the north of Kowloon, where we lived part of each year while I was in primary school. I boarded at school during the week and rode a bus home to the farm on weekends. From age eight to twelve, I was separated from my family during the week and reunited with them on the weekends. Strangely, I never felt homesick. Boarding school taught me a sense of stoicism and independence, yet I cherished the fact that I could be with my family on weekends, wrapped in a rural landscape that felt like a kind of nirvana on earth.

At the farm, we raised the loveliest little chickens and grew beautiful flowers such as hibiscus. We brought to life the sweetest fruit trees, such as papayas, dragon eyes and lychees. Today, I hold dear the pictures of me and my sister Brenda, born one year after we arrived in Hong Kong, taken in our sprawling vegetable fields. And while I couldn't swim, I enjoyed playing in the water of the stream running through our land. On the weekends, my mother would sell chickens at the nearby farmer's market. My parents did whatever they could to support our family, finding the most creative ways to ensure there was enough food on the table and everyone we could ever want and need as small children.

My mother gave birth to two more girls, Vickie and Yu-San. I was the eldest of the four sisters. We ate traditional Chinese food at home but, in my parents' encouragement of adventure and education, they gave me a little pocket money to spend at the food stalls nearby where hawkers sold delicious snacks and small dishes that smelled of sweetness and spice. This gifted me with a lifelong diverse palate. In that, and in every other way, my parents were most generous. As the eldest, I received a little more money than the others, but I always shared it with my little sisters.

The separation from my family during the week made coming home on weekends ever more special, and I am eternally grateful for the boarding school years, which fueled my sense of self-reliance and autonomy. I learned early on to live and solve problems independently with courage and curiosity. In addition, my parents taught me and my sisters to think for ourselves and stand on our own two feet, and to never let ourselves be victims of circumstance. Even though we were poor, we never felt that we were underprivileged. We may not have had a Rolls Royce and or designer clothes or a fancy mansion to call home, but my sisters and I were blessed not only with love, but with every opportunity to make something of ourselves in this life.

As the eldest child at home, I had my own room with a bunk bed, and when my best friend Connie Chen came to stay, she slept up top. It was a small but well-lit space, with one of my father's cherished paintings on the wall. His paintings were all traditional Chinese natural themes and his use of color was always subtle, whether flowers or a bird on a twig, a couple of fish in water, or a praying mantis on a bamboo stalk, they are always colorful but with subtly – and they were light and exceptionally beautiful. All the birds and insects came alive under his skillful eye and brush stroke. My father's flowers and sentient beings looked authentic, as if you could reach through the canvas and stroke them – the magical product of his dedicated horticultural training.

Next to the window sat my wooden desk with a tiny lamp. I spent most of my time there studying and gazing out into the changing seasons when I was at home. A large wooden clock sat on top of a credenza between two mustard-yellow sofas in the living room alongside an upright piano.

My childhood teemed with love, even if circumstances were not always easy. In 1956, when I was nine years old, I was infected with the deadly disease diphtheria and subsequently riddled with fatigue, chills, and struggling to breathe, before the vaccine common today was prevalent in Hong Kong. I spent five weeks in one of the city's most equipped public facilities, Queen Mary Hospital. The illness was terrifying because the disease was very contagious. My parents were not allowed to visit my bedside. I still remember their fearful faces in the tiny window outside my room, where they were allowed to watch me for small increments of time. They brought me my favorite treat, imported grapes, despite their being really expensive and considered a luxury at the time. Whenever I see grapes now, I recall my parents' soft faces in that tiny aperture in the wall, and I am flooded with their love and generosity.

At the height of the illness, doctors warned my parents that

I probably would not survive. Yet somehow, I defied the odds and made it through. Much later, my father reminded me that it took ten months to make a full recovery. Perhaps it was all for the greater good: "One who survives a great disaster is destined for good fortune," my father later wrote about the incident.

Despite our low economic status, my parents gave us girls everything they could. If something was needed, they made sure we somehow received it. We were a family that loved deeply and cared intently for one another unconditionally.

My father taught at a high school and later joined the Hong Kong Department of Education as an inspector. Meanwhile, my mother always exercised an entrepreneurial flair, unique at the time. She and a few friends she played mahjong with pooled their monthly money and invested in the Hong Kong Stock Exchange. The pot kept growing, and if one of them needed extra funds, she could sell out her share and take what she needed. Soon, my mom moved into property investments, resourcefully diversifying and teaching me good money habits by example.

My mother and father had very defined ideas about our upbringing. They insisted that we sisters got along and did not tolerate us fighting and arguing. It was imperative to them to know that after they were gone, we could rely on each other. My parents cautioned us never to buy anything on credit and always to remember everything anyone has done to help us. My mother always said if someone showed us an act of kindness, we should repay them twofold. The tenants of humility and graciousness were constantly instilled in us, principles that lie at the foundation of the charity work that would later become a prominent portion of my life.

My parents discovered I possessed a natural talent for music, singing and dancing when I was around six years old, observing me move around the house always on the beat. I begged for the chance to learn more and was struck with a desire to learn to play this grandiose construction they called the piano. My parents hired the best female piano teacher they could find. Every year, I participated in the British Royal Music Piano Examination, and I passed all seven grades by the age of fifteen. My piano teacher, Mrs. Wang, entered me into competitions, and I always won. I still remember how she pridefully boasted to our neighbors about my wins, wins that came even though I didn't practice as much as I should have.

At the beginning of my musical journey, we did not have a piano at home, so we had to rent time on our neighbor's piano for me to practice. Each practice session was supposed to last one hour, but I often adjusted the clock forward half an hour without my mom ever finding out. At that time, I yearned to go outside to play and felt cooped up in a small room with stained keys and notes and the demand for concentration.

However, my last piano teacher in Hong Kong was a well-known Russian named Harry Orr. This small, white-haired man was filled with sassy jokes and made each lesson fun. He taught me how to make a dancing doll using a handkerchief, a trick I still employ to impress kids. Mr. Orr's lessons were undoubtedly expensive, but my parents would sacrifice whatever they could to ensure we got the best. Mom would pick me up from school in a white Volkswagen to take me to my lessons with Mr. Orr every week, and for the first time, I could not wait to sit beside him in front of that illustrious instrument, wishing the hour would never end.

My parents never forced me to study or do anything I didn't want to, yet their support and confidence helped me develop my hobbies and interests. That doesn't mean they spoiled me. When my interests and hobbies conflicted, they offered advice and allowed me to decide. For example, at one point, I was so busy attending ballet classes and piano lessons that my mom finally put her foot down and told me to choose the one I wanted to learn the most. After some deliberation, I packed away my little ballet tights and blush shoes. To reconcile my anguish, my mother gently explained that I could make a living by teaching piano even when I was old. Sure enough, later on, I supplemented my income during college by teaching kids piano.

My parents also warned us not to spend money on useless things. They cautioned against five-cent chewing gum because it was terrible for my teeth and inelegant. On the other hand, if I wanted Beethoven's piano pieces, they would find the money to buy the record, no matter the cost. And every weekend, my parents took us to a restaurant. This was usually Chaozhou cuisine (潮州菜), a seafood meal on one of the outer islands accessible via a ferry ride from Hong Kong Harbor, or we went to a vegetarian food in a nearby Buddhist temple. As the adage goes, "the stomach has memory," which makes sense to me as my favorite foods still are those I ate in Hong Kong – especially wonton noodle soup or fish ball rice noodles with spicy sauce and vinegar. These were dishes worth sneaking out of school for, and I would sometimes slip into a little restaurant nearby to fill my stomach. Other times, our housekeeper, Little Piano, one of the sweetest women I would ever know, brought them home to keep as midnight snacks.

My father sometimes reminded me that I was a little naughty as a kid and often slithered out to play with the local boys. Once, a car hit me when I was walking home from school, sending me to the hospital for ten stitches to close a gash above my left eye. If the cut from the fall were just a tenth of an inch lower, I would have lost my vision. The scar awakens the memory of how lucky I am, reinforcing the notion that someone above is watching over.

But on many occasions when I did something wrong or disobeyed my parents, a feather duster with a bamboo handle emerged from the dark depths of the kitchen closet. I always knew why, and a light smack over the rear typically ensued.

Thinking back, their approach to discipline set guidelines on how to live. The beatings were never terrible and proved helpful in setting boundaries and enforcing life lessons. Although I chose not to have children of my own, I passionately believe that children need to be given limits, and to understand limitations and the consequences of veering wrong when there is a right. It is almost funny to think that a feather duster, of all things, was my parents' disciplinary tool. I can't quite understand why people today think it is so wrong to issue a mild physical punishment when a child knowingly exhibits unruly behavior. The measured but not severe pain inflicted was a perfect reminder not to repeat the mistake.

My father often pointed out that for someone of my young

age, I had amassed quite the abundance of friends, and when I wasn't engaging with others, my strong sense of curiosity kept me busy. Once, my father bought me a toy fish, and in less than an hour, I had dismantled it, intent on discovering what was inside. Rather than scold me, my parents encouraged my curiosity and spirit of exploration. Recently, someone asked me what I felt was the most crucial attribute to living an interesting life.

"Curiosity," I answered without hesitation.

When you no longer have curiosity, you're no longer the driver of your education; your life is over.

The two schools I attended in Hong Kong were the Heep Yunn Primary Girls School (协恩中学), an Anglican school where I boarded Monday to Friday, and then, in high school, the Maryknoll Convent School, which was Catholic. They were both girls-only, making my adolescent years rather simple. The only contact we girls at the Maryknoll Convent School (玛利诺修院学校) had with any boys took place when the students from Lasalle College next door joined us to sing under the watchful eyes of the nuns who taught us.

My parents sent me to these schools not because of their religious affiliations but because they were considered the best girls' schools in Hong Kong. My parents always ensured we got the best of everything, and education was paramount for them.

"After she graduated from primary school, she was admitted by Maryknoll Convent in Hong Kong, which was not far away from our home," my father wrote. "From then on, Yue-Sai made huge academic progress, especially in English."

At Maryknoll, I was Sister Rose Virginia's little pet and was chosen to be the school prefect, which is a student class leader, carrying out her orders among my peers. It was at Maryknoll that I also learned basic etiquette. When we saw a nun approaching, we stopped to say, "Good morning, Sister." Or if a sister was descending a staircase we were climbing, we stopped and let her pass. No respectable young woman ever chewed gum. There was a wealth of rules and regulations, but learning and executing them made me more of a lady.

"Her unique independence and strong personality were formed when she was a kid," my father said of me. "Once she had decided to do anything, she would just go for it and do it perfectly. As parents of all our children, we were most worried about Yue-Sai because she was always the most adventurous, doing what we thought were crazy things. I was always afraid she would be so disappointed if she didn't achieve her goals."

MOTHER

My mother, Li Hui-Gen, always wore simple cheongsam (旗袍) of high-quality fabric and stitchwork with matching purses and shoes. Her skin was smooth, her hairstyle a simple silky black bun, and, most memorably, she always carried this fresh scent of cleanliness.

My mother's influence in my life is foundational. She was exceedingly kind and spoke to us in soft, rhythmic tunes of Cantonese. My mother was very ladylike and never raised her voice, even when my sisters shrilled at the top of our lungs.

To my young eye, my mother seemed like an ethereal figure, an angel, who calmed my soul when I cried and kissed away the hurt when I tumbled to the earth and needed a gentle hand to guide me back onto my feet. My mother was always there when I needed her, and even in the times when I did not realize that I did.

Before my parents moved to Hong Kong, my mother asked one of my father's sisters, who was relocating ahead of our family, to hold on to a few pieces of her jewelry for safekeeping. When my mother arrived in Hong Kong and went to pick up these heirlooms, my aunt shrugged and said, "What jewels? I never received any jewels from you."

The whole family knew the truth, yet, through the years, my mother always treated my aunt very well and never brought up the issue again. Learning how big and forgiving my parents' hearts could be served as a profound lesson. If someone did something like that to me today, I don't know how I would be able to look at them ever again. But my mother seemed the impeccable human form of Grace Incarnate.

At our Po On Road home in Hong Kong, someone we called "Uncle Zhou" lived with our family for a while. I thought he must be a relative, however, much later I learned he was just a friend of my parents whose business had failed. He had nowhere to live, and my parents invited him to live in our home as he put himself back together again. Uncle Zhou stayed for two years. Whenever someone needed assistance, my parents were there to offer a warm hand.

One of the people my parents supported the most was my mother's maid, Little Piano. She traveled from China to

Hong Kong with our family and lived with us from my earliest memory, helping my mother with cooking, cleaning, and caring for me and my three younger sisters. I didn't know much about Little Piano's life before she joined us, except that she came from a family so destitute that they couldn't afford to keep her, so they sold her to my mom's sister as a servant girl. Little Piano always kept her dark hair short, and possessed a beautiful wide smile that gave me immense comfort as a small girl.

When my parents married, my aunt gave Little Piano to my mother as a wedding gift, tasked with serving my mother for the rest of her life. Though slavery in China was abolished as a legally recognized institution in 1910, the practice continued until much later, at least till the 1950s. Only Little Piano was not a slave to us but an integral member of our family. She did not know her family name, so she took our family name. Through the years, Little Piano worked hard, was extremely loyal, and we all adored her and could not have imagined life without her presence. One day, in 1959, Little Piano came to my mother and told her that she had fallen in love with a farmhand who worked on our farm in the New Territories and asked permission to marry him. My mother not only agreed but also cried with joy and gave Little Piano a large dowry to start her new life.

Before my mother passed away, she told us that she expected us all to watch over and take care of Little Piano. We did. Little Piano died on June 7, 2018, and through shattered hearts we all chipped in for her funeral. It was the least we could do. To this day, my sister Yu-San, who lives in Hong Kong, keeps in remarkably close touch with Little Piano's children, and when any of us are there, we always have lunch with them and with her grandchildren.

My mother influenced me and my sisters through her kindness, gentleness, and common sense. However, I also clearly remember her saying that women must be financially independent to avoid marrying a wealthy man. This fundamental lesson served me well in later years. Since my mother was versed in fiscal management, she always made us feel that we had enough money and never needed to worry about where the next meal would come from. My mother taught us the actual value of money and how to use every penny wisely. When we were in Hong Kong, she invested in real estate, and later, when I was ready to go to college in the United States, my mother sold a property to finance the cost. She did the same when my three younger sisters needed money to go abroad. I learned a lot about managing my finances from her, along with the gift of generosity, qualities that have been a lifetime benefit for me. My mother was my first home, my connection to the earth.

After her stroke in 1987, my mother was never the same. She required full-time care and was in the hospital for the last two months of her life. Yet my mother remained an incredibly proud woman. Whenever she knew a friend was visiting, she asked the nurse to help her comb her hair and put on lipstick. She always looked as good as she could to show respect to her guests and was elegant to the end.

My mother, the beautiful Li Hui-Gen, died on November 13, 1994. I am so grateful to have been raised under the tutelage of her great wisdom.

"You are young, and it seems like you are successful, but your life can only be judged by what you do with your last twenty years," she often told me. "In those twenty years, are you healthy, happy, and financially independent? Are you surrounded by people who love you and who you love? If you can say yes to these questions, then you have lived a successful life."

Furthermore, my mother always stressed to me the importance of remaining healthy enough so that you do not spend your twilight years in great pain or confined to a bed, and to have accumulated enough wealth to sustain a roof over your head without hardship and stress, enough food to fill your stomach and to cover all medical expenses without dependence on others. My mother believed that we all should take responsibility for our lives and outcomes.

Indeed, the older I get, the more I fully understand all of what my mother meant. This acumen was her most profound advice, words that have guided me daily for my time on earth. My quest for financial independence started very young, and I continue to eat healthily, exercise frequently and surround myself with all the wonderful human beings in my life today. Some people become very rich and successful but die lonely, bitter, and miserable. In the end, the quality of our lives hinges on the depth of our friendships, and I have never discarded the importance of kindness and appreciation for the incredible beings in my orbit.

FATHER

My father, Kan Wing-Lin, taught me to appreciate the beauty of color. As a painter of the Lingnan school, a storied style of painting founded in the 19th century in Guangdong Province with a focus on complex strokes and bright coloring influenced by impressionism, he created traditional Chinese paintings that also borrowed techniques from Western watercolor and oil painting, boldly using vibrant and subtle colors in his work. My father loved nature, and his college study of agriculture and horticulture fueled him a comprehensive understanding of topography and the natural world.

As a small, wide-eyed girl, I often watched him paint, asking questions as he worked. While continuing to grace the canvas with an intricate blend of color, my father explained how just one single brush stroke could create both dark and light and how the amount of ink he used in a stroke determined if the objects painted were closer or further off. My father showed me that his bamboo stalks were made in rapid single strokes, as was his fish. I was amazed at the results, as if magic had been performed. Furthermore, I admired his discipline. If the last stroke of a painting were even the slightest bit off, he would tear the whole thing up and do it repeatedly until he was satisfied. My father demonstrated to me what striving to improve and striving for perfection looked like, along with the self-awareness required to achieve such greatness.

In 1979, both my parents fell sick while all four daughters lived in the United States. We felt helpless, eight thousand miles away, as the people we adored most in the world struggled to regain their health, and we couldn't help them. My sisters and I could not care for them across the ocean, so when they were well enough to travel again, we brought them to live in New York City. It was not easy for my parents to leave their friends and belongings behind and once again settle into a foreign place. Moreover, my mother was not thrilled by the thought that she would have to do the cooking, a pastime she never really enjoyed. But when she arrived, she amazed us all. Before mom left Hong Kong, she took a comprehensive cooking course. She delighted us with exquisite dishes like braised chicken and chestnut, mushroom and sea cucumber, and spare ribs simmered to perfection. But while my father spoke good English, my mother did not. So, before leaving for America, she also took English classes to improve her language skills.

Once in New York, my dad devoted himself to his art and to the promotion of Chinese culture, in the way of exhibiting time-honored Chinese painting. My father's work has been displayed in many art exhibitions, prompting the ABC and NBC television networks to interview him. A number of famous galleries in the United States, including the Hammer Gallery in New York, the Hartman Gallery in Dallas, and the Shogun Gallery outside Washington, D.C., staged personal exhibitions of my father's works.

As a renowned master of traditional Chinese painting abroad, he was the first overseas Chinese invited by the Chinese Ministry of Culture to hold an art exhibition in China. In August 1981, his touring exhibition caused a sensation in

Beijing (北京), Shanghai (上海), Guangzhou (广州), and Nanjing (南京), with scores of people falling in love with his graceful brush strokes and vivid ability to bring visions to life. And then, in what would mark the first joint venture hotel in Beijing, the Jianguo Hotel (建国饭店) invited my father to create five paintings for permanent display. One of them, a large-scale landscape, was hung in the lobby, in prime position over the reception desk.

In my eyes, my father was the consummate gentleman. We all noticed and valued his thoughtfulness towards my mother – always helping her before she even needed to ask, and the selflessness he demonstrated toward us children. As his illness worsened during later years, we were fortunate to find a great nurse from Sichuan province, Lisa, who lived with him and cared for his every need. Lisa had been a "barefoot doctor" (赤脚医生) in China, tending to the sick in remote villages, thus she had extensive knowledge of alternative medicines. Lisa was hardworking and especially gifted at working skillfully with minimal medical information and technology. Barefoot doctors were the saviors in many rural parcels of China, where there weren't enough formally trained physicians operating. Given her short but stocky and strong build, Lisa was able to lift my father off the bed in a single huff.

Lisa quickly became an especially important person in my dad's life. But more than that, she was a very important person in all our lives. Lisa was genuinely fond of my father. To this day, she goes to the cemetery to visit my father more often than my sisters or I do. Lisa remembers that dad was always kind and gentle. Unlike some ailing, older people who tend to take their pain out on their caregivers, my father, she says, was never once rude to her. Even when he could no longer get around without a wheelchair, my father would still meet me for lunch in a suit complete with a tie, pocket handkerchief, and sometimes a hat – ever the beautifully dapper man even in the waning twilight of his life.

I was the only daughter beside the lauded Kan Wing-Lin when he passed away on February 7, 2007, in his beloved Manhattan home. He was 91 years old. I held my father's hand the whole time and felt his heat slowly escape my palm. I squeezed his hands tight, trying to warm him again because I still had more to say about how much we loved him and how thankful we were for his sacrifices for our family. We would never have come so far if it were not for this great gentleman. Even right through to his dying days, my father donned his best suit and tie just to come to myself. It was his unfailing sign of respect to himself and to others, a dignity that nobody could take away from him.

I sat there for some time after his soul left us, holding on to the sleeping shell of this incredible life, recognizing that in the flash of time, a part of my heart had passed, too – something I could never bring back.

I will forever be my father's daughter. There isn't a day that goes by that I don't think of my father and miss him with everything I have to give. and one of his teachings in particular – one that has stuck with me and influenced every facet of my being. My gratitude goes out to him for all the knowledge he shared.

"Always be the first to land on the moon," my father once

told me. "Because no one will ever remember the second."

His powerful words influenced every significant step I took in my life. After all, I was the first to produce a TV series about Asia, the first to do a broadcast for both CCTV and PBS, the first American to do a TV series on China Central Television and the first to start a foreign-owned cosmetics company in China. Furthermore, if I look at the books I have written, most of them were the first of its kind. Almost everything I have done in my life was a first, right down to the advertising model to fund programs. Perhaps in my own way, I did pioneer my way to the moon – and back – many more times than one.

SISTERS

Just before my father died, in the last letter he wrote – at the request of a journalist doing a story about me – he noted, "Although I had nine brothers and sisters, we did not have a great relationship. They were sometimes jealous and selfish and sometimes argued about money. As a result, I taught my kids to be the opposite. Luckily, this never happened with my four daughters, which makes me blessed and proud."

The words and deeds of our parents taught us one thing above all else: that we sisters must always love and protect and help each other through thick and thin and the ups and downs that life projects.

I was not incredibly close to my younger siblings throughout my youth in Hong Kong, as I lived at a boarding school and only saw my sisters on weekends and during the summer holidays. But being the eldest child in a Chinese family comes with privileges and obligations – more critically, the inherent responsibility to take care of your parents and younger siblings.

Brenda (羽东) with her short hair and immaculately arched eyebrows is the second oldest. She is a mature, extremely kindhearted single mother with two intelligent, wonderful kids. Jaimie, her daughter, works in Kuala Lumpur for her father, and her son – my beloved nephew – Jamieson Chew also lives in Kuala Lumpur with his gorgeous Taiwanese wife Karen and works for his father, Sing Chew. Then there is their son, Brenda and Sing's grandson, Adrien, who is the world's cutest boy and the youngest of our family. Although Sing and Brenda are no longer married, he remains utterly charming and a generous member of our family. Sing works harder (and drinks more Coca-Cola) than anyone I know!

Every year, I take time to be with them, whether in Kuala Lumpur or New York. As we live oceans apart, we make sure to carve out lots of time for fun when we do get together, enjoying meals and scouring the city.

Number three is Vickie (羽平), who dons a classic bob and a wide smile, is the most energetic of all my sisters. She is very socially active and constantly travels the globe. Vickie has many homes and many friends worldwide; thus, it is never dull to be in her presence. Vickie talks fast and thinks fast. If she wants to understand something, she will labor tirelessly to get to the bottom of it. Almost thirty years ago, Vickie remarked that she loved Italy's culture, history, and lifestyle. So, she learned

Italian and moved to Rome. Today, she speaks perfect Italian, albeit with a Cantonese accent. I admire her quick learning ability, and her ability to stay ahead of the curve in everything from fashion to medical trends. Everyone who knows Vickie loves her for her charm, kindness, generosity, and humor.

IN THE WORDS OF VICKIE KAN

I never call Yue-Sai by her name, but rather always address her with the respectful Cantonese term for elder sister, Dai Ga Tse (大家姐). As the firstborn, she was always our role model. She always dresses city-girl chic, and because of her, I love fashion, design, and beauty and appreciate handsome men. Her life has always been flowery, filled with rich, famous, and handsome suitors chasing after her. It seemed like her destiny.

I married a boy I met at UC San Diego. Our parents could not attend the NYC wedding, so Yue-Sai hosted our wedding. First, she arranged for a famous judge to marry me in her apartment, then threw us a big and lovely banquet in Shun Lee Palace in Manhattan.

When our mom passed away, we four sisters sat around a table with a bunch of her jewelry from a safety deposit box. Yue-Sai told the three of us just to take whatever we wanted. None of us made a move; we just cried. Yue-Sai then commanded: "Close your eyes, put your hand into the jewelry and take anything your hand touches." That was how we split my mother's jewelry together, and fairly.

In 1990, I suffered a near-death experience on the ski slope in Aspen, where I almost broke my neck. I looked terribly pale, semi-conscious from painkillers when Yue-Sai came in. She took one look at me and ran to the toilet to vomit. When she had recovered, Yue-Sai returned and sat beside me for a long time. I was touched. She drove two hours daily to be with me for about a week.

In December 2018, Yue-Sai was in Hawaii, and I was in New York having a regular health checkup when I received the terrible news that I had breast cancer. It was a frightening time. My big sister asked me what she could do for me, and I told her I needed to get an appointment to see the top breast surgeon in New York as soon as possible. She hung up and called me back almost immediately. Yes, she had arranged my appointment for the very next day. Typical of Yue-Sai, she was always ready to use her extensive connections to help.

Sister number four is Yu-San (羽姗) – we call her San-San and she will forever boast a thick head of raven hair and porcelain skin. She was a big-time banker at one time, and we all gave her the reins to take charge of some of our stocks and bank accounts. Then, San-San fell in love and married a fabulous Hong Kong man named Lincoln Leong, a prominent real estate developer, developing more than 40,000 apartments in Vancouver. San-San willingly and wholeheartedly took on the role of a devoted homemaker after their son Alexander's learning challenges demanded all her attention. San-San now lives in Hong Kong most of the time and works with many non-profit organizations, enjoying a fulfilling, exciting and meaningful life. We don't often see each other in person, but frequently connect via video chat. Whenever I go to Hong Kong, I stay with her family. When I was ill on one visit, San-San was as anxious as a mom, checking on me every few minutes, giving me pills and water and ensuring her chef cooked me my favorite meals. I slowly regained health. She pays great attention to health issues; we do acupuncture therapy together.

IN THE WORDS OF YU-SAN KAN

My childhood memories of Yue-Sai are vague because I was only four when she left Hong Kong to study in the United States. We were very proud that she went abroad because, in those days, it was a big deal in the eyes of our friends. Due to our age gap, Yue-Sai has always been less of a sister to me and more of a guardian and a nurturing figure, as our parents entrusted her with the responsibility of looking after all her siblings early on. Nevertheless, there is one incident that stands out clearly in my memory.

I was four when I started kindergarten. The responsibility of taking me up the hill to school and picking me up afterward fell on Yue-Sai's shoulders. One day after school, she didn't show up. Reluctantly, I made it down the school steps by myself and waited by the roadside. I remembered that mom warned me not to cross the street by myself. I waited and waited, not knowing what to do. Pretty soon, a young girl approached me and took me across. Back home, Yue-Sai was embarrassed as it had slipped her mind because her best friend was visiting.

Our mother was not amused, and I distinctly remember the apologetic look on Yue-Sai's face and felt sorry for her and how upset she was that she had let her responsibilities falter.

During our fourteen years apart, Yue-Sai wrote home often, advising on our future education and career plans. She brought two of my sisters to the United States to study, but the U.S. consulate turned down my application for a student visa. I cried and cried. Then Yue-Sai sprang into action! She managed to get Senator Ted Kennedy to write a letter to support the application. When we returned to the consulate, the Consul-General received us, and my visa was approved immediately. He asked Yue-Sai to say something nice about him to the Senator.

Yue-Sai was the first of our immediate family to leave Asia. In choosing America, she followed in the footsteps of her great-grandfather and great-great uncle. Fourteen years after she left Hong Kong, we finally lived in the same city again, this time in New York. Our parents had retired, and Yue-Sai also brought them to the U.S. Once again, she shouldered the responsibility as the eldest child. She became my father's most ardent advocate as a prolific and leading Chinese artist of his time. We traveled a great deal together on his exhibition tours. As his manager, Yue-Sai went on TV interviews with our father. He gave live demonstrations of classical painting while our mom sat at his side grinding ink for his brush. Supporters and friends used to envy my father as he was always in the excellent company of two good-looking women.

Since our four sisters don't live in the same city or country, we don't get to connect in person as often as we all would like. But we constantly make video calls or visit each other in different cities. When one of us endures a crisis, we join forces to solve the problem.

The most challenging time for all of us collectively was when our parents were seriously ill. When my mother suffered a stroke, we decided that at least one family member should take care of her in addition to a nurse. Since Vickie and I traveled a lot for business and Brenda had two small children, San-San, who had just graduated and was working in banking, shouldered the duty of caring for mom and did a remarkable job. She took an entire year off from work to devote herself to the task, and I made it up to her by giving her a whole year's salary.

Furthermore, our father was seriously ill for the eight years before his death. Although he had full-time nurses, dad still needed someone from the family to supervise his diet, oversee the plethora of examinations, and ensure he consumed the twenty-five pills he needed each day at the right times. At that point, Brenda lived in New York and took on the heavy task of caring for him. For her convenience, I bought an apartment in Midtown East with large French windows overlooking the vibrant life below for our father, just opposite Brenda's residence.

It was inconvenient for him to go out from that juncture; however, he would just as happily sit happily in front of the big windows, soaking in the sunlight and the electric bustle of the busy streets down below. Still, we could all feel Brenda's pressure as the primary caregiver. In many respects, she took on the role of the elder sister when dad was ill. I appreciated all the things she did for him and us, as the glue that held our family unit together as our father ventured into his final swansong.

Some years ago, I was invited to record a "Thank you, My Family" (谢谢了, 我的家) segment for a Chinese state television show, which provided me an opportunity to review all the moments that I have spent with my family. To my surprise, the program included a video made by my sisters in which they called me a "Modern Mulan" who served as guardian of the family in my father's place. I was humbled and embarrassed by the clip because I knew that without their unrelenting support, I wouldn't have been bold enough to do what I had done – to tread where no woman had stepped before me.

Ancient anecdotes tell us that siblings are friends you cannot choose. However, I am glad that I didn't have to choose. My sisters came into my life as the greatest of gifts. They eventually went to study in the U.S., following in my often uneven but always forward-charging footsteps.

My father once said: "I think Yue-Sai had a great impact on them."

I can only hope it was the positive parts that they adopted.

TWO YOUNG MEN WHO CHANGED MY LIFE

Like many people of Chinese heritage, my parents were not religious but were brought up with Confucian philosophy that imbued their lives with a code. Confucius was a teacher around 2,500 years ago who devised an ethical framework of rules governing relationships. Confucianism provides a clear hierarchy for society, and because of his teachings, so deeply ingrained in the Chinese way of life, we know how a child should behave towards parents, a student towards teachers, and one sibling to another. We understand the cycle of holidays and festivals and how to behave in all circumstances. Confucius teaches us to respect our ancestors and to clean their tombs on a specific day every year. We are not religious according to the Western definition, yet most Chinese people embody a profoundly ingrained, clear understanding of the world order. Effectively, this is our rendition of religion – an Eastern underpinning that accentuates the importance of personal and governmental morality, justice, kindness, and sincerity and enhances social relationships without lavishness.

The teachings of Confucius are alive and well today. Our family, the Kan family, hail from a village in Panyu, near Guangzhou, where everybody's surname is Kan. The village beholds a 14th-century temple where we have worshipped our ancestors for countless generations, in keeping with Confucian beliefs.

In 1961, when I was fourteen years old, two young white men rang the doorbell at my family's apartment in the densely populated Hong Kong enclave of Kowloon.

My best friend Connie and I answered the door to two men donning white shirts and black trousers. They were very friendly and greeted us politely, greeting us and reading scripture from the Bible in Cantonese! The men then explained that they were missionaries of the Church of Latter-Day Saints, the Mormon Church. We learned that they were Elders Barton and Elder Conley, both only 19 years old, had traveled from the United States on a mission to spread the word, before which they immersed themselves in six months of intensive language training.

I was intrigued and impressed that these young men had mastered the Chinese language and left their families on a mission they wholeheartedly believed in. Beyond that, I recognized how much their families had to sacrifice for their children to depart on an expedition on the other side of the world. However, the most remarkable learning aspect for me was the emphasis the Mormon culture placed on families, togetherness, and unity.

At their invitation, Connie and I later visited their Mormon place of worship called a Ward, which occupied the whole floor of a commercial building in midtown Kowloon. There was a large room with chairs, a podium and a piano, and a few smaller rooms on the side used as classrooms.

Right away, Connie and I started attending services at the Ward every Sunday. My parents knew about my new pursuit and believed that religion was good for society and never objected to their daughter's newfound devotion to the Mormon church. Another young Mormon missionary we met was Elder Don Conley. When he arrived in November that year from a small Welsh community in southern Idaho, Hong Kong must have seemed like another planet. Still, the Mormon community there opened his eyes and his heart and filled him with a sense of community.

"I was 20 years old but looked 15, and my brain was probably about 12 years old at that time," Conley told me over the phone from his home in San Francisco in 2021. "There I was, bringing something to the Hong Kong people to change their lives for the better. That was the intent of our mission, but, in truth, I found that in my heart of hearts, so many of the people I contacted were already morally superior to me, and they didn't need to change to become better than what they already were."

In two and a half years of work all over Hong Kong, Conley came to see that – in his words – although few people there had ever been exposed to Christianity, there was still "a huge moral compass in their lives and their culture, and in the way that they lived."

He marveled at the memory of his introduction to Confucian ethics when he moved to Hong Kong, so ingrained in the people he was just then getting to know.

"There was enormous generosity and kindness from people who had nothing," Conley continued fondly.

Following our telephone reunion, he penned a letter testifying to maturity beyond my years when we met.

"You were already a serious human being," Conley wrote. "There was a tension that revealed both your drive, confidence and extraordinarily high standards."

Not long after I became a member of the Mormon faith, I was "called" to create a branch choir for the Lai Chi Kwok branch. The majority of the choir members had little if any musical education. Conley recalled an incident during a branch choir practice when my youth caught up with me.

"Your idea of what the choir should sound like and what it did sound like turned out to be worlds apart," he noted with a gentle laugh. "You needed to find a place to vent your frustration, so you stowed away in a supply closet inside the chapel until you could regain your composure."

Next, I was asked to translate some Mormon hymns into Chinese and subsequently threw myself into the daunting task. I became highly active in the Mormon church and, at one point, started a percussion instrument band for the kids. Soon, the Elders Conley and Barton asked Connie and me if we wanted to be baptized. Imagine me, a Catholic girls' school prefect, being baptized as a Mormon. I was never a christened Catholic, yet I was still the favorite of the nuns and teachers. Without hesitation, Connie and I accepted the Mormons' invitation. I did hear sometime later that the nuns had gotten wind that I had "converted" and were incredibly disappointed.

Two years after the baptism, Conley and Barton asked if I wanted to attend a Mormon school in Hawaii, then called Brigham Young University Hawaii, a private research university founded in 1875 in Utah and sponsored by the Church of Jesus Christ of Latter-Day Saints (LDS) and later renamed Brigham Young University (BYU). The elders explained that I would be eligible for a cash scholarship to cover my tuition and two additional work scholarships on campus to cover my other expenses. This was not an opportunity that saunters by every day. I begged my parents to let me go, and I seized the moment.

"After school graduation, Yue-Sai aspired to further her education in America," my father wrote in his memoir. "At that time, she was only sixteen, and no family members or friends, in this generation, ever went abroad to study, especially girls. We were nervous to leave her alone, but she was determined. Yue-Sai finally persuaded us. Her resolution helped her to go out into the new world. As expected, she worked hard to get a degree in music and did well."

By traveling across the Pacific, I was merely pursuing the path of countless other Chinese people, my grandfather included. But I was the first in my generation of the Kan family to leave for the United States. In those days, venturing to America for school was considered a very noble undertaking for a Chinese family, the ideal steppingstone to a wonderful and prosperous existence.

Nevertheless, my mother was extremely nervous as I was only sixteen. She was concerned that I could not adjust to a new life by myself in Hawaii. Yet nothing could dampen my enthusiasm, and once Mom finally understood that my zest and excitement would not atrophy, she decided to do everything she could to help me on my journey. Our family had very little money, so my mother sold the small apartments she had invested in, borrowed some more money to collect enough cash to buy my airline ticket, and, with tears of pride in her eyes, placed a little spending money into my palm. My parents were enormously proud that one of their children was going to school in the illustrious and mysterious United States of America.

So, there I was, a mere 16-year-old fresh-faced teenager at the crowded Hong Kong Kaitak airport on a hot August day, saying goodbye to everyone I knew and loved most in this world – my parents and my three younger sisters, some of my father's brothers and sisters, and a few of my schoolmates. It was incredibly emotional because all of us quietly knew that, due to financial limitations, I wouldn't see any of them again for at least four years. My parents repeatedly instructed me to write to them as soon as I arrived. I pretended to be calm and replied, "Got it!" over and over again, trying not to let tears catch hoarsely in my throat.

As I passed through the gate, I dared not look back. I was afraid I would burst into an ugly sob. Only the tears welled up as soon as I was on the plane. I pressed my nose against the window seat as we took off, rising into the sky and watching the island of Hong Kong becoming smaller and smaller until it finally disappeared. I prayed hard to God that He take loving care of my dear mom and dad and my sisters, whom I idolized more than I could articulate. I drew a deep breath and wiped away the tears that had smudged my cheeks. I straightened my back and reminded myself of the astonishing new chapter I had embarked upon.

I landed in Honolulu, teeming with curiosity. I had no clue what was ahead of me and what life there might be like. All I knew was that Hawaii was an island like Hong Kong or, more accurately, a multitude of islands. We touched down in broad daylight; thus, I could see Hawaii from the plane in all its tropical splendor – the ceaseless blue-green waters, long stretches of pale sands and palm trees that stretched elegantly into the cobalt skies.

I was met at the gate by church representatives and escorted straight to Laie, a small town on the north shore of

Oahu, an hour's drive from Honolulu, home to the school and my dormitory. It was a remote island parcel where you could walk a mile and not see another person. Further, the university was small – no more than a thousand students. All the lush greenery enraptured me, the vast open spaces and the cloudless umbrella that allowed slithers of golden light to highlight the colorful homes scattered among the shoreline.

My mother had packed my luggage, so when I flung it open in my little dormitory room, a few packages of my favorite noodles fell out, and I was crying all over again.

During the first three months in Hawaii, using the most westernized name of Yvonne for my non-Chinese counterparts, I was admittedly very lonely. I was known at the University as Yvonne, my English name, and I felt far from home. The most popular song that year, in 1965, was "500 Miles" by Peter, Paul and Mary. Every time I heard it, which was every day, I wept. I was the youngest person in my class and missed the gentle touch of my parents profusely. Nonetheless, I still felt their love and concern. Every few months, I received an oversized parcel from my mother filled with goodies, such as the shrimp noodles I adored, clothes she purchased from the Hong Kong streets, and a lovely letter updating me about the happenings of the family.

After accepting the initial spending money my parents gave me before I left Hong Kong, I never again asked them for financial help. I knew how difficult it was for them, how much they had given up in order to send me to Hawaii, and I didn't ever want to become a burden. Instead, the moment I started making earning from the scholarship and jobs set up in advance by the Church, I sent them money back – not because I thought they needed it, but because I knew my mother and father would then rhapsodically tell their friends and relatives that their daughter was making money and was a responsible child who was thinking about her obligation to repay them.

Once I had worked through the homesickness and learned to navigate the American university system, my new life in Hawaii became much easier than I initially envisioned. All my schoolmates were from abroad, and they, too, were experiencing an emotional rollercoaster. All were Mormons, and like me, none of them were from families with money. Nobody tried to show off, and everybody was very humble and authentic. I so valued these new individuals in my life and felt that every person surrounding me was honest, pure, and eager to grow and experience everything the island had to offer.

LIFE AT BRIGHAM YOUNG UNIVERSITY HAWAII

Hawaiians are as solid as the Earth and as sincere as they come. It was in Hawaii that I learned to love people, really love people, and the beauty of what humans can do to support one another. I will never forget the kindnesses extended to me from many different walks of life, especially during school holidays. We overseas students had nowhere to go because our families were so far away. Still, we were constantly invited to join one particular family, the Goo family, who owned a general store in Laie and enthusiastically invited us for holiday meals.

Their home-cooked meals were such treats for a poor student such as myself, and the Goo family's kind gestures were not lost on me. Nowadays, on holidays, I invite students to have dinner at my home, hoping they will enjoy and appreciate the opportunity as much as I did. While the Goo family elders, my hosts when I was a young student, have long since passed away, their son Charles Goo and his wife, Helen, are still in Hawaii, remain my close friends and carry on his parents' generosity.

Brigham Young University Hawaii was a very small college comprised of less than one thousand students. I reveled in meeting and getting to know my schoolmates, consisting of roughly four groups: Pacific Islanders, Asians (mainly from Hong Kong, Korea, and Japan), Hawaiian natives, and Americans from the U.S. mainland. Even though the student body was sparse compared to most U.S. universities, the school spanned extensive grounds, all of which were immaculately crisp, green, and well-maintained. No building on campus was taller than two floors, which, coming from crowded and vertical Hong Kong, took a little adaptation.

I was assigned a second-floor dorm room with just enough space for a single wooden bed, a desk, and a small closet. Each dorm unit had seven rooms around a communal area with a kitchen. This very simple setup was my home for four years. Outside my little window were lawns and palm trees and, far off, other buildings. I had been independent in Hong Kong and lived in school dormitories, but this was a whole other level of self-sufficiency. With my family thousands of miles away, I was truly on my own, a notion that at times induces a sense of both freedom and fear.

Perhaps making life a little less daunting, Brigham Young University promotes strict moral standards and an environment of innocence. Mormons do not believe in sex before marriage, so if we girls went on a date with a man, we understood that we were not likely to end up in bed together. Mormons follow well-heeled rules of conduct for their young men and women, and despite being ridiculed for being prudish, I liked the Mormon code: clean living, volunteering, philanthropy, tithing ten percent of all income to the church, and, of course, regular worship in church every Sunday. I believe in the unity of the family and the sanctity of marriage, and I very much respect the Mormon code.

But there was one incredibly terrifying occasion. One weekend, when I was practicing piano on an empty campus, a male student knocked on the practice room door. The tall and lanky man – and not a person I would describe as good-looking – marched in and, without saying a single word, tried to kiss me. It was the scariest moment of my life, and once the first few seconds of shock dissipated, it took all of my strength to kick him out. It was the first time I comprehended how some men treat women as objects and think they can do that with free will. I never forgot it.

My seven-unit mates and I took turns cooking in pairs, with our duty to prepare meals for the group for a whole week, which was quite a challenge as I didn't know how to cook. I'm Chinese, and yet I couldn't even make good rice.

"It was always either too wet or too dry," Helen Goo recounted with a laugh over lunch near Laie in 2021.

One afternoon, a handsome boy named Brian – the President of the Turtle Club for fishing and diving – came to my dorm room and excitedly gifted me a large fish that he had just caught. I put it in the freezer until my turn to cook came up. I could barely use a knife. When I tried to cut up the frozen fish myself, I managed to put a giant gash into the palm of my left hand and ended up with eight stitches.

In that first year, my budget only allowed for spending $25 a month on food. It is incredible how little I had and how careful I had to be. None of the food anyone cooked was especially desirable, so the real excitement came on the weekends when we went into the heart of Honolulu, which we called going to town.

There was no alcohol at BYU, and I still do not drink alcohol today. The Mormons also disapprove of caffeine, so there is a ban on tea and coffee. It is difficult to tell Chinese people not to drink tea, and some Chinese Mormon friends and I have long opted for healthy herbal tea without caffeine.

Once each week, a group of us BYU students would take a minibus taxi seating twelve to Chinatown in downtown Honolulu, where we could have a decent meal. Chinatown in those days was primitive, but there were dim sum (点心) restaurants that served us our best meal of the week. We would stock up on all the Chinese goodies we needed for the next seven days.

We also made a point of going to the Ala Moana Center, the largest outdoor shopping mall in the world with over 350 stores. There, we could buy anything we needed.

As I was studying for a degree in music, the classes were all small, no more than fifteen students, and I used to spend hours practicing the piano, perfecting every tune and willing myself to improve. When I wasn't in the practice rooms, I studied hard and worked in the university library, fulfilling one of my two work scholarships. My other vocation was to teach small children to play the piano. Every couple of months, we put on a recital for them to perform for friends and family. There were next to no free moments in the day between music and work, classes, and study. Thus, I never learned to surf, scuba dive, or fish in the deep sea. Yet, I was perfectly content navigating the music rooms and smelling the sea breeze as I shuffled from place to place.

All of the Pacific Island students worked at the Polynesian Cultural Center, a place that had been a popular tourist attraction in Hawaii for decades. Their college education was made possible by the Center's regular employment. It was also a wonderful place to educate people about the Pacific Islands and their cultures. Beautiful dancers with a deep understanding of their cultures were a joy to watch.

The Center put on a marvelous show every sundown, brought to life by fantastic Hollywood producers. The superb sound-and-light visual and auditory feast illuminated all the features of the Pacific Islanders' heritage. I especially loved the last fifteen minutes, when a waterfall at the back gushed down, and the lights and sound dazzled. I would trek to the Center most nights after work just to enjoy that part. From my lens as a little girl raised as a poor immigrant in Hong Kong, this was Hollywood – it was glamor, light, life, sparkle, and stimulus. I had never been exposed to such a thing. It enlightened me to the notion that the world out there was incredibly huge, and it was a world I wanted to clutch with the first of my hand and explore as much as was humanly possible.

IN THE WORDS OF HELEN GOO _____

I first met Yvonne, as she was then known, in 1964 when she moved into our apartment in Hale 1 at Church College of Hawaii in Laie, Oahu. There were four of us girls from Hong Kong in the apartment. Yvonne was roommates with Angela Chan, and my roommate was Wendy Chan. Since we are Chinese, we decided to eat together. Mind you, that was before we knew that Yvonne had zero experience in the kitchen. She was the youngest, so we just took her under our wings. As far as she was concerned, she would have been okay eating a bowl of instant noodles daily. One day, she received a box from her family in Hong Kong, and inside was a bag of dried duck gizzards. She was so excited because she loves duck gizzards. She said her parents said to share with us, and so we all wrote thank you notes to her parents.

One afternoon, when I came home from class, I found Yvonne in the kitchen struggling to cut the gizzards into pieces to eat for lunch. I asked her how long they had been boiling, and she said maybe half an hour. I told her these dried gizzards would need to be cooked for several hours before it is tender enough to eat. I then put them in a big pot, added water, rice, and a few drops of oil and made congee for dinner.

In our apartment, we sometimes had issues with each other

when chores were not done to keep the apartment clean and orderly. I once told her she needed to get it done today. She is very good-natured and does as she was told, but she can sometimes be stubborn. Sometimes, she insisted on doing things a certain way, and when we overruled her, she didn't get upset. The following day, she would smile as if nothing had happened. The truth is she is seldom home during the day. Most of her time, besides working and attending classes, is either at the library studying or practicing piano in the music room. Every evening, right after dinner, she would gather her sheet music, toss her hair back, and say, "I am going to practice!" We would say, "Yeah, go!"

Music was her passion, and once she told me that she wanted to be a concert pianist and become rich and famous. I never doubted her because she was so focused and driven in her work ethic. She was an accomplished pianist, and every day, she spent hours on the piano to continue to sharpen her skills. She was well-known on campus because she was asked to perform many functions. I wish I were that focused and didn't get distracted. Come to think of it, she didn't get too involved in campus activities, but she did date a few times.

After she became a Narcissus Princess, for a whole year, she went to town most weekends to attend various community functions such as charity events and the Chinese chamber of commerce functions. That was her job as a Princess.

I am not that good at music, but I enjoyed listening and watching her play because her body movements showed how in tune she was with her music. She has great talents and is a talented artist in her own right.

Many years later, Yvonne hasn't become a lauded concert pianist, but she is rich and famous. She is also doing a lot of humanitarian work and loves what she can do to make a difference in the world.

I WAS CROWNED A PRINCESS!

In 1967, my third year at BYU, I turned nineteen. One morning, when I was sick in bed in my dormitory, the President of the student body knocked on the door.

"I know you have a cold, but can I come in to talk to you?" she asked eagerly.

I untangled myself from the knot of sheets and let the young woman in, and she sat down on my only chair, almost bursting with excitement.

"This morning, at the student body assembly, the students voted for you to run for the Narcissus Festival beauty pageant as a contestant to represent the university," she quickly gushed, unable to hold back.

"What is the Narcissus Festival?" I questioned blearily.

"It's a prestigious beauty pageant in Hawaii," she replied, clasping her hands together. "The narcissus flower epitomizes the purity of heart and soul, and since the 1950s, the Chinese Chamber of Commerce has organized it yearly to create awareness of Chinese art and culture."

I was shocked. I never expected that I would be issued such an opportunity.

"What do I have to do?" I asked tepidly.

"You will go through a training program," the student body

president explained, her tone turning a little serious. "And in three months, you will compete in the event."

"Wow, I have never done anything like this."

"Don't worry. The whole school will be behind you, rooting for you. The teacher is a famous lady called Helen Richardson. You will learn a lot."

The student body president giddily revealed that long learning list, which would entail everything from makeup, stage-walking, and hairstyling to posing for pictures, training the voice, and answering questions in-person and on-camera. There was also a talent performance portion, which I immediately viewed as a chance to share what I'd learned slaving over the piano for the past twelve years.

"But I am not an American," I pointed, my heart sinking a little. "I am a student from Hong Kong. Does it matter?"

"Well, it will be tough for you to win the Queen title, but we hope you will still compete," she pressed on. "If you end up as Princess, it wouldn't be too bad, would it?"

I had no idea what the student body president was talking about, and I had little idea then, still barely out of my teens, how participating in such a monumental event would impact my life. But I felt flattered and shyly agreed.

The following weekend, and every weekend for the next three months, a young man representing the Junior Chinese Chamber of Commerce picked me up from school and graciously drove me three hours back and forth across the island to training classes.

The concept of competing in a beauty pageant was totally new to me, and I was inquisitive about the whole thing, whether or not I could win. Above all, I was most excited about the learning process and the experiences I could never have imagined as a poor girl from Hong Kong. As it turned out, the event had far-reaching consequences for my life.

My coach, Helen Richardson, was a very chic lady – always outfitted in classy, tailored clothes with immaculate hair and makeup. Her husband was the Attorney General of Hawaii. Helen taught me how to apply makeup for the first time, an act that was as captivating as it was strange. I had never used such a thing before. Helen watched over me, issuing instructions as to what went where and guiding my shaking hand to compliment my finest features. Under Helen's guiding light, I discovered the magic of these various sticks and pods and palettes of color, how they could all be used to enhance our outward appearance and our inside confidence. Further, Helen coached me on how to walk the stage and present myself in public, and, most importantly, she taught me what to do in front of a camera. All these teachings had an extraordinary influence on my future life when I chose to go into television production and, later, the cosmetics business.

Although my family could not be in Honolulu for the Narcissus Pageant, they supported me wholeheartedly in my new venture. My parents ordered dazzling garments made by a talented tailor friend in Hong Kong named Anita Szeto. I wore a long, ornate beaded dress as white as snow, satin gloves for my piano recital, and glittering earrings that dropped several inches from my lobes. For the final appearance, I emerged in a stunning beige cheongsam made of French lace. I don't know how my parents afforded them, but somehow they did.

Once again, they sacrificed their only happiness and rest time to ensure their daughter had the best chance of succeeding at whatever opportunity unraveled before me.

The night of the contest, I sat alone wedged in the backstage corner, pretending to be busy. The other contestants had many people around them – their sisters, mothers, and aunties. There was no one to fuss over me. I felt so lonely but did not want to show it.

"Everyone ready now!" a production manager called. "Come out for the first lineup on stage."

We lined up and, one by one, strutted out and under the spotlight as our names were declared over the speaker. Later, backstage workers rolled a piano onto the stage. I drew a deep but measured breath and took my seat to perform. I played "Seguidillas" by the Spanish composer Isaac Albéniz. It is a complicated piece to perform, and I still don't know why my piano teacher, Professor Peter Corragio, chose it. It is not particularly melodic, and its degree of difficulty is not always appreciated. In other words, it was the wrong choice for an event like this. The experience taught me to always be in control of everything I do and use my instinct to decide no matter what anyone else thinks. I am the one responsible for my actions in the end.

Then came the question-and-answer part of the pageant. I can't remember what they asked me, but I thought I did well because I got the most applause. Then came the announcement that I had been chosen as Princess! I knew I could not be Queen because I was not American, but I was ecstatic to be labeled a Princess.

The year that followed was terrific. I traveled as a Narcissus Princess to many places, including San Francisco and Victoria on the west coast of Canada. People paid a lot of attention to us as we were the ambassadors of the Chinese community of Hawaii. We were driven in parades through Chinatowns, waving our hands demurely like Queen Elizabeth to the crowds lined up to welcome us. The whole experience was exceptional for a naive nineteen-year-old.

In Honolulu, there was a lady in the audience named Beatrice Ching. She was very active in the Chinese Chamber of Commerce and was also the sister of then-Senator Hiram Fong (邝友良), the Republican Senator from Hawaii, who, in 1964, became the first American of Asian descent to run in a Presidential primary. She took an immediate liking to me as we talked. And from that day, she became something akin to a surrogate mother. She subsequently wrote a long letter to my parents to document that evening for them.

"Though she had the highest score, the Queen had to be a Chinese American, so Yue-Sai took second prize," my dear father wrote.

My last performance at the university was a solo graduation piano concert. I started the concert with a piece of Bach's organ music, transcribed beautifully for the piano by Liszt, and then played pieces by Chopin and Debussy. Despite the applause, after the show, I felt a strong pang that I would never be a great pianist; I would never be a Rubinstein.

Deep down, all artists know at a certain point whether or not they can succeed. You are probably stupid if you are not incredibly in tune and sensitive to your craft. The piano is an immensely disciplinary art, and the classical piano is even more so. You must play every note with colossal rigidity and expression at the same time. Every one of your ten fingers has its own masterpiece to remember, yet the two hands must still come together in a sort of unity that makes magic.

It was when I started to learn Franz Liszt's "La Campanella," which translates from Italian to "little bell" and is widely considered one of the most challenging pieces of classical to acquire, that my friends knew – I knew – I would never be the virtuoso I had once hoped.

But I don't regret the years and the dedication, not at all. The arts brought so much to my young life, from discipline to ingenuity. With a love of music and the craft, I don't think I was ever truly lost or lonely. Piano lessons were greatly beneficial to my character development. Piano practice taught me how to discipline myself. It also brought me into contact with some of the most beautiful music ever written by human beings for posterity. The study of music, in general, is excellent for the development of the soul, and while playing any instrument well is difficult, playing piano is an extra challenge. It is the most demanding instrument for a musician because it requires memorizing so many notes played simultaneously by all ten fingers.

My years at BYU taught me to let go of bias and be generous with all. It was a place populated with very selfless and supportive people. Once I found my financial independence some years later, I set up two small scholarship funds to help Chinese students get to BYU, and I still give ten percent of my income to various charities.

IN THE WORDS OF ANGELA CONLEY _____

I first met Yvonne in a dorm room at the end of summer 1965. That was her first year, and I returned for my third year. I learned right away that she was only sixteen, where she went to high school, and so forth. I asked myself, "I wonder how we will get along?" She's what I called a Hong Kong girl, and I was a transplant from mainland China. I was from Guangzhou, and when I moved to Hong Kong, I was 13. Yvonne could have been one of those phony, unkind people who judge you only by your appearance – are you good-looking, or do you have money or whatever? That's quite common in Hong Kong. Pretty soon, I was reassured.

Our dorm was right next to the campus. There was a clock bell that rang every hour. One morning, we were asleep, and the bell rang "ding-dong," at about the third dong, Yvonne suddenly jumped out of bed, grabbed whatever clothes she could find, put them on, got her books and ran out of the room. She got stopped because part of her clothing was caught on the doorknob. So, then she untangled herself and ran down the stairs. I smiled and thought, we'll get along just fine, no worries. Her hair was in a vertical position. No brushing teeth or washing face. That was Yvonne in those days.

One thing that was very obvious to people who were around her was that she was very devoted to her music. She was very disciplined. At night, Yvonne would take an incense stick to the empty campus music room because the mosquitoes would eat her up. She would go alone, leaving these warm, funny, fun friends in the dorms. She would go all by herself. That's very impressive to me. Yvonne devoted so much time to practicing, and also, on the weekend, she found a teacher all the way downtown, and she had to figure out how to get there from Brigham Young University Hawaii. The bus would only drop her off at the Ala Moana Shopping Center, and she had to find her way to wherever she wanted. It was expensive, but he was supposed to be one of the best teachers. Yvonne followed that route. She told me she searched for him and heard he was recommended as the best piano teacher.

Music was such a big part of Yvonne's life that I couldn't see there being anything else. And she was so young, you know? Just sixteen. She was friendly, but she was very selective. With boys, the only ones who impressed her were those with intellect and ambition. She succeeded in making me go out with a boy she thought highly of, and I said, "he has a girlfriend," but she still would not give up. Then I said, "I have a boyfriend," and she still didn't give up. Yvonne worked on me for a long time. Finally, it was easier to say yes. I can't remember this name. Anyway, we went to a special dance, and afterward, his girlfriend and her friends gave me dirty looks for a month. They didn't know that Yvonne was the culprit, you know? You see, I am a very stubborn person, right? And she was able to make me change my mind. That's how convincing Yvonne was. It was a fact that she would not give up. She would work on it until I said yes.

RETURNING TO HONG KONG _____

After I graduated from Brigham Young University in 1967, my mother urged me to return to Hong Kong. My family had not seen me for four years. Nowadays, quite a few Chinese parents go so far as to go with their kids to high school or college overseas, buy an apartment and live with them, prepare their meals, and shop for them. We didn't have that kind of luxury.

So, finally, I returned to Hong Kong at the dawn of summer to see my family. Four years was a long time to be apart from them, but we didn't have the money for intermediary trips back and forth. It was so wonderful to be around them all again, to see my baby sisters all grown up and emerging as lovely young women in their own right.

My parents suggested I find a job in Hong Kong if only to be close to them for a temporary window of time. My uncle worked at the Hilton Hotel, which was the top hotel back then, and helped me score a position. I was only there for four months, but it was a delightful experience. I entered their trainee program, which gave me a little experience in all hotel departments. Initially, I worked as a telephone operator. I'd answer the phone saying, "Good morning, the Hilton Hotel. How can I help you?" I enjoyed its simplicity and found it helpful, as I learned the best way to ensure that words related to messages are spelled correctly. "A" for Apple, "B" for Boy, "C" for Charlie, and so on.

After one week, I was assigned to the Public Relations

Department, and I also had a ball there, meeting some of the most interesting guests. We took care of the VIPs, which included actresses, politicians, singers, and famous entrepreneurs. It was such fun. I was so naive that my colleagues had to tell me who our first-class guests were coming to our first-class hotel.

At four months, the Human Resources Manager, Larry Chu, asked if I would follow him to another hotel. The Hyatt Group was setting up its flagship hotel across the harbor in Kowloon, and he offered to double my salary. It was very flattering for somebody as young as myself, barely twenty years old, so I went from the Hilton to the Hyatt.

My first job at the Hyatt was in the banquet department, working for a supervisor named Mr. Herbert Ebert from Sri Lanka, a patient gentleman who took me with him when he made client calls all over the city to drum up business. It was not a difficult job, but it took courage. We went to offices without knowing anybody and requested to see the public relations manager or anyone in charge of booking hotel rooms and special events. We pitched our services and offered special room rates and restaurant and banqueting facilities for special occasions.

It may sound simple, but this was the first time I had done anything like it, and as daunting as it was, I valued the opportunity to learn how to do cold-call sales. This experience helped lay a foundation of skills I would use in future work – cold-calling advertisers for my TV shows. I learned early on that success is a numbers game. Almost nobody wins on their first try, yet you must drum up the will to keep going. I learned to go into a call well-prepared and, when it went wrong, tap into a growing ability to dust myself off and do it again with the confidence that soon, my fortune would change.

I also learned that in the hotel business, many vendors and suppliers, such as tailors and gift shops, will do anything for you if you introduce VIP clients to them. Eventually, I ended up in the public relations department working under Marla Chorengel, a beautiful Filipina married to the hotel group's vice president. She taught me a lot, most importantly, how to write eloquently in the specialized realm of public relations and marketing.

After working in Hong Kong for a year, I decided it was not where I wanted to stay. Hong Kong was a British colony, and the official language at that point was not Cantonese but English, even though the overwhelming percentage of the population was Chinese. Moreover, I constantly witnessed instances of racial discrimination. The British made it clear they were in charge and that the Chinese were second-class citizens. They took all the important government jobs, even if an individual wasn't so great at their position. I found this all very disturbing and decided that I wanted to live back in the United States, but this time in New York City.

I am not entirely sure why I was so fixated on the Big Apple. I had heard a lot about the city that never sleeps while I was in Hawaii, and it seemed like it would be an immense but welcome challenge to carve out a life there. New York felt like the center of the universe, and I longed to be right there in the middle of all the magic and madness.

During a lunch party for a friend in Hong Kong, I met a

well-dressed American man from Manhattan. He knew I was preparing to leave for his home city, and he told me he would call me, which he did. The stylish man invited me to lunch a few days later, in what would be one of the most devastating experiences I have ever had. Initially, he was a little hesitant, beating around the bush, and I wasn't clear about what he was saying. Finally, the visitor from New York informed me that he owned a clothing company and wanted to offer me a job as a designer.

"But I have no experience; I am not a clothing designer," I responded, perplexed.

"Well, you don't have to know how to design," he continued sheepishly. "Your job is to take care of my clients."

"So, what is it I have to do?" I asked.

"Well, you will just go to dinners with the clients and keep them company. And if you stay the night with them, they will pay you HK$1,000," he said. "If you do it for ten years, you will have made enough money to quit, and you'll be able to live very well for the rest of your life."

My jaw dropped to the floor. The man was offering me a job as a call girl. I couldn't believe it. Ashen-faced, I headed straight for the bathroom to vomit and made a hasty exit from the restaurant.

I wept all that afternoon but managed to pull myself together enough to attend dinner with a close friend of mine, Larry Goodman, a friendly man who was something like a big brother to me. I relayed the traumatic experience.

"Do I really look like a hooker to you?" I asked as tears streamed down my cheeks.

"Of course not! You don't look like a hooker," he assured me.

Larry explained that the going rate for prostitutes was about HK$100 a night, and I was being offered ten times as much, or the rough equivalent of US$165 a night, in 1969.

"If you looked like a real hooker, you wouldn't be able to make that kind of money," he continued gently, amused that I was so concerned.

Larry's consolation made me feel much better, but I had learned a valuable lesson. Just because somebody is a friend of a friend doesn't mean they are a quality human being. The guy looked good, prosperous, and professional – however such types can deceive. As a young woman, I was learning to be more discerning, to see people for what they are, and not to be fooled by appearances. Sadly, I discovered that my experience was not unique. Young women – especially those considered "exotic" to the Western eye – are preyed on worldwide. I was steadily figuring out how to avoid dangerous paths in life and make careful choices.

The designer's money offer would be very tempting for many young women to take the uncomplicated way out; thus, I am grateful to have been imbued with the strength to understand that prostitution was no solution. Thank God I had my head screwed on straight, and this unpleasant experience was an opportunity to learn that I would want a future I could control instead of being a servant to someone else's fantasies or money.

Before I departed for New York City, I returned to Hawaii to spend a little time with my sister, Brenda, who was studying at the University of Hawaii. As much as I revered the laid-back attitude and the scent of the salty ocean, I felt reassured that Hawaii had nothing to offer me at that primitive stage in my life. So, I hugged my little sister goodbye and boarded a plane bound for New York City.

NEW YORK, THE CAPITAL OF THE WORLD __

Recently, an old friend from Hawaii reminded me that during my time at college there, I always said I would go to New York City, the enclave I believed to be the greatest on earth. The City seemed like the epitome of excitement and glamor, but in reality, I knew nothing about it.

On January 2, 1972, my sister Brenda and George Kanahele, a Morman friend, drove me to the airport in Honolulu. George was the Lieutenant Governor of Hawaii and a scintillating writer whose many books about his beloved islands, and especially Hawaiian music, are among the most captivating ever written on the subject. George was the Honorary Consul-General for Indonesia and routinely invited me to fancy events where he educated me in Hawaiian political life, teaching me lessons for which I remain grateful for today. He was just one of those rare individuals who happened to cross my path, so rare in his brilliance and ability to grasp and disseminate so much wisdom and knowledge.

Sometimes, I regret that I didn't continue my relationship with George. He was an extremely cultured person who enriched my life with constant awareness and education about the political and societal landscape. He connected me with incredibly interesting individuals and provided a beautifully detailed history of the islands – a history that I could not have gleaned from a textbook. However, I was young and naïve and didn't appreciate his gift of friendship as much as I wish I had. George was not a boyfriend but could have been if I'd stayed in Hawaii. There was a unique, unspoken spark that zapped between us. Brenda later told me he cried the whole way back from the airport following my departure.

Finally, I touched down in New York on a frozen January day. I wore the warmest clothes I owned, including the thickest wool pantsuit I could find. Yet, the frigid air still whipped and guttered every bone in my body as I stood outside, trying to weave my way through the dense and stern-faced crowd.

I didn't know anybody in New York City except for Connie Chen, my best friend from boarding high school, whom I hadn't seen for years. She and her sister Jane invited me to stay with them for a couple of weeks and, as I only had $150 in my pocket and a small suitcase with very few belongings, I gladly accepted and went straight from the airport to their tiny apartment in Queens.

First, I needed a better coat, a proper New York winter coat. Connie allowed me to use her credit card to purchase a beautiful padded black coat with an elegant Persian fur collar. Although that took me a year and a half to pay back, and at the time I bought it I had next to no money to my name, I insisted on having the best quality and investing in items that would last me a very long time. That coat saved my hide for at least fifteen New York winters and remained just as intact and elegant through every season.

Nevertheless, I was immediately overwhelmed by how different New York was from the distant islands of Hawaii. I noticed that in my new city, most people were of European descent; I saw no Polynesians anywhere and hardly any Asians outside the small neighborhood of Chinatown. It quickly occurred to me that I had better learn to speak English very well and very quickly. Pidgin wouldn't fly.

In China, if a foreigner speaks a few Chinese words, locals get overly excited no matter how bad they sound, amazed that they've tackled the bare minimum. On the other hand, Americans often peg you as a second-class citizen if you don't speak English well. While my English was not that bad, I realized I had to speak the language much more fluently and articulately to succeed in New York. I immediately signed up for English and diction classes in a little nearby classroom.

I was living in Queens, but my classes and work were in Manhattan, so I had to ride the subway for more than an hour every day, braving the sardine-like crush of people at rush hour. Twice, I fainted because the airless cars were so packed. Fortunately, on both occasions, passersby and subway workers carried me off to a platform seat, gave me some water, and helped to wake me up, debunking the stereotype of New Yorkers as unsympathetic and rude. I was hustling with the rest of the metropolis, and when I stumbled, there was always a helping hand.

I adored New York City. I learned to love root beer, especially with a big scoop of vanilla ice cream. I gobbled down delicious hotdogs on street corners, enjoyed pastrami corned beef on rye, and smoked whitefish in the Jewish delis. On my first weekend in the Big Apple, I attended a concert featuring the Boston Symphony led by the famed Japanese conductor Seiji Ozawa at the renowned Lincoln Center. I visited the green room as the guest of an oboe player whose parents were friends of mine in Hawaii. The very next night, I saw "Death of a Salesman" on Broadway and sitting in front of me was the playwright Arthur Miller. I couldn't believe my fantastic fortune. These artists were demi-gods in my book. I'd only just landed, and here I was, mingling among the stars. It all felt so surreal.

The wide variety of opportunities New York had to offer blew Hong Kong and Hawaii out of the water. There were always symphonies and operas to attend. Tickets were expensive. However, I befriended an usher at the Metropolitan Opera who would sneak me into a seat that he knew would be empty for a mere five dollars. I saw outstanding performances by some of the greatest artists in the world: Renee Fleming, Beverly Sills, Joan Sutherland, Luciano Pavarotti, and Placido Domingo. Mondays were especially exciting as it was a black tie for men, and the women got really dressed up in their most lovely and dazzling ballgowns. Today, when I occasionally notice people wearing t-shirts and shorts to the opera, I become nostalgic for my first years in New York, when the audience showed their most profound respect to the performers by putting their best foot forward.

New York City was the stuff of strangeness and dreams. I learned to embrace the ceaseless clattering of footsteps on the streets, the first and last snowfalls of the season, like white tissues that kiss the earth and immediately disappear, and how it is never really dark – with illuminated buildings that seem to be sucked into a misty, vibrant sky. New York felt like the center of the universe and the capital of the globe, and the bedrock of romance and influence.

But what I appreciated most was that New York City teemed with cultured people knowledgeable about such a wide range of topics. I thought I was a pretty worldly, wise young woman, but often, I found myself at a dinner table where someone would comment that the Berlin Philharmonic was coming in September and that they'd be performing Beethoven's Ninth before diving into the history of the world-famous composition. And then someone else would reply, "Yes, the last time I heard this Choral Symphony, the choir was brilliant! Von Karajan was conducting it, and the Ode to Joy part was particularly amazing!" Everyone seemed so in tune with the arts and the happenings of the planet, and I was a little intimidated as I grasped the depths of my ignorance.

During that first year in New York, I kept my mouth closed and tried to absorb as much as possible from the personalities around me. I read the newspaper every day to soak up information so I would have something to say. New York was full of people rich not only in knowledge and talent but also in material wealth that often was hidden away in high-rise apartments filled with great art collections and exquisite treasures. Outwardly, most of the real New Yorkers I got to know were relatively low-key. The longer I walked the New York streets, past the towering buildings, flashing lights, stern-faced bankers, and flamboyant artists, the more confident I was that it was where I wanted to live, the place that felt like home.

Shortly after I arrived in New York, I met a man called George Lang, a Hungarian at least twenty-five years my senior. He was a consultant to many revered restaurants worldwide and had a hand in a few famous ones in New York, such as The Four Seasons and the Café des Artistes. Short, stocky, and filled with boundless energy, George was not especially good-looking nor excessively wealthy on a material level. Still, he lived very well in a stunning duplex apartment on Central Park West and was a true Renaissance man adored by many.

Further, George was a fantastic violinist, an extraordinary writer who authored many books and upheld an exceptional network of famous friends such as the designer Milton Glaser, the cosmetics executive Ronald Lauder, and a bevy of politicians, famous chefs, hotel developers, writers, and entrepreneurs. George hosted the most fabulous parties with the most delightful flowers and the most exciting and magnificently presented food, always accentuated by the most spellbinding tunes flowing through the rooms. His piano was the centerpiece of every occasion.

Through George, I had the honor of meeting a string of well-known musicians, including the Hungarian American cellist Janos Starker, conductor Lorin Maazel, violinist Pinchas Zukerman and one of the greatest American classical pianists, Gary Graffman. George often invited me to play the piano with these legendary figures during his soirees, and I was flattered by his attention. There was no time to be nervous, and I giddily accepted. I learned a lot from George about how to live life, excel in what you do, write enchanting prose, love music, and, most of all, how to entertain and nurture deep and lasting friendships.

One afternoon, George beckoned me to follow him. He wanted to show me the drawings he had commissioned from an architect to redesign and remodel his apartment – and announced that he had carved out a special part of his apartment just for me. I gasped. I knew George was very keen on me, but this was not what I expected nor what I wanted.

George proposed then and there, which sadly led to our friendship's end. Until then, I was not aware that a brave gesture could hold and destroy so much. It marked the first time anyone had offered me their hand in marriage, and while it was done with such care to detail and with such an incredibly touching romantic flair, I did not love George and could not possibly marry him. Besides, I was still in my early twenties. How could I get married so young? I was far from ready to settle down.

After I declined, George did not talk to me again. His friends told me he wept every time my name was mentioned in conversation. I felt so rotten for his heartbreak and missed his friendship and guidance terribly, but I had no regrets about my decision. I could not marry him, nor anyone else at that time. I was determined to remain unattached, a free spirit navigating the adult world through my own time and space, and to figure out who I was and the journey that awaited me.

LEARNING IMMIGRANT WISDOM

1970s New York City was vastly different from what it is today. One rarely ever saw Asian women around town. Thus, we were considered unfamiliar and exotic. No matter where I went, I stood out. Many men would not go out with us Asian girls, but a growing number were curious. Just because they were intrigued about Asian women, however, didn't mean that they were genuinely interested in me as a person.

Given that I resembled a China doll, exhibiting the classic feminine features of an oval-shaped face, plump lips and an obtuse jaw angle, men often expected me to be like the characters they saw in movies: subdued, with a painted perfect smile and walking three steps behind men. Once, I sat next to an immensely powerful man on Wall Street during a dinner at the home of a very esteemed Manhattan couple.

"You mean you are young and beautiful, and you are not kept by any man?" he asked, genuinely surprised.

This wasn't the first time such a phrase was tossed my way. It never offended me. I was proud of my single status as I maneuvered through my young adulthood. Moreover, such an attitude towards women was probably not reserved exclusively for Asians. Still, since I would always have a Chinese face, I resolved then and there to always represent my heritage well. I paid meticulous attention to the way I dressed and presented myself to others. I made sure to speak English well, to read extensively, and to keep up with the newest trends. As a new immigrant, I was adamant not to give anyone reason to look down on me.

I also paid close attention to other newcomers' successes in New York. Among the city's most thriving and established immigrants were the generations of Jewish people. They began arriving in large numbers in the late 1800s, fleeing discrimination in Europe. This was around when my paternal grandfather and great-great uncle set sail together from Canton to seek their fortune in San Francisco.

I looked around the city and could not help but notice the outstanding contribution Jews made to the very foundation of New York. I quickly learned that at the beginning, when they first reached the shores, they were treated as inferior, barred from certain clubs and from living in certain buildings in New York. Nonetheless, the Jewish arrivals worked extremely hard to elevate themselves into positions of power and influence. Rather than grovel for acceptance for the snooty-nosed others, they started their own clubs, built their own buildings, and established their own positions of leadership.

I also noticed that Jews held many important positions in media, financial institutions and public office and were some of the countries' leading doctors and lawyers. I had never met any Jews before, not in Hong Kong nor in Hawaii, so I decided to educate myself. I visited a bookstore, and the first two books I bought were "A History of the Jews" by Abram Leon Sachar, the American historian and former President of Brandeis University, and "The Joy of Yiddish" by the American humorist Leo Rosten.

My eyes were opened to the stories of family-oriented and philanthropic entrepreneurs, whose names adorn some of the city's most significant buildings from concert halls and theaters to libraries, hospitals, and museums, all built with the visions and donations of Jewish benefactors. It was imperative that I learn from them. Soon, my Rolodex was replete with more Jewish names than Chinese names. I memorized a number of Yiddish words and found they came in very handy.

One time, in 2009, the Sheba Hospital of Israel honored me for being their ambassador, a "special bridge between East and West." At the awards dinner, I was asked to give a thank-you speech to a completely Jewish audience. I first apologized for my "chutzpah" for using Yiddish at all. Then, I told the crowd that when I schlepped to Israel several years earlier, I came to be known there as "Yoshi Cohen" in a nod to how much I loved to nosh cream cheese and bagels. I shared that I knew I was definitely a "shiksa" (a term for a non-Jewish girl) and that, like the Chinese, Jewish families have a lot of "mishegas" (crazy folks) because they are so close.

The audience laughed hysterically, and after the event, a little lady came up to me, beaming from ear to ear, insisting that she had to meet this Chinese "shiksa" who received an award from the Jews. I hit it off right away with this woman, who turned out to be world-famous sex therapist and television host Dr. Ruth Westheimer, who remains a very dear friend to this day.

MY GREEK MOTHER

Another of New York's immigrant communities I came

to admire was the Greeks, whose diners served me my first delicious spanakopita – a savory Greek loaded with layers of crispy phyllo dough shielding the rich spinach and feta cheese filling – and carried the most astoundingly thick menus with something for everyone.

One afternoon, I was enjoying lunch with a friend at such a restaurant when she motioned for me to follow her, whispering, "Let me introduce you to someone." My friend led me to a man who she introduced as Mr. Jacobson. My friend explained to him that I was looking for a job. Mr. Jacobson replied that a Greek lady with whom he served on a charity board was looking for an assistant. He made a quick call and instructed me to immediately head over to the office of Mrs. Kakia Livanos, the Director of the United Greek Orthodox Charities.

I knew nothing about charities and even less about the Greek community. I was dressed in orange short-shorts under a long skirt split in the front, the in-fashion at the time, but so inappropriate for a job interview! I nervously followed the man's cue and walked straight over to her small but pleasant office. An incredibly refined-looking lady greeted me. She was around 60 or so years old with big, beautiful eyes and shining white hair. She donned a simple, dignified dress, accompanied by rings and earrings made from elegant stones and emboldened with a family crest.

This most extraordinary woman was the former wife of the late Greek shipping magnate George M. Livanos. Mrs. Livanos hired me on the spot to be her personal assistant, confessing later that she was taken by my innocent smile and chic outfit the moment she saw me.

"Cute as a button," she exclaimed with a broad smile.

I started working with the Greek community and had the most wonderful time. Mrs. Livanos often discussed charity events we would hold with Greek Orthodox priests dressed in long black robes. I traveled to Chicago and New Hampshire, where many Greeks lived, to choose suitable locations. Mrs. Livanos was kind and thoughtful, taking me under her wing and treating me like a member of her own family. Every Friday, she invited me to join her family for dinner, and I was always invited to join them at Greek Easter and other special occasions.

Through Mrs. Livanos, I learned a different degree of sophistication and elegance. She always dressed, spoke, and wrote with a beautiful, delicate hand. The consummate host, she entertained in her lovely, not-too-big, but tastefully decorated Upper Eastside apartment and always served her guests delectable food and drinks, making every visitor feel wanted and valuable.

During those few years working with Mrs. Livanos, I learned to dance the Sirtaki – a group of traditional Greek dances of the "dragging" style – and to fall in love with Greek food. I could eat Greek salad every day and never tire of the fresh feta drizzled in olive oil on a bed of crispy lettuce and cucumbers. I was also blessed with the opportunity to meet influential Greeks such as Twentieth Century Fox Chairman Spyros Skouras and shipping magnate Aristotle Onassis, who, later on, would be my neighbor on Sutton Square, where he lived with his longtime girlfriend, the world-famous Greek

American opera singer Maria Callas.

Moreover, Mrs. Livanos helped me cultivate the habit of embracing demanding work. She was so well off that she didn't have to work. Yet, she did so seven days a week, running charities and incredibly mindful of the people she wished to assist. Mrs. Livanos surrounded herself with the nicest people, who were always ready to give generously of themselves. I felt fortunate to be in her orbit.

During my tenure as her assistant, Mrs. Livanos watched over me like a hawk, protecting me from men who expressed interest. One man I met during this period was a Greek who owned one of the biggest cruise ship companies in the world. He was tall, dark, and handsome – the walking epitome of a Greek God – and always impeccably dressed in carefully tailored designer suits. One evening after dinner, we returned to his apartment, and he showed me his fantastic wardrobe of probably two hundred suits. I had never encountered a man with such a closet.

The shipping tycoon invited me to have dinner with him the following night, too, and I agreed. He showed up at my apartment with a robin's-egg-blue box from Tiffany containing a beautiful silver bracelet. While charming, something about the lavish gift made me nervous. The following day, I showed the bracelet to Mrs. Livanos, and she instantly put words to my concerns.

"Beware of Greeks bearing gifts!" she exclaimed.

Still, I couldn't help but be a little mesmerized and didn't listen either to myself or Mrs. Livanos – accepting the handsome Greek's invitation to join him and another couple for the weekend on the Caribbean island of St. Martin.

Soon after the early morning flight took off from New York, my date started drinking a lot of vodka. During the flight, he was jarringly rude to the flight attendants and generally obnoxious to everyone else. By the time we landed, he was smashed and intolerable.

At dinner, he became even more crude and abusive. I had never encountered a drunk like this before, and I was so concerned that I tip-toed over to the other couple's suite and stayed the night with them. I bought a ticket for the first flight off the island the next day. I was so inexperienced with men and was terrified by expectation and what might happen next. For a long time, I didn't accept invitations to go anywhere with any man, scarred by the illusion of outward perceptions and always assuming the worst. People can appear exceptionally charming from the outside, and I did not want to be fooled again.

Not long after that ill-fated weekend, another hurdle surfaced. I received a letter from the United States Immigration Office informing me that my visa, granted on the basis that I was doing Practical Training in the United States, was about to expire and that soon I would have to go back to Hong Kong. The authorities only gave me two months' notice to pack and leave. I felt a sense of dread and panic rise in my throat. I did not want to leave my beloved city and could not imagine returning to Hong Kong.

When I told my friends, every single one of them tried to find a solution for me. There were some interesting proposals. One friend even suggested I marry her autistic brother for a little while and then divorce once I had secured a green card. In the end, Mrs. Livanos sponsored my residency application, which marked one of the most wonderful days of my life.

Another glorious day dawned in 1978 when I retrieved a letter from my mailbox inviting me to be sworn in as a United States of America citizen. I was over the moon. I love America, and becoming a citizen was a great honor for me and remains one of the most noteworthy events to unfurl in my life. My dear friend Margery Liechtenstein, the wife of a notable physician, threw a delightful party at her apartment in my honor. There were American flags everywhere, and the cake was adorned with the stars and stripes, too. It was wonderful and incredibly emotional to have so many friends come by to congratulate me.

Not long afterward, Mrs. Livanos told me she was leaving her post at Greek Orthodox Charities. It was the closing of another chapter. Never one to hold on past the expiration date, I decided to do the same, thus beginning another period in my ever-winding life.

A few months later, in 1979, I went to work for Robert Taplinger. He was a very dapper and polished man with a vast collection of tailored suits, and one of the most famous public relations executives in the entertainment business at the time. I often joined Mr. Taplinger and his notable clientele, including Cary Grant, at dinners and parties. I was also tasked with hosting dinners for them in Chinatown, showing them the best of a part of their city that they barely knew.

Mr. Taplinger was certainly a lady's man. While technically single most of his life, he was known to cavort with some of the most famous ladies of his time, Oscar-winning actress Bette Davis among them. He bestowed a lengthy list of wealthy clients whom I was always intrigued to meet. Sometimes, I was invited to fly cross country on their private jets when they had events in Los Angeles. Mr. Taplinger liked the fact that I was willing to work well into the night no matter the circumstances, and that I never counted the hours, including the weekends, or made a fuss about overtime.

"Why not?" I figured. "These experiences don't come along every day."

That's how I learned so much quickly. I was unafraid to give the position everything I had to offer. The highly connected Mr. Taplinger rewarded my tenacious work with introductions to his fancy friends, including June Martino, the ever-powerful Secretary-Treasurer at McDonald's. She was then the highest-paid female executive in an American corporation. When the fast-food chain founder, Ray Kroc, hired June as his first bookkeeper, he had no money, so he paid her in stock. When I met June, McDonald's was a top-ten global brand, and her fortunes had soared.

Through my work with Mrs. Livanos and Mr. Taplinger, I developed an understanding of what it meant to work hard and stay humble enough to study a lot and absorb all I could. My employers noticed these qualities and were eager to support and connect me with all kinds of opportunities to prosper and grow. Apart from reinforcing my work ethic through rewards, I also learned shorthand – essentially, how to write a press release and follow up on all my work. Whatever skills I acquired in one job transferred to the next, and I steadily built upon my knowledge base. The time spent working and studying relentlessly was never wasted.

When Mrs. Livanos passed away at 82 in 2002, I was heartbroken. I was in Shanghai when I received the devastating news, and I flew back to New York for her funeral. I could not pass up the opportunity to pay my respects to the woman who, after my mother, had the most considerable influence on the woman I was becoming.

Mrs. Livanos taught me so much, from the quiet power of a simple, classy appearance to the magnitude of advocating tirelessly for causes that matter to the dynamism of elegant penmanship. Mrs. Livanos had the most exquisite handwriting I ever knew.

LOOKING TO THE STARS

In the summer of 1982, I was invited to stay at June Martino's sumptuous white mansion in Palm Beach, Florida.

At one of her lavish soirees, I met an elderly gentleman named Norman Arens, a pleasantly plump man with white hair and a captivating smile, then considered the most famous astrologer in America after departing a 44-year career as a high-profile banker to pursue a more profound spiritual calling. Norman took an instant shine to me and said he wanted to do a reading for me, although he usually didn't make charts for anyone other than his students.

I visited Norman in his West Palm Beach residence. He drew my chart and, bubbling over with excitement, told me that he had not seen one as exciting for a long time. I asked Norman if I should be in the TV industry. He replied without hesitation that not only should I be on the screen, but that it would catapult me into a hard-to-fathom level of fame. Norman explained that the "career house" in my life chart (there are twelve houses in astrology, each representing various parts of life) contained the sun and three of the most potent planets – Neptune, Jupiter, and Mercury. The sun represents the top of the universe with the creative life force; Neptune influences beauty, cosmetics, TV, and movies; Jupiter influences expansion; and Mercury affects communication.

Norman stated reassuringly that I could be expected to do well in all these areas.

I desperately wanted to believe every word and started checking in with him each time I wanted to make a big move. Almost everything Norman told me over the years, right up to his death in 2006, came true.

By the time I first met Norman, I was no longer an active member of LDS. I had lost the enjoyment I once had for attending Church, but I remained very spiritual and open to the messages of God and the religion, finding solace in my journey. To this day, I continue to adhere to the Mormon practice of donating at least ten percent of my income to a greater cause, and I do not drink alcohol or smoke. While no longer officially Mormon, the movement still holds a special place in my heart.

Little me with Mum and Dad in Guangxi

In Hong Kong with Little Piano and my best friend from high school Connie Chan

Leaving for Hawaii in 1963, saying goodbye to friends and family in Hong Kong

Japanese event at Brigham Young University Hawaii

At 19, I became a princess in the Narcisus Festival Beauty Pageant

With Greek "mother" Mrs. Kakia Livanos. Board members of the United Greek Orthodox Charities

I threw many fun parties in my tiny New York studio apartment

My extended family, the Rizzutos

With Luciano Pavarotti, Andy Warhol, LeRoy Neiman, Dr. Arthur Sackler, and Iris Apfel

Dr. and Mrs. Jill Sackler and Mum and Dad; with Hubert Burda and Dr. Ruth

Reunion with my college roommate Helen and Charlie Goo family in 2020

With my sisters Brenda, Vickie, and Sansan

Family get-together: Vickie, Brenda, Dad, Mom, me, and Sansan

The house where I was born in Yan Shan Garden in Guilin will be made into a museum

Sergio Orozco with my brother-in-law Lincoln Leong and my nephew Alexander

All my sisters with my wonderful Malaysian family

Yue-Sai Kan's life straddles the East and West as an Emmy-winning television producer, best-selling author, entrepreneur and humanitarian. Scan the QR code to access Yue-Sai's YouTube channel and find some of her earliest television moments and most captivating celebrity interviews.

CHANGING THE
FACE OF CHINA,
ONE LIPSTICK
AT A TIME

The New York City winter of 1990 was the warmest and the coldest of my life.

I finally met my Prince Charming – a dashing, muscular, articulate redhead named James McManus. He was a marketing extraordinaire, thus exceptionally equipped at selling himself from the moment we locked eyes at a dinner party. I didn't know then that we would be married in a lavish ceremony just a couple of years later.

Afterward, we went on our honeymoon to China. The first stop was Guilin (桂林), where I was born. I wanted my husband to see firsthand this beautiful place in my native country's lush southwest. With my "One World" celebrity as a calling card, the mayor of Guilin greeted us at the airport and escorted us to a suite at a lovely local hotel. The mayor celebrated our arrival with a special round of firecrackers that took James by surprise. No matter what my husband had read about me, he was unprepared for all the attention I drew everywhere we stepped foot in China.

Next, we visited Beijing, entering a near-empty hotel. After the previous year's tragedy; most foreign investments and businesses got cold feet. They rapidly withdrew from China, and nobody had re-entered to take their place.

Feeling a little gloomy, I received an upbeat welcome phone call from the Office of the Vice Premier, Tian Jiyun (田纪云), who invited us to meet with him for a private dinner of just four – he and his assistant, James, and I – at the Diaoyutai State Guesthouse (钓鱼台国宾馆). At that time, Tian was responsible for all foreign investment across the country. At the dinner, he turned to my new husband.

"You are now a Chinese son-in-law, and you should do some business in China," Tian enthused. "If you want to invest in China, we will help you."

Tian then looked me in the eye and noted, "As you know, many foreign companies and investors are spooked by the incident and are leaving China. You are very famous, and if you register a company in China at this time, it will help our image tremendously."

I paused. This was something I had not even thought about. Later that evening, James asked me, "If you could do business in China, what business would you do?"

"Cosmetics," I replied without pause.

I had been wearing makeup on television for years but could never find any cosmetics suitable for Asian faces and thus our relatively small deep brown eyes with heavy lids, black hair, flat noses and the yellow skin tone and texture of our skin. In the U.S. and many other developed countries, women used cosmetics every day – painting their faces and applying lipstick was and still is as routine as brushing teeth, and I believed that with the opening, Chinese women would one day do the same. I wanted to design cosmetic products specifically for Asian women; and I wanted them to fall in love with this transformation process as much as I had.

Immediately after our thought-provoking honeymoon, I registered the brand Yue-Sai in March 1991, with a square logo designed with my Chinese name, Yue-Sai (羽西), hand-written by my father. The decision to turn from culture to business disappointed many of my friends. Some felt my decision would diminish my status in China as a cultural ambassador and dilute society's respect for my work, which pivoted on helping educate Chinese society through television. Back then, those who started companies were not lauded or known names and the career was considered far less esteemed than being the television personality. However, I was not fazed by the negative response. I remained steadfast in my vision to create a brand that was more than just a product but a means of transformation for millions of Chinese women.

How perceptions have changed since then. Today, successful businesspeople are the stars of Chinese society and very much admired and looked up to, as much as any silver screen sensation. Yet back then, China was not a major cosmetics market – not even close. Most Chinese women wore gray, blue and black clothes with no makeup on their faces, essentially visceral representations of the historically stark struggles through years of revolution and famine.

The fact that Chinese women did not use cosmetics was precisely why I wanted to enter the market. I knew it would be difficult because most did not even have a rudimentary understanding of cosmetics or what to do with them. It would undoubtedly take tremendous education and promotion, but that did not scare me. It made me all the more excited. As I mentioned earlier, my father always urged me to be the first person to the moon.

During that time, cosmetics were limited to actors on stage. Such use was considered bourgeois, even criminal, for ordinary people. The country was physically dreary, dull, and colorless. The word "beauty" was not part of the vocabulary. Everyone looked the same – the same clothes and the same hair.

Only after China's doors opened following the Revolution in 1978 did people's imagination of beauty begin to emerge. For the first time, some Chinese people dared to consider wearing clothing a bit more colorful, but no one person or entity led the way. I longed for Chinese women to have a tool to assist them to look their best. Cosmetics could help to emancipate and to empower.

"If you can change your appearance, you can be and do anything you wish!" I would often tell my friends.

This was a novel idea, and it was the very spirit that I wanted to inject into the psyche of Chinese women. With regard to raising the capital to get Yue-Sai Cosmetics moving, I was extremely fortunate to have James by my side, working ardently to bring the financing aspect to life. By 1996, just five years after I registered the business, Yue-Sai Cosmetics was the number one brand in China, proving that the message was heard loud and clear.

To reach that apex, I had to overcome many obstacles. The first of them was personal. I knew how to put makeup on myself but had yet to do it on others, so I needed to learn how to do makeup as beauty experts do. The first time I did it, drawing eyebrows on people and contouring their cheekbones, I was so nervous my hands shook. After much practice convincing my friends to come over and act as my guinea pigs, my makeup technique got to be good and very fast.

Many Chinese women I met repeated a familiar refrain, confessing to me as if I were a long-lost friend, "Yue-Sai, I'm embarrassed to tell you that I'm nervous because this is my first time holding a lipstick!"

While building the company, I also gave countless lectures around China. At Fudan University (复旦大学), Shanghai's number one institution of higher education, my address sparked an intense debate among the students as some of them proclaimed that women should learn how to use this tool to improve their appearance, while others argued that cosmetics was "spiritual pollution" and should be banned, and that we should be proud of su mian chao tian (素面朝天), or "wearing a naked face."

On another occasion, I talked with a group of high school teachers in Beijing, and one of them remarked: "Teachers should lead by setting a good example, and we should demonstrate the virtues of frugality and zero vanity by not using makeup."

"What you say is only half true," I replied. "Teachers should definitely lead by example, but on some occasions, putting on some makeup shows your respect for others. You don't want to embarrass yourself and your host at a more formal event by looking messy. As a leader, your image is important. Your students will follow your lead and learn to create a good image for themselves."

Not long after, that same group of high school teachers helped me host China's first teachers' makeup competition. To further open up the market, I worked relentlessly to educate consumers, publishing a book entitled "Yue-Sai's Guide to Asian Beauty," (《亚洲妇女美容指南》) which taught Chinese women en masse how to do makeup. I supplemented the book and lectures by writing and interviewing for countless articles, appearing on television programs, and personally teaching large groups of women how to apply such aesthetic goodies.

My company proved a turning point for the entire cosmetics market in China, which I essentially opened and dominated. In showing millions how to improve their appearance, I imparted a crucial message: "If you can enhance any part of the face you were born with, you can enhance other parts of your life, too."

My message of self-improvement eventually played into the government's new policy to encourage Chinese people to become consumers in the model of many advanced societies worldwide, although the brand did take a little time to really resonate with the political powerhouses of the time. But the concept was something of an instant success to the broader Chinese community, a concept that truly spurred a consumer revolution in China and inspired a generation of women entrepreneurs. Noting my success, many Chinese women probably said to themselves: If Yue-Sai can do it, I can, too! Every time I heard this; my heart sang with joy.

I wanted to empower other women to shatter the ceilings and take the throne as a top executive. Not only are multitudes of Chinese women today starting their own companies, but they are also heading major foreign companies. For example, Angela Dong is the top brass of Nike in China, while Isabel GE takes the helm at Apple. Chinese women have been lucky in the sense that they haven't faced the same level of discrimination as other women in developing, and even Western countries, when it comes to excelling in one's career. While I felt very alone when I launched my television jaunt among a sea of all men, Chinese women today are calling the powerful shots anywhere and everywhere.

Nonetheless, it takes a special skill set to become an entrepreneur, and it simply isn't a path for everyone. To make it work, one must really want it – want it from a place that rattles their bones, and they must strongly believe that this is the way and the only way for them. A true entrepreneur at heart is one who is willing to dangle most of their body outside of a high-story window, merely grasping the window ledge for support. He or she knows that they could fall at anytime, but it does not to deter them from cowering away from the thrill of possibility.

I have to thank Vice Premier Tian Jiyun, whose inspiration and support for Yue-Sai Cosmetics proved invaluable. Secondly, I have to thank my then-husband, James McManus. He had a lot of business experience and provided vital advice on finances. James was most helpful in setting up the company, helped me to find a few initial investors, and was also an excellent sound board. For anyone, especially women, starting in business, the most significant need is someone who can give smart and sensical business advice. Men often have trusted friends and associates with whom they golf or drink, share confidences, and exchange thoughts and ideas. Women of my generation simply did not have that kind of support circle.

Thirdly, I have to thank Sam, a former member of the Chinese delegation to the United Nations. He spoke good English and had robust connections in China. The year we decided to delve into the cosmetics business, Sam had just graduated with a master's degree in International Economics from Johns Hopkins University, and we offered him the general manager job. Gleefully, he accepted. Sam was willing to learn accounting and how to run a business from James, and quickly took off like an absolute pro.

As his first duty with the company, I asked Sam to research the best city in China for us to register Yue-Sai Cosmetics Ltd. We visited factories in Beijing, Tianjin (天津) and Shanghai and were surprised by the antiquity of the equipment used for cosmetics production in China. We applied to various local governments for investment breaks for a cosmetics manufacturing operation, but all of them, including Shanghai, turned us down. Then, through his wife, Sherry – who also worked for the China section at the U.N. - Sam contacted someone in the new economic zone of Shenzhen (深圳), next to Hong Kong. He was advised to visit a local government official named Li Hao (李灏), who turned out to be the Mayor of Shenzhen. When Sam arrived at the office, Li Hao exited a meeting early to greet him and said with enthusiasm: "We have received a call from Mr. Tian. Let me introduce our staff to assist you."

As it turned out, Shenzhen was the best place to start the company because it offered many tax breaks and great flexibility, and we applied for a business license. Cosmetics, we were informed, was a restricted industry, and therefore we would have to partner with a local Chinese company. Through Sam, I told Mayor Li that if that were the case, I would withdraw my application. I needed to do this alone. Having a partner is essentially the same as having a boss; you never really have true freedom. My fame and backing from on high in Beijing made it nearly impossible for him to turn down my request.

The next snag arose when Sam regretfully informed me that the wholly foreign-owned manufacturing entity I was setting up would only be approved if I could guarantee that 90% of our product was for export.

"But my product is specially designed for Asian women!" I protested. "How can we sell it in the United States when we don't even sell in China?"

Sam delivered Mayor Li's position: a joint venture to sell into China, otherwise, export-only.

"NO! NO! NO!" I shouted to nobody in particular.

I insisted on sole proprietorship, which I knew was nearly impossible. I had a name, and I believed that China was where things could be worked out as nothing is allowed and everything is possible. Sam, the former diplomat, found a way. He argued eloquently before the officials that Yue-Sai's goal was to change the image of Chinese women and make them international. Shenzhen was synonymous with "reform and opening up."

"How can you let her down?" Sam asked the officials.

Finally, the approval came through on August 15, 1991. I exuberantly traveled to Shenzhen with James and Sam to formalize the first cosmetics business license issued to an American business in China.

At the subsequent banquet given by the Shenzhen Municipal Government, Mayor Li pointed out that the Yue-Sai Cosmetics project was only approved as a special dispensation because of my name, Yue-Sai. I felt that all my years of tireless work, from a low-income family to coming to America and rising through the ranks, came to fruition at that very moment. What I was doing felt like a much deeper calling than anything I had ever done, that I could play a transformative role in an ever-changing China.

The company was registered in seven working days, probably still among the fastest registrations ever for a WFOE, a Wholly Foreign-Owned Enterprise, a company set up without a Chinese partner. Due to favorable policies in Shenzhen, we could import machines and other equipment without paying the usual exorbitant import duties.

In those days, Shenzhen was an oversized fishing village of 875,000 people, a far cry from the boomtown of nearly 18 million that it is today – China's Silicon Valley and home to Internet giants such as Tencent. Shenzhen in 1990 was a radical concept, an experiment called a Special Economic Zone, designed by Deng Xiaoping. China's Open Door Policy started there, with manufacturing. Officials leased the land inexpensively to attract manufacturers, especially those from neighboring Hong Kong. Workers from all over China flocked to this new frontier town to work, forge a new life, and become pioneers in the hopes of making real money. "To Get Rich is Glorious" was Deng's slogan for the people.

Sam worked quickly on his toes and managed the fast-growing business exceptionally well. He possessed a sharp mind with a can-do attitude, and the logistics and manufacturing side grew strongly under his leadership. James went to China every two weeks to pore over the numbers with Sam then play golf. Thank God I had Sam to entertain him because I was always busy.

Moreover, Sam's wife, Sherry, is one of the brightest and most intelligent people I have ever met in China, with a remarkable ability to navigate the country's red tape and political inner workings. In Sam's first two years with the company, she stayed in New York. I suggested she move to China and work with Yue-Sai Cosmetics, too, first as our new business development manager, a role that would lead her eventually to become head of sales and marketing. Shen had an uncanny knack for understanding the politics of any situation, was highly articulate and able to negotiate well with store managers, ensuring our counters got the best locations. I traveled constantly and extensively with Sherry all over the country. She was great at landing our products in stores, but no matter how much I taught her, she could not seem to learn to put makeup on her face with any skill. Like her inability to speak good English, these were things we always made the butt of our inside jokes.

Without Sam and Sherry, Yue Sai Cosmetics could not have developed as fast and as well as it did. While I was the face of the company that bore my name and the front person, they held my back up and were my unconditional, solid support. China was – and still is – a tough place to do business due to its language, unique history, opaque laws, and politics. Westerners who plan to succeed in China need a guru, a trusted guide to navigate the minefields and misunderstandings. This couple served as that for me. I am forever grateful for their devotion, hard work, and guidance.

We purchased the whole top floor of a most sought after industrial building in Shenzhen at that time, and we turned it into a small office, factory, and warehouse. However, initially, we shipped all products – from lipstick to skincare – pre-made from U.S. cosmetics factories, so all we needed to do was re-package them. No research and development (R&D) were required because there were no technical staff to develop cosmetics in China then.

I returned to Shenzhen in the late summer of 2023 and saw the building that once housed my first factory. It exists in an area now deemed the "old" industrial town and if you drive a few jagged miles down the same street, you will see the "new" industrial town which is amazingly modern and smart. The scale of change still blows my mind.

In addition, trademarks are essential, and when we applied to register the Yue-Sai logo, we found that a farmer in a remote area had already registered the name. As annoying as that was, he was a pretty smart guy. I sent Sherry to talk to him. She found him standing half-naked in the doorway of his farmhouse, flanked by a large mastiff.

"What do you want?" the farmer croaked fiercely.

Sherry later divulged that she had never been more terrified in her life. In the end, we successfully bought the trademark from him. However, it was an unpleasant experience that led me, especially in those early days of China's foray into the global marketplace, to advise my friends to trademark their brands to protect themselves immediately. Thankfully, China today has a trademark law that allows celebrities like me to protect our names automatically. No one can register my name or the name of a high-profile person without their consent.

Having learned such a lesson the hard way, I quickly

registered my name in every category except armaments – not an industry I ever planned to dabble in – and alcohol because I don't drink. Unbelievably, someone later developed a medicinal wine called Yue-Sai. However, still today we see beauty salons in small towns using my name and image, and we have to exercise a tiresome amount of resources to go after the misleading profiteers.

During the startup and launch phase, another major problem Yue-Sai Cosmetics faced was discouragement from Chinese government departments. After decades of deprivation, cosmetics were still considered non-essential. Yet, I refused to give in. I understood that Chinese women were slowly starting to explore skin care after such "materialistic" concepts had been suppressed for decades. This was also an important part of the "One World" television series and the cosmetics company aimed at ordinary Chinese people.

I was very grateful for my father's blessing. As it turned out, he was an exceptionally devout supporter of my cosmetics business because he was extremely sensitive to how the dominant white society in the United States sidelined Chinese people, something he experienced for many years in Hong Kong.

"Yue-Sai witnessed the lack of makeup among Chinese women," he wrote in a letter to a journalist profiling my life. "Compared with Western women, there existed a huge difference in appearances. She believed that for Chinese women to stand up, they must first pay attention to external beauty. Sure enough, with Yue-Sai's hard work in a relatively short period, she achieved so much, from fundraising to product design, from building factories to training personnel, publishing books, and educating Chinese on how to use makeup. She has amazed us with her determination and flawless timing. It's so admirable that she has gone so far without any of her parents' aid. I'm so proud to have a daughter like her."

Nevertheless, starting a company takes an almost unfathomable amount of work. You need confidence in your vision and must be determined to go through all the difficulties to reach the goal. I aimed to create a product that combined the best ingredients from the West and the East to enhance the status of women. Each product had to contain traditional Chinese herbs. My first lipstick smelled deliciously of jasmine. Formulas had to be suitable for sensitive Asian skin, and colors needed to be ideal for Chinese complexions.

As the company began to take form, I leased an old building in Shanghai's Pudong (浦东) district, renovated the rundown and dusty interior, and transformed it into a clean and ready-to-go factory. I needed a manager to set it up, but I couldn't find a local suitable for the task. In the United States, I was introduced to an American couple who owned a cosmetics factory that had just sold to Shiseido, the Japanese cosmetics brand. I invited them to work in Shanghai to train our Chinese employees, and they worked relentlessly for over a year.

While I knew how to use cosmetics, I did not know how to make them. So, the first act I undertook after my decision to start the Yue-Sai brand was to learn from the experts how to bring these tiny but prized items to life. I located the best cosmetic laboratory in the United States, which happened to be nearby in New Jersey. Then, I spent many hours with the chemists, learning about the various ingredients and the precise art of formulating these products.

I also became something of a student under the tutelage of the best Chinese doctors, developing a stronger understanding as to how medicinal Chinese herbs could be incorporated into our formulas. This part of the work was exciting, and I absorbed as much knowledge as possible. However, the most riveting aspect for me was testing the colors to bring the most suitable shades to life. There are colors that Chinese and Asians generally cannot wear. We have black hair and a yellow-tinged skin tone, definitely different from the blue-eyed, blonde-haired, white-skinned girls. I spent months experimenting with shades and colors on all kinds of Asian skin. During this time, my Chinese friends complained that the moment I met anyone, I would ask them to sit down facing the natural light so that I could trial colors on them. Of course, I tried them on myself first, matching hundreds of assorted colors and textures in coordination with skin tones unique to Asians.

Additionally, I learned early that to start a new business, I needed to come to terms with all the things that I did not know, and then dutifully set about conquering those mysterious parts. A critical key to success is a willingness to find the best teachers, and then to study as though your life depends on it.

I could not lose sight of the fact that my customers were uneducated about colors and the use of makeup, let alone how to coordinate the various components when they got dressed. To make it easier for them, I created a unique color chart. This was pivotal to the prosperity of the business – bringing to life colors especially for Asian skin tones, which nobody had done before. I researched dutifully, ensuring a palette as close to perfection as possible.

On either side of the chart was a group of fabric colors carefully studied and chosen to make Chinese skin look younger, brighter, and flawless. Yes, colors are magical. A certain color can make you look either dazzling or dull, so as Asians, with our particular skin tone and hair color, we must choose carefully. For example, I have yet to see an Asian look good in mustard-colored clothes. This color brings the sallowness in our skin to the surface and makes us look tired.

After I chose my favorite clothing colors, I grouped them into three families: orange, pink and neutral. I created nine perfect lipstick colors and two rouges in orange and pink to coordinate with them. For one, if I wear a pink dress from one side of my color chart, I look across the chart to the corresponding cosmetics and see I will be wearing lipstick from the pink family. I have three different pink lipsticks to choose from, ranging from darker to softer pink, all of which have been tested for the Asian tone. On the chart, neutral clothing like black, deep brown, or deep blue would match lipstick from any of the three groups. Moreover, eye products such as mascara, eye pencils and liquid eyeliner all belonged to the neutral family and could be used by anyone to match all clothing colors.

This chart made getting dressed simple and easy, removing the intimidation of using makeup. I understood that our customers sought guidance, and our easy guidelines became an instant hit. The first group of lipsticks we released on October 1st, 1992, consisted of nine shades. To this day, they remain the most beautiful shades of the Chinese face.

From the beginning, I felt very strongly that product names are important. Therefore, I named all the products myself and wrote the beauty consultant training manual. It struck a chord. My buyers at that time were all inexperienced users, and I wanted them to become sensitive to colors by associating them with world destinations, which was also a nostalgic nod to my TV series "One World."

"New York Orange" couldn't possibly be a mild shade; it had to be formidable and vibrant like the city itself. "Iceland Pink" needed to be pale and cool, not too strong, and then there was "Paris Pink," which was a sexy and sassy rose hue. I wanted customers to come to the makeup counter asking for the colors by name. Even today, after all these years, customers will visit a Yue-Sai Cosmetics counter and request the "Bangkok Orange" lipstick, an evocative burned orange inspired by the saffron robes worn by Thai monks.

We later developed a lotion called "Extraordinary," which sold out primarily because of its oozing-with-confidence name. I always told my team: "If we keep copying and don't innovate, the brand is doomed to fail." It was the job of the beauty consultants running Yue-Sai Cosmetics counters all over China to persuade hundreds of thousands of customers daily to buy our products. I understood from the get-go that our business would fail if the beauty consultants were not well-trained.

While not everyone needs or even wants cosmetics, my

idea was that if a woman did buy lipstick, I wanted her to know how to use it correctly – whether to enhance her lips and/or coordinate with her clothes. The spirit of my brand was to encourage women to accentuate their favorite features and then, inspired, feel confident to improve other aspects of their lives. I wanted each woman to feel empowered to be herself, and not necessarily to conform, which back then meant donning the same dark clothes and the standard haircut of everyone else. I imagined each Yue-Sai customer as developing her own look, expressive of her unique personality. Cosmetics are just a tool for putting forth your best, individual self.

However, cosmetics, as they existed then, were created for Caucasians, whose eyes and face shape are different from Asians. And that is the gap that Yue-Sai Cosmetics was created to fill. Our eyes are smaller and often slant, the very shape of our faces is different, with mostly flat noses, and we tend to be more monochromatic because our eyes and hair tend to be a shade of brown or black. With these specific characteristics in mind, I created the "Three Color Contour Powder" with off-white, medium brown, and dark brown colors, all that was needed to highlight and recess an Asian face. The medium brown is an eyeshadow for shading the sides of the nose to make it taller and for shading the two sides of the face to make it look narrower. The deep brown further deepens the eyes, especially their outer corners. The white is for the highest corners of the eyebrows and for highlighting the middle of the nose. A mix of dark brown and medium brown is used for drawing the eyebrows. All three shades are matte.

The "Three Color Contour Powder" fast became the single

most-used product by all makeup artists in China. It was a revolutionary product specially designed for the Chinese. Back then, one would be hard-pressed to find a single makeup artist without this product in their makeup bag. This little compact quickly became the industry standard in China. It lived up to our slogan, "The Best the World has to Offer to Asian Women," a saying so famous that a male taxi driver once gleefully recited it back to me.

In preparation for the Yue-Sai Cosmetics launch, I read many books. The two most influential were "Don't Go to the Cosmetics Counter Without Me" and "Blue Eyeshadow Should be Illegal," both by Paula Begoun, founder of the Paula's Choice cosmetics brand. Nicknamed the "Cosmetics Cop," Paula was correct about blue eyeshadow, especially for Asian women whose black hair, dark brown eyes, and gold skin tone clashes with blue. Once, I was fortunate enough to have dinner with Paula in a restaurant in Honolulu. I was thrilled to meet this cosmetics icon, and we became good friends. Paula is among the sweetest, most generous, hard-working women I know and with the most radiant and youthful skin.

My colleagues and I also spent a long time designing the Yue-Sai Cosmetics product. It was pivotal that the packaging reflects my personality. My shiny black bob hairstyle was my most famous feature, so all the packaging was made in that shape. Our powder boxes and even our nail polish bottles were made to resemble my hairdo, designed by the famous packaging designer George Gottlieb, who won an award for cosmetics packaging design at the London International Advertising Awards in 1993.

Once we had the ingredients down pat, colors, and designs, it was time to start manufacturing. We started with a small factory in Shenzhen, and while we lacked R&D personnel, I hired the best chemists in New York to formulate semi-finished products, which we then shipped to Shenzhen for processing and packaging. Our employees were very enthusiastic and profoundly serious about their jobs. To ensure that the products met the best standards, they always followed my lead and tested the products on themselves. I did not import powder products, working instead with Mr. Ge Wenyao (葛文耀) of Shanghai Jiahua Cosmetics (上海家化联合股份有限公司), the biggest state-owned personal care products company, whose brands were Liu Shen (六神) and Meijiajing (美加净). Mr. Ge allowed Yue-Sai Cosmetics to make all our powders without investing in the expensive machines needed. I used to call him "my benefactor" or "enren" (恩人) as a token of my gratitude.

However, I do believe that an undeniable factor of my success was due to my practice not of examining how to make a company triumphant, but analyzing and thus mitigating all the ways it could fail. Too many people develop these grandiose ideas of extreme wealth before they even got started, falling prey to false pretensions and selling a certain image, and end up in dismal debt trying to pay off their fancy office suites and flashy sports cars.

Seeing my vision spring into existence was as exhilarating as it was heart-pulsating. Naturally, I dragged my mind through the multitude of ways that I could ultimately fail and did the best I could in the start-up process to remedy the grousing worries in my head. But when it was ready, all I could do was hold my head high and birth Yue-Sai Cosmetics into the world, accepting that much like launching "One World," I had reached a part of the galaxy that no person before me had tread – and there was no turning back.

IN THE WORDS OF SAM

Yue-Sai likes adventure. She wants to do new things while not being forced into anything by somebody else. As we were getting into cosmetics, she'd say, "We are the blind leading the blind," a famous Chinese idiom: 盲人带盲人. I was blind, too. Sure, I'd just graduated from Johns Hopkins and, in theory, knew something about macroeconomics and all this conceptual stuff, but I'd never built a company.

It was a very rare opportunity. I'd graduated and was looking for a job. I was in New York, and one day, Sherry received a phone call from Yue-Sai; I think it was late February of 1991. Yue-Sai called Sherry to ask her if she knew somebody who could work on a cosmetics project. I was the first candidate, but Yue-Sai was worried about the visa. I was on an F1 Student Visa, but after the Tiananmen Square incident, every Chinese in the United States was offered amnesty and had an atypical status. If I wanted to return to China, I could get a pre-approved return visa to the U.S.

I reassured her: "The visa is not an issue, okay? I can get a visa in three days."

Yue-Sai's husband, James, I called him Jim, was a strategic

planner. He was responsible for getting the money, raising the funds and pushing the business in the right direction, not for supervising not the day-to-day operations but the financial stuff and the business plan and production strategy. Overall, Yue-Sai was on product development and all the ideas while I was the one to go to China for the implementation. We just started our journey on March 5, 1991, Lei Feng Day, celebrating the birthday of China's most famous Good Samaritan, the young soldier and martyr Lei Feng (雷锋).

I asked James, "Why don't you hire Estee Lauder or L'Oreal – big bosses and marketing people with experience?"

He took a moment to think and then answered me.

"It's the four of us. You, Yue-Sai, and Sherry have zero business experience. I am 100 percent of the business side, and you three are zero, okay? If I hire very professional people to do this company with me, then who's the boss? But look at Yue-Sai," he said. "She did another job in China, television, without knowing anything. Well, the Chinese market for cosmetics is brand new; it's at exactly zero. So are we, but we can make the market."

James McManus was the CEO of the Marketing Corporation of America. He was a marketing expert. He decided he would not hire any professional management in China at the beginning. First, Jim only had a million dollars for investment at that time, so how could he afford to pay a professional manager? Secondly, how would he work with Yue-Sai if he hired a professional to come to our team? It wasn't an option.

Getting to know the market was most important. Yue-Sai had first-hand knowledge because she'd aired TV programs in China. She spent a lot of time with the Chinese people, especially Chinese women, during the process of producing her "One World" show. She had a very important perspective.

Because we were the blind leading the blind, to get a little bit better acquainted and familiar with some cosmetics ideas, Yue-Sai brought me to the Estee Lauder factory in Long Island, one of the most advanced in the industry at the time. During one of her programs, she interviewed Leonard Lauder and asked the Estee Lauder PR department for a visit to the factory. It was early 1991 when we went to their warehouse. What I saw was amazing. It was an automated factory with little electronic vehicles to move materials from one location to another without people. And also, everything had a barcode. Every shipment would arrive, move along a long conveyor belt through the warehouse, and be checked at every point on its way in and out.

What does a cosmetics factory look like? I needed to know because I was responsible for starting manufacturing in China.

We couldn't tell them why we were there. We just went for a visit, okay? So, I was observing and watching, for example, the pick-and-pack process in the warehouse. Computerized pick-and-pack nowadays is very modern, but at that time, it was new and had already been installed in their Long Island factory. Five lipsticks? Done. The computer made the order, and five lipsticks disappeared from the inventory. This was 1991. America was so advanced already. China's only done this in recent years.

Yue-Sai realized that to live up to her dream, she needed the right product design. She spent a day and a night researching to narrow down products for the first batch we would introduce in China. Secondly, we needed production because these were consumer products for which we could not rely on imports. After all, Chinese women couldn't afford them at the time. Yue-Sai was very clear: she would never bring finished goods into China. My target was to find a location. Beijing, Tianjin: out because they were not advanced in industry. Shanghai was out, too, because the Shanghai government was a very conservative hotbed of China's centrally planned economy. Shanghai said, "We'd love to have Yue-Sai's investment, but cosmetics is on a list of industries to be discouraged." I went to the authorities on her behalf to figure this out.

In Shanghai, we met one of our best friends, a legendary figure in the Chinese cosmetic industry called Ge Wenyao. He had a particularly good vision and offered a lot of help to Yue-Sai Cosmetics in manufacturing. Mr. Ge was the General Manager of the Jiahua Cosmetics factory. He suggested in our first meeting that Shanghai was too conservative and that we'd be better off going to Shenzhen. When he said this to Yue-Sai, James McManus and me, Jim asked, "Where's Shenzhen?"

Shenzhen, of course, is the special development zone in south China next to Guangzhou. Yue-Sai said, "Okay! Questions? We can go there tomorrow." Oh my gosh, so, all of a sudden, I needed to go to Shenzhen, about which I knew nothing. I knew nobody there. I didn't even know where Shenzhen was. I had no knowledge. Nobody knew about Shenzhen.

Shenzhen had just started up. We spent a little time studying what we could about it. However, the next day, Jim and Yue-Sai left to return to the United States. We got nothing from this trip except the knowledge that I needed to go to Shenzhen. I spent one week in the city and did everything. I got the product established and a contract signed, all in three days. The night I flew to Guangzhou, I stayed in a Dong Fang Hotel (东方宾馆), and I called Sherry and said, "They wanted me to go to Shenzhen. And now I'm in Guangzhou, and I know nobody."

Sherry suggested, "Why don't you call the office of Tian Jiyun?" So, I called the Vice Premier's office and his secretary, after conferring with Mr. Tian, came back to me to say, "Sam, tomorrow, when you get to Shenzhen, you go to the government office and speak to a guy called Li Hao.

Li was a mayor who had become Party Secretary. In China, a Mayor is below a city's Party Secretary in the power hierarchy. Subsequently, I made it into the Shenzhen Government office, which in those days was small, without even a military guard. There was just an old man in a shirt who inquired, "Who are you?" and "Who are you looking for?"

"I'm looking for Li Hao," I said.

"Oh, Li Hao is the boss. I'll call him. What's your name?" the guard responded.

"I'm Sam," I said. "I'm here from America."

He sent me up to the second floor to Li Hao's office, with his secretary. I go in, and Li Hao is on the phone.

"I'll be with you in a moment," he told me.

I sat. Mr. Li hung up the phone and turned to me.

"Mr. Yi has told me to expect you," he said, referring to Vice Premier Tan Jiyun's secretary. "We're going to help you, okay? Don't worry. So just go to the investment center and talk with so-and-so about the foreign investment, okay? He will help you."

That was it. Five minutes. Amazing. I exited Li Hao's office, walked to the Bureau of Economic Development, and knocked on the door.

"Oh, we just got a phone call. Welcome, please," was the greeting.

And just like that, I was led to the conference room where I was asked nothing short of one hundred questions about the cosmetic business and cosmetic products, and I simply said, "I know nothing."

"Okay," the Economic official replied. "I understand. You just stay in your hotel and tell me exactly what you want, okay?"

"Yue-Sai wants me to set up a factory here to produce cosmetics for Chinese women," I explained, adding that we also wanted a Wholly Owned Foreign Enterprise license.

The official said, "Yeah, okay, give me 24 hours. I'll call you tomorrow. You stay in your hotel. The guy who was the Foreign Investment Center's Deputy Chief was a Tsinghua graduate with a major in aerospace engineering. He made airline engines. He even visited Rolls Royce."

He took only 24 hours. It could have been a big stack of papers, but it was a thin stack. This was the feasibility study. Yue-Sai became the first foreigner to own a cosmetic factory license in China. She offered me a platform to work for her and to learn. Many Chinese who were lucky enough to study abroad at that time ended up working for American companies, like Citibank or something, in some area of Chinese business. Instead, I became the General Manager of Yue-Sai Kan Cosmetics. This was a "big sky" opportunity for me. I was not a business major, but I learned from doing business.

It worked because China's situation then was a blank slate. We were allowed to make mistakes, to navigate, and to grow. There was so much opportunity. We made mistakes, adjusted, and moved forward. Here and now, make a mistake, and you're out. This is a big difference. Because of that everything-is-new environment, we could succeed as the blind leading the blind. Today, that wouldn't apply. For example, Sherry started her own business five or six years later and knew nothing about the fashion garment business. But because she learned about cosmetics, she had the courage to learn about the garment business. Only in China could you have this kind of market opportunity. You could make mistakes and not only survive but thrive.

IN THE WORDS OF SHERRY

My mother was from a large, well-to-do family. She was quite the young lady, so of course, she used cosmetics before Liberation. During the Cultural Revolution, my mom managed to acquire cosmetics from England and America, but she had to hide them because, at the moment, she could not use them or talk about them. Me? I had no idea about cosmetics growing up.

In 1983, I came to America. This was my first-time using makeup. I was working for the United Nations. I couldn't go to work without makeup, but I honestly didn't really know how to use makeup. In China, I asked many people how to apply makeup on my face, and the answer was always, "No. We don't know." The Cultural Revolution cut us off from knowledge about this stuff.

Yue-Sai and her husband, James McManus, needed somebody to research cosmetics in China. He was a master planner, but he needed help. So, Yue-Sai asked my husband, Sam, to be the first General Manager of her cosmetics business.

China's market was zero. If they'd hired a super marketing person and a CEO from America, they might have understood America's market, but I am sure they had no know-how about operating in China. Knowing the cosmetics world was different from knowing China's situation or understanding what China thought of cosmetics at that time. It would have been challenging for a foreigner to come to China and understand how to sell cosmetics in China at that time.

When I started working for Yue-Sai, she told me right from the beginning, "Sherry, the most important thing about this business is going to be education, above all else." "

Education? What do you mean?" I asked her.

She replied, "From the start, I want to give them the rules." She asked me, "What's the thing you want the most?"

I said, "I want to be pretty."

She said, "Wrong. You need to learn about color."

I said, "Fine. That's enough."

She said, "No. Wrong again. You are an Asian with yellow skin. You have a flat nose and small eyes. Yue-Sai Cosmetics is a start, a foundation."

This way, she got everybody's attention. They identified with what she was saying about accentuating and working with their flat noses, small eyes, and yellow skin. That was the first step. Second, they learned to match their clothes and coloring with cosmetics.

The challenge was to introduce the idea of cosmetics as consumer goods. How do we get Chinese women to have these new ideas themselves? This was a challenge because there weren't that many stores in China at that time. What to do? Yue-Sai said she'd go on the lecture circuit. Her first audience was a government group of 2,500 women. She had two hours with them to teach them by herself about color swatches and clothes and color cosmetics. "Match this color with this one," and "Match these clothes with this lipstick," Yue-Sai would instruct.

We gathered a lot of Beijing teachers in the Great Hall of the People and had a competition to see who among these influencers could get the training and education around cosmetics.

Yue-Sai knew she had to influence the influencers. First were the journalists, second were the teachers, and third were the ordinary female government officials. They didn't always fully understand Yue-Sai's lecture, but we knew she had to start with them. China has 4 provincial-level administrative regions in China, including 23 provinces, 5 autonomous regions, 4 municipalities, and 2 special administrative regions (Hong Kong and Macau). Yue-Sai went to 24 of them, and I went with her. In each place we went, we found the women journalists, the women teachers, and the women cadres – women who influenced the local culture.

Yue-Sai was teaching Chinese women the value of wanting

to make themselves more beautiful. For instance, I learned that my husband occasionally liked a little makeup on me. More than that, we all learned that if we didn't like how we looked, it was harder to believe that others would like how we looked. This was revolutionary thinking for Chinese people. Revolutionary.

So, after Yue-Sai gave these lectures and imparted this education, this way of thinking, Chinese women woke up to learn to think of themselves. They began to think that these products would help them improve themselves, and this self-care was the opposite of what we'd been taught up to this point in our lives. This was Yue-Sai's personal beauty philosophy.

If you asked me, "What's an influencer?" Firstly, to Chinese people, the influencer must be natural and authentic. Secondly, they have to be appealing and friendly. Thirdly, they have to model being good to themselves and others. This was very important to selling cosmetics. Once people saw Yue-Sai, they started to question their behavior and thinking and said, often, "She's right."

I asked my mother, "What do you think of Yue-Sai Kan Cosmetics?" My mom responded, "She has taken American and Western things and put them together with an understanding of the Chinese people's culture and given this to Chinese people." She felt that Yue-Sai was coming up with something even better by taking American things and adding a Chinese twist.

Yue-Sai built a unique brand with a robust corporate culture. All our beauty consultants are skilled makeup artists because of Yue-Sai's meticulous training. All our regional sales managers are men, but they also must have makeup skills. If Yue-Sai saw that employees in a particular city had poor makeup skills, I heard about it as the National Director of Sales. Each time Yue-Sai visited a counter, she paid the utmost attention to the staff's appearance. If she saw anything wrong, she pointed it out immediately. She spot-checked the staff's makeup bags to see if they used Yue-Sai products. "If you don't use Yue-Sai products yourself or don't know how to use them correctly, how can you recommend them to others and persuade customers to buy?" she'd ask. "If you find better products, you are welcome to report to us, and we'll improve our products accordingly."

Yue-Sai Cosmetics' corporate culture nurtured the first generation of professional managers in China's beauty business. Revlon China's General Manager, Zhao Lixin (赵立新) (who is now national director of sales for Tom Ford), Jenny Chen (陈涓玲), the PR Director of the Jala Group, and many others, all got their start at Yue-Sai Cosmetics. Yue-Sai personally trained them all. Other beauty companies all have Yue-Sai to thank for her pioneering leadership.

The Yue-Sai Cosmetics brand was established in the early 1990s and, by Chinese standards, has lasted a long time. Over three decades of breakneck growth and change, and while many other brands have come and gone, Yue-Sai Cosmetics has prevailed into an old and trusted name. It is a testament to how well we built the foundations of the brand that still exists today. But above everything, witnessing Chinese women's stunning rise and transformation sends chills through my spine even today.

The fundamental ingredient in my recipe for success was sharing this knowledge of demonstrating and training women to carry on the cosmetic legacy independently of me. My well-trained consultants were the spirit and the substance of the company. I ensured that the message we dispersed was that Yue-Sai Cosmetics was more than just a cosmetics product to enhance one's appearance; it was a transformational tool empowering women of all ages and levels of society. I did not want to sell people a product; I wanted to teach them how to do this themselves and take on the world with a refreshed lease on life.

In 2022, we celebrated Yue-Sai Cosmetics 30th anniversary. It felt like yesterday, yet so long ago, that it was still a vision slowly coming to fruition in my mind. The brand continues to do very well, although sometimes I cannot help but ponder ways I might have run it better, especially in some of the early years after the sale. Nevertheless, I have to dim these thoughts from my mind.

Before I eventually sold my company, I asked Vidal Sassoon, the hair products giant, for his advice.

"If you are going to think that the company you sell is still yours, then don't sell because it's no longer yours," he replied bluntly.

This is among the best pieces of advice I ever received.

When we started Yue-Sai Cosmetics, there were no experienced beauty consultants in China; thus, we had to start from scratch and train new people ourselves. The first batch of thirty trainees arrived with absolutely zero understanding of cosmetics and makeup, yet neither myself nor my close-knit team were deterred.

Our first training camp occurred at the five-star JC Mandarin Hotel in Shanghai. The trainees, most of whom were in their early twenties and not even from moderately wealthy backgrounds. Given China's isolation from the world, they certainly had never been inside such an opulent place before. All of a sudden, there they were, living in luxury for a whole four weeks. These young women were lovely and pure but had no understanding of how to dress, carry themselves, and adopt the mannerisms of a lady.

With that, it didn't take us long to discover that the young women had many inappropriate habits we needed to correct. Every time they used the bathroom, for instance, they left the sink wet and the floor saturated. Many had no idea how to use a Western toilet, having come directly from homes with only a hole in the ground for squatting, and had never been instructed to eat with utensils or closed mouths.

Nevertheless, every single trainee was very eager to learn, and our incredibly in-depth, three-month curriculum not only taught them how to use, demonstrate and sell cosmetic products but also etiquette, from how to select a suitable hairstyle for themselves, to how to talk with great articulation and carry themselves with poise and grace. We spurred an entire generation of young women with the skills and know-how to stand apart, value themselves, and impart that wisdom to every customer who entered their orbit. I placed training as the company's number one most crucial component, a tenant that paid off and paved the way for the company's distinguishable success.

Our training camp was similar to the current K-pop idol training approach, minus the singing and dancing. Throughout the training session, each consultant was coached on presenting themselves with elegant manners and exquisite makeup. I designed special uniforms for the consultants that included earrings, scarves, and cosmetic bags, rounding out their professional demeanor.

Yue-Sai beauty consultants soon stood out from the women at the other makeup counters across China. Our employees dressed in stylish, neat Yue-Sai Cosmetics uniforms, usually black, amplified by immaculate grooming and perfect posture. They looked different and sounded different from almost all the other sales assistants. You could instantly see and hear their professional training. The customers called them "Little Yue-Sais. 小羽西" After all, they were my representatives, upholding the spirit of my brand as it was impossible for me to be present at every counter and tend to every customer myself.

Everything my employees did had to reflect the energy I endeavored to put into the world. The young women gave customers the most knowledgeable and attentive service, ensuring every person felt valued and emboldened, and the success of my cosmetics venture had a great deal to do with our sharp focus on their training. From day one, the trainees were equipped with a spirit and an attitude to convey beauty and project the elegance synonymous with Yue-Sai Cosmetics. Customers received superior service from our consultants, which made me immensely proud.

I also put a lot of effort into educating consumers to help open up China's primitive, almost non-existent cosmetics market. The Chinese media dubbed me a "beauty educator." Given that beauty was not a concept familiar to this closed country, it needed to be taught. Adhering to such a label felt like a tremendous responsibility, but one I wholeheartedly embraced going into this project. I knew that for my company to succeed, I had to really popularize cosmetics and the power that physical beauty could bequeath inside and out.

IN THE WORDS OF HOLLY YAO DUNCAN (姚红)

I worked as Yue-Sai's assistant from 1992-1995 in China and 1994-2000 in New York City. Once, we were in Hangzhou (杭州), and, as usual, we had a jam-packed schedule. Yue-Sai visited stores in the morning, standing at our counter for hours demonstrating how to use her products. Then we had lunch with our local press agency, and in the afternoon, she met with the provincial governor and the mayor. That evening, Yue-Sai did a TV interview. The general manager of the TV station pulled me to the side and asked me quietly: "Holly, you are Yue-Sai's assistant; you must know the answer to this question. We are all very curious – what kind of drugs or supplements does Yue-Sai take? After this long day, we are all exhausted, and we are only the onlookers. How come Yue-Sai is still so full of energy?" I laughed and told him, "She does not take any drugs or supplements. Yue-Sai gets her energy from being active."

Working with Yue-Sai, I learned to catch up to her speed. When I lived in her Manhattan townhouse, we often worked late into the evening. When I got up the next morning, I'd find a to-do list already waiting on my desk.

I officially launched Yue-Sai Cosmetics in 1992, on China's National Day, October 1. My team and I selected Shanghai, a bustling city of twenty-six million, as the first stop because of its rich history as China's most cosmopolitan and, therefore, most fashionable city. New fashion ideas were more readily accepted and absorbed by women in Shanghai. We opened the first counter in the top department store (第一百货) in Shanghai on Nanjing Road (南京路). I figured that if Shanghainese women rejected Yue-Sai Cosmetics, I might have to quit then and there, as there would be little hope for the rest of the country. However, I need not have worried. The counter was instantly swarmed with people curious to learn more about us from the moment it opened.

Our pre-launch promotion was superb. I undertook scores of interviews and press requests. My team and I labored unremittingly to put Yue-Sai Cosmetics on the map and inside the minds of hundreds of millions. But again, it was the attention given to the pre-debut training that cemented our triumphant start. Our expertly trained beauty consultants were energetic and enthusiastic, providing each customer with a valuable introduction and helpful tips on applying every product. Many women saw a considerable change in their appearance in the mirror after visiting our makeup counter – pleasantly shocked by the transformed faces reflected through our illuminated mirrors. And word travels fast.

Typically, a new company needs months, if not years, to adjust production, logistics and sales, to then coordinate all of its various departments and refine the entire process as society adjusts to the new product, or in my case, an entirely new movement. It was a welcome surprise when our launch was overwhelmingly successful right out of the gate. Customers flocked to my products, which flew off the shelves.

My premature fear of failure was groundless and launching in only three stores in Shanghai turned out to be the right approach. It gave us the leeway to adjust and polish our teaching methods, observe our customers, and work out technical kinks in our system. We quickly did ten times more business than any other cosmetics brand at any department store, an economical equations that continued to proliferate across the country.

I invited veteran Bloomingdale's designer Rolando Seinhart, a larger-than-life stylish character, from New York to China to develop an overall design for my makeup counters and department store windows. He was a visual genius, able to create some of our most alluring and classy window displays in China within the limitations of the time and place.

The other person that I was most grateful to was New York makeup artist Donna Fumoso. She knew artistry and the accentuation of facial features better than anyone I had ever encountered. She was a brilliant makeup teacher with all the patience in the world with the girls, who were starting from a zero-knowledge base. Donna and I worked together in New York for two years while I was preparing the first line of products. I performed color testing with her, and we prepared all the promotional material together, both print and video. This visual element was critical. I ensured all the models featured ranged from their twenties to their sixties, making up half their faces so potential customers could see the jaw-dropping transformation and reiterate that these products were for all women from all of life's domains.

I learned so much from Donna. Later, when we started training and selling cosmetics in China, Donna visited China numerous times to help me train, prepare and implement new products. It was terrific to have Donna close to my side. She was constantly upbeat, ready to work and never once lamented that she was tired.

IN THE WORDS OF DONNA FUMOSO

I worked as a makeup artist with Yue-Sai from 1990-1997. Yue-Sai has endless energy, and it was hard to keep up with her. One great memory of this was when she would hold "town hall" meetings with consumers. The halls would always be packed, and this is where she would explain her ideas. It was an incredible experience. She had a good instinct for zoning in on the worst-dressed people, picking them out of the audience and explaining why their clothing was wrong for their body type. Then, Yue-Sai would detail how to match clothing colors and styles that best show off your figure. We would transform them in front of the crowd. We had clothing for them to try on, and I would cut their hair and give them a new look with makeup. We showed the audience how to look before and after in just a few minutes. This little knowledge changed how they felt about themselves and gave them confidence. It was awe-inspiring to see how the crowd responded. They all wanted to get a chance to be on stage.

With Steinhardt's help, we were ready to develop the market elsewhere. Six months later, in Spring 1993, we launched Yue-Sai Cosmetics in Beijing. I was nervous because Beijing is a relatively conservative city and political too. I was worried that someone would stand up and condemn women for using cosmetics. Beijing women, it turned out, accepted my cosmetics, too, and our sales were surprisingly good.

We continued to expand our team and set up counters in major department stores, peaking in 1996 at 800 counters nationwide. Our "Little Yue-Sai" makeup consultants working in significant stores in China soon earned the highest income in the industry. If their sales were high, they could gross more than RMB 3,000 a month, roughly $US450 per month, while the average salary of civil servants at that time was only about RMB 300 a month, around $US45. The parents of some of my beauty consultants told them that they must work hard to ensure they could stay on with Yue-Sai Cosmetics, and the positions became highly esteemed and sought after. I was proud to offer such a source of self-esteem and stability to so many young women in China.

During this period, I revolutionized the cosmetics industry in China in other ways, too, by changing the way cosmetic counters look. Before I entered the market, all sales counters in Chinese department stores looked exactly alike throughout the store; all lined up one after another in a large room.

I was determined that Yue-Sai Cosmetics needed to stand out. But it wasn't a straightforward objective, with department stores initially refusing my requests to brand and decorate our counters differently, to feature televisions with promotional materials, which was entirely unheard of, and to allow our sales consultants to wear a unique, tailor-made Yue-Sai Cosmetics uniform. Back then, everyone working at the store wore the same dull outfit regardless of the brand or company they represented. It took quite some convincing, yet I did get my way and effectively sparked an industry-wide transformation.

My beautiful and well-trained beauty consultants were the talk of every town. As they performed their pivotal part, I crisscrossed the country, giving lectures in jampacked halls, providing demonstrations at department stores, and promoting the brand and my book "Yue-Sai's Guide to Asian Beauty." Through this multi-pronged approach, I pioneered a comprehensive cosmetics business category – a business that was more than just a product but expanded into the realm of a fully-fledged brand – which, in China, had not previously existed.

To keep all this going as we rapidly expanded, my team and I understood that we had to address increasingly complex logistics. Initially, we shipped products from Shenzhen to all parts of the country by rail, but the availability of space in freight cars was not always reliable. I sent a staff member to the train station each morning to book the first available container. Yet, several times when our products arrived at their destination, we found that the containers had been opened and the products stolen. We were all so frustrated.

I was a novice in company management, with little experience handling those challenges, and making it all the more difficult was that my Mandarin was still not very good. Business dramatically improved when I learned to rely on solid support from my management team and not try to handle everything from the top down.

With an outstanding team who were just as passionate about the brand as I was, the products kept flying off the shelves. Our billboards were prominent in all the big cities of China, and supplies were always tight. One day, I received a call from our accountant in Tianjin saying someone had brought a large suitcase of cash to the office and wouldn't leave until he got the Yue-Sai products he wanted. Keeping the supply up with the demand was at times very daunting, but it was my job to do whatever it took to deliver – and I did.

If a store announced that I was going to make a guest appearance, hundreds of fans arrived early to meet me. Doors were often blocked off, and department store security staff had to surround and protect me from the somewhat aggressive members of the audience. Customers lined up to ask questions. "What color lipstick should I wear? What product should I use for my wrinkles? How can I get rid of these pimples?"

They were eager to meet me, and there was never resistance to whatever I recommended. Whatever I suggested, they bought. It felt very gratifying to have earned such trust.

In the early 1990s, there were still very few top-notch hotels in China. Large cities such as Beijing and Shanghai were better, but there were few good places to stay in the second and third-tier cities. I had to get used to living in less-than-pristine places, and when I flew to China, I packed a plastic bag containing gloves, a brush, soap, Ajax, and a bottle of shampoo. At every hotel I stayed at, I first cleaned the bathroom, toilet, sink and shower. In those days, as Yue-Sai Cosmetics was opening up new counters, I was running frantically across the country and cleaning hotel toilets. Who says there isn't dirty work in the beauty business?

A TV crew accompanied me to Inner Mongolia to launch our products. It was the most fantastic trip, as there is something so fun and spontaneous about people from that region. After dinner, as soon as the music started, the mayor of the capital, Hohhot, and the city's other leading officials jumped up and started dancing. What wonderful, hospitable, and open people, I mused to myself. Mongolians are people whose character embodies their homeland – a physical landscape described in the chorus of a popular local song: "Wide open skies, extensive grasslands, and the horses running free."

At a dinner held in my honor, the hosts presented a giant roast lamb and the expectation that I would eat one of its eyes, which is considered a delicacy among ethnic Mongolians. I drew a deep breath, and I did so with a smile. How could I not? A giant billboard of me was positioned next to the banquet hall, overshadowing us all and stretching down the whole block. I had to live up to this larger-than-life image, if only for a few squidgy bites. One must step outside one's comfort zone and adapt when doing business abroad. Never underestimate the power of small gestures and how much they are appreciated.

While in Inner Mongolia, I rode horses, watched traditional wrestling, and visited nomadic families living in tents. When it was time to leave for my next stop, Japan, on the way home to New York, an extra bag I had to check in at the last minute was lost, or someone stole it. The tragedy was that it contained all the footage we shot in Inner Mongolia. I lost some fabulous jewelry, too, but I was more upset about losing the footage, which felt like a window to the inner workings of my company's soul that I could never again replicate.

My staff arranged my schedule so tightly that I had little time to breathe. From meeting store managers, providing interviews, holding press conferences, and greeting local political and women leaders and the wives of premiers and mayors, there was barely a moment to rest my tired eyes. I was utterly exhausted by the end of each day, but I was informed that I needed to be ready to get up at 5 a.m. the following morning to visit another town two hours away.

One time, I protested, refusing to rise before dawn. My body was in breakdown mode. I insisted to my team that I must sleep a little longer and that we leave at 8 a.m. When we arrived at the next town, I found the mayor and a giant children's orchestra and choir there to receive me with a flag-raising ceremony. I had kept several hundred people waiting for two hours. I have never felt more ashamed and vowed I needed to keep it together at all times, even when it felt like I was falling apart.

Life on the road was arduous work. While I had endured an intense schedule filming television shows from country to country, the demands of running a company felt like I wore the world's weight on my fragile shoulders, working days and weeks and even months on end without a single moment, let alone day, off. When I landed in a new place, I was on the ground running. I could not say no when my staff required me to solve a complex problem. I remember driving across the country in long and winding road trips in temperatures that exceeded 100 degrees, intent on visiting five stores in two days and almost throwing up because of the heat slapped over the fatigue. These days, traveling around China is much easier thanks to improved air travel and the high-speed railroads that now cover the whole country.

In each new city, I met with my local office staff, led a training session with my local consultants, held a press conference, and then had dinner with the regional brand manager and their team to help solve problems. My staff told me, "Yue-Sai, you must meet with the store manager because we would like to have this location for our counter, and now they are unwilling to give us." They knew that store managers would grant their wishes if I showed up in person. Besides, our products were top-rated and quickly sold out. We drove so much business that almost all of our makeup counters were eventually poised in the most prime locations. No matter how drained and sleep deprived I was, there was no time to rest. I caught colds all the time but pushed through the fatigue and pain. I understood what I needed to do to accomplish the goals I had set for myself and my company, large and small, and this was not a time to slow down even when every morsel of my being screamed for just a tiny sliver of reprieve.

Compounding the challenges of entrepreneurial work in the early 1990s, China needed to gain more understanding of trademarks and my name was often widely used illegally by others. We found knock-off cosmetics pirating my brand sold in supermarkets. Sanitary napkins, wine, and many other items bore my name without my permission. Overcoming such a hiccup required comprehensive monitoring and due diligence, which could never be put to rest.

During those days of building my cosmetics company in the early 1990s, my mother became especially ill. It pained me to be on the road, thousands of miles from her. Each time I returned to New York City, I hurried from the airport directly to my mother's bedside. And she was always the last person I saw before I left. My mother was bedridden for six years following her stroke, and each time I left her, I wept into my hands. I never knew if I would see her alive again.

Then, on November 13, 1994, my mother – the beautiful and gracious Li Hui-Gen – took her last breath.

I used my colossal workload to numb and force myself to forget the pain. But one can only dull the mourning for so long before it comes rushing back two-fold.

TEACHING THE INFLUENCERS

One afternoon in 1994, not long after we launched in

Beijing, I received a call from Zhu Lin (朱琳), the wife of the then Premier Li Peng (李鹏), inviting me to a private lunch with several of the vice premiers' and ministers' wives in Building 17 of the Diaoyutai State Guesthouse. Several American presidents had stayed in this stately residence, from Nixon to Clinton to Bush. Madame Zhu Lin explained that when she received dignitaries to China, she tried to wear the most appropriate clothes for each occasion. Cocktail attire for early evening drinks, a simple yet stylish dress for a visit to a kindergarten, and a formal gown for a traditional state dinner. Sometimes, she had to change multiple times daily and lamented that doing so had drawn condemnation. Some critics called Madame Zhu Lin vain. Wives of top leaders anywhere are the targets of rude comments, and China is no different. Still, Madame Zhu Lin owned who she was and never apologized for being wholeheartedly herself, a trait I could resonate with and greatly admire. The country might have still been stuck in a backward mindset that such self-care and respect was self-indulgent, but Madame Zhu Lin knew better.

Over lunch, I asked how long Premier Li Peng courted her. She explained he gave her a pair of Chinese-made HERO fountain pens, a touching gesture as they were the height of extravagance in those days, marking the beginning of a magical romance. Madame Zhu Lin, born Shanghainese, was a good-looking, gracious, gentle lady.

"How do we use cosmetics to help Chinese women become more modern?" Madame Zhu asked me, with the other ladies listening intently.

"First, a woman should look closely at her own body

and face," I answered. "She should analyze herself without prejudice or preconditioned ideas. Once she understands her most beautiful and least attractive features, she should learn by turns to enhance or correct them. That is where education comes in. You need to be taught how to be beautiful."

I gifted each of them a copy of my book "Yue-Sai's Guide to Asian Beauty," and I started to demonstrate some of the lessons. Firstly, I did Madame Zhu Lin's makeup. She was delighted. I pulled my one-of-a-kind 'Tri-Color Shadow Powder' box from my makeup bag and showed Madame Zhu Lin and the other guests how to enhance their Asian features. I described each step of the makeup process.

"The lips are the heart of the face because you constantly move them," I explained. "You need to know how to make them as attractive as you can."

I taught the ladies to put lipstick on first then outline their lips with a pencil. One of the wives confessed that she had never touched lipstick before, and her hand trembled as she brought it to her mouth.

"A woman really only needs two shades of lipstick to go with all her outfits; one is orange, and the other is pink," I continued. "The intensity and shade of each is totally up to the individual, what color they are wearing where they are going."

In 1995, the semi-governmental All-China Women's Federation (ACWF) was set to host the Fourth United Nations Women's Conference in Beijing. Established in March 1949, even before Mao declared the foundation of the People's Republic of China, the All-China Women's Federation is an official body tasked with assisting women in all aspects of their lives. For decades, the Federation has taken on the most important and pressing women's issues, supporting women who perhaps face the prospect of poverty due to divorce or assist women caught up in the painful and barbaric ring of sex trafficking.

To prepare The President of All-China Women's Federation, Madame Peng Peiyun (彭佩云) and all the ladies of the Federation, I gathered them in a conference hall. After I had painted Madame Pang's lips, she commented, "How about my eyes?" So, I educated her on how to do light but alluring eye makeup. Then she asked, "How about my skin? Some rouge?" I ended up completing a full face of makeup, and Madame Peng was delighted with the result.

Soon, Madame Pang's secretary called to request I go shopping with her to help her choose clothes for her boss to wear at the Women's Conference events. I could not find anything I could recommend for her to wear from the stores in China. Therefore, when I was back in New York City, I visited stores specializing in clothes for women who were a little on the larger side and purchased several outfits.

When I returned to Beijing, I took them along with a tailor to Madame Pang's home. We made some alterations, and I guided her on how to wear her new garments. She looked ravishing. I was most happy to give her the clothes, but the next day, her secretary called and insisted on paying for them. So, I had to submit a small bill for her as, at least back then, corruption was largely frowned upon and I did not witness any such maleficence firsthand. Sadly, this would become a very different story years later.

On the opening day of the conference, I saw the All-China Women's Federation leaders who had participated in my training session up on the podium, all beautifully dressed and with immaculate makeup to match. Madam Pang made quite the statement by sporting the red jacket I purchased on her behalf, standing out in a way Chinese leaders did not do back then. I was very proud.

Having helped the ACWF leaders and women, my next opportunity was to help a particularly important man in China learn about cosmetics. In 1996, when Chinese President Jiang Zemin (江泽民) visited the United States, I noticed that his face was always very oily. I sent him a Yue-Sai Cosmetics transparent powder along with an explanatory note.

"Image is particularly important for politicians," I wrote to him. "When President Clinton goes to a major event or does a TV interview, he will always use some makeup or at least some loose powder to avoid looking shiny under the lights on his face. You can also use some."

Surprisingly, his staff confirmed that Jiang heeded my suggestion before speaking at a United Nations conference and applied a touch of powder to his face. They said that I was the only woman who had ever asked a leader of China to de-shine his nose. By the third year in operation, Yue-Sai Cosmetics achieved the mind-blowing annual sales of over $27 million, an unheard-of dollar for the era and a brand new concept for a closed country. There was a brand recognition rate of 95 percent, which stirs pride in me even today, and furthermore, my brand boosted all of China's consumer cosmetics market.

Chinese domestic media and international press took

notice. Forbes claimed that I "changed the face of China, one lipstick at a time," and TIME called me "Queen of the Middle Kingdom." Other publications dubbed me the "Most Famous Woman in China."

My father's encouragement that I should always aim to be "the first on the moon" drove me. The television series "Looking East" and "One World" broke so many records, and as an independent producer, I'd learned that I could achieve whatever I set my mind to. Even though I was competing against myself, I always wanted to improve, and to win. Winning requires immense dedication.

When I was developing my lipstick line, we tested each color on a minimum of 500 Chinese women before picking the most flattering shades. In 1995, we launched a fragrance called "First Love," using the slogan "First love, how can you forget?" I used a stopwatch to time the lasting power of the top, middle, and bottom notes. I sprayed it on my arm and noted how long the fragrance lasted.

"Yue-Sai, don't be too serious," our general manager Sam protested. "No customer will test how long it lasts with a stopwatch!"

"I hate not being able to support our claims!" I replied.

Before each new product went to market, I tested samples my lab sent me on myself. No matter how busy I was, I made sure I personally tried everything. I would green-light mass production only after my own trial use was satisfactory. I always said, "The product has my name on it. It must be good. I have to be sure of that!"

I visited department stores constantly, observing the

Yue-Sai Cosmetics counter and staying as long as possible to interact with customers. I wanted their feedback on our products and to listen to their needs, so I understood what improvements were needed and what products to develop next.

"Each Yue-Sai counter is a billboard," I told the staff repeatedly.

The counter has to be both attractive and functional. Every inch must serve the purpose of selling. What kind of mirror to use, where to place it, where to put tissues, and how to arrange products so our beauty consultants could reach them easily, were just some of the crucial factors to take into consideration. I paid close attention to all the minute details, things many people in China didn't think were a big deal at the time. There was no professional help locally because exhibition designers did not exist in China in the early 1990s, thus I took charge in taking the counters to an entirely new level.

I repeatedly informed my staff that even though not all of them worked in sales, they all were salespeople for the company. No matter their job, I insisted they all know the products inside out and back to front. If a store manager was male, he needed to learn to do makeup with the women.

By 1997, only five years after launch, Yue-Sai Cosmetics reached the pinnacle of all personal product sales in China. Years of overdrive had paid off. The business was a success, ultimately, because of the products. Each formula we released was one-of-a-kind, and the quality was top-of-the-line. It's not an exaggeration to say that by 1997, the year Britain returned Hong Kong to Chinese control, every makeup artist in China had a Yue-Sai Tri-Color Powder in their bag of favorite contraptions.

In revolutionizing the beauty landscape of China, we also brought several new concepts, such as sunscreen, previously unfamiliar to Chinese people, to the market. We designed a marketing and PR campaign to introduce sunscreen by giving it away to traffic police on the street. We were training a whole new generation of Chinese in skincare.

Once, my friend Leonard Lauder, who – with his brother Ronald – ran the famed cosmetics brand Estee Lauder that their parents founded that I've long admired, came to Shanghai. He asked me to lunch, but I told him I was at a training session, so our meeting would have to wait. I invited him to the hotel banquet hall, where we trained our beauty consultants. I had 150 trainees from all over the country in the room that day, each professionally decked out in long white blazers trimmed with red. Lauder appeared most impressed, smiling and nodding enthusiastically.(At lunch afterward, he told me that personally he believed that like me, training is the most important for a cosmetics company. Then he asked me what he had to do to buy my company.) I was flattered, and meeting and talking with him was a great honor.

While I was curious to learn more, the bold proposition did not result in an immediate sale. Executives routinely approached me about selling the company, or at least about selling shares, and although I didn't feel ready at that particular point, I always entertained the requests. And from a legend like Leonard, such an inquiry solidified how hard I had worked to bring such a company – and concept – to life from scratch.

I was keenly aware that people purchased Yue-Sai Cosmetics not just because of my name but because the products were superior. Fame cannot sustain the longevity of a brand. Brilliant products amplified by top-notch training are the first keys to success in cosmetics. People might buy my products once because I'm famous, but if they are no good, they won't repurchase them. I had to ensure that my products were the best. Returning customers is the lifeline to any business.

Each product we launched during that period was so on target that it sold out instantly. Our research and development department needed to work faster to keep up with the rapid growth in market demand. As the company grew more prominent, I needed more input from those close to me. My assistant, Stephanie Jacobs, helped me see through some intense challenges in that period. Again, I was blessed that the universe surrounded me with the greatest gifts: incredible humans.

IN THE WORDS OF STEPHANIE JACOBS ———

I started work as Yue-Sai's assistant in November 1994. In my time with her, I witnessed the highest of the highs and the lowest of the lows, both for Yue-Sai Cosmetics and Yue-Sai personally. A few days into the job, I learned Yue-Sai and her husband, James McManus, were divorcing. Yue-Sai was entitled to half of James' assets. She could live comfortably for the rest of her life as a wealthy lady, but Yue-Sai, an independent, modern woman, didn't want anything from James. Everyone thought she was silly.

Without his support and that of his company, the Marketing Corporation of America, Yue-Sai and Yue-Sai Cosmetics would suffer a heavy financial strain. Her cosmetics firm was taking off, and her products were gaining immense popularity and selling very well in China. As the Lunar New Year approached, many Chinese department stores urged U.S. headquarters to deliver more of Yue-Sai's products to meet increasing Chinese demand. But by then, Yue-Sai Cosmetics had run out of money.

Everyone was apprehensive and on edge. Yue-Sai Cosmetics was a huge success and couldn't be closed because of a cash flow problem. Yue-Sai's cholesterol level rose so dangerously high that doctors warned her to slow down, relax, and care for her health. Finally, Yue-Sai's little sister, San San, saved the day with a loan to pay for production and shipment just in time for the New Year.

To learn how to avoid repeating such a crisis and to save her company and its employees, Yue-Sai hired Bill Kahane, a competent consultant, to look for a partner who could help Yue-Sai Cosmetics grow and expand to the next level. Many companies, including Estee Lauder, L'Oreal, Coty and others, were interested in Yue-Sai Cosmetics and its massive presence in China. Three to four months after Bill came aboard, I met Leonard Lauder of Estee Lauder, Coty's executives, and L'Oreal's executive Gilles Weil, among many others.

When Weil and his people arrived at Yue-Sai's Manhattan

townhouse to meet her for the first time, they asked if they should take off their shoes. I remember Yue-Sai's quick-witted and ice-breaking reply.

"Oh, yes," she said. "Take them off. Take everything off!"

After a few months of intense back-and-forth negotiations, Yue-Sai, Bill, and their trusted inner circle decided to go with Coty. Though it was not Yue-Sai's first choice, Coty made her the best offer. I remember Yue-Sai being very disappointed that L'Oreal hadn't offered a proper partnership. Bill reassured her: "Yue-Sai, you need a partner who really loves you!"

Yue-Sai and her investors quickly came to see the Coty deal as good. Tenfold profits were returned in just a few years and made Yue-Sai a rich woman. She paid James every penny he put down on the Manhattan townhouse and exchanged her engagement ring for a happy yellow diamond ring. Everything Yue-Sai owned; she had paid for herself. James delivered a beautiful BMW wrapped in a big red bow that Christmas to show Yue-Sai his gratitude. Everyone was happy, and it was a very good holiday.

In the couple of years that followed, everything went smoothly. Coty was in charge of the expansion and production of Yue-Sai Cosmetics, and Yue-Sai was head of creative and marketing. We shot many commercials and added many new products to the original Yue-Sai Cosmetics line, keeping us busy testing and re-testing.

In July 1998, my husband and I attended the opening of Coty's newly built, state-of-the-art Yue Sai Cosmetics factory in Pudong, Shanghai. It was so clean and beautiful that everyone wore protective clothing. I felt so proud to be part of it.

The partnership with Coty was not without conflict and disappointment, especially when the company management made decisions without consulting Yue-Sai, sometimes doing things that contradicted their working agreement. Yue-Sai's responsibilities were limited to the creative arena, a vastly reduced workload that didn't sit well with the woman who finds it challenging to sit back and relax. Thankfully, she was always thinking ahead to her next adventure.

She quickly went on to create a jewelry line for QVC, design a line of Chinese dolls called the Yue-Sai Wa-Wa ('doll' in Chinese) (羽西娃娃) and sold them to prestigious outlets such as FAO Schwarz in New York, and open a beautiful home decorating store in Shanghai, The House of Yue-Sai – all while writing several books on etiquette and beauty.

I finally reached a tipping point where I knew that I needed a partner to meet the vision I upheld for the company's future. It was a tense period, and I was nervous. Major financial institutions such as Goldman Sachs and Morgan Stanley came to us asking to buy into our company, but I turned them all down; the fit didn't feel right.

Money was not my primary concern. I truly needed management expertise, especially regarding R&D. There were so many decisions to be made, and it needed to be exactly right. I birthed this brand with my bare hands, and I was well aware that a partnership had the potential to reach a whole other stratosphere – but it needed to be the right partnership.

At this point, it was well known that Peter Harf was the

aggressive and successful leader of the Paris-originated, now Amsterdam-headquartered multinational beauty company Coty Inc., founded in 1904 by French perfumer François Coty. Peter was also extremely interested in stepping into the Yue-Sai Cosmetics fold in whichever way he could and personally supervised the negotiations.

My plan was not to sell the whole company to them but merely to sell a part and to take out my five partners, George Valassis, George Lindeman, Charles Diker, Samuel Fang from Hong Kong, and my by-then ex-husband, James.

The Coty investment in 1996 was a lifesaver. With their investment, Yue-Sai Cosmetics was guaranteed continued success. True to their promise, Coty helped me build a substantial second factory in Shanghai, in addition to running the original flagship in Shenzhen. The third factory – the most stunning of all – would come later.

For the third, we found a rundown building in the Pudong area of Shanghai accessible only via a dirt track. We undertook extensive renovations and established it up to an impressive code to produce cosmetics. I was dazzled by the result, and when I saw my name inscribed across this incredible facility, I burst into tears. Further, we laid a proper road to the factory and requested the government's permission to allow us to name it Yue-Sai Road, but they said no. Possibly in the United States, it would have been a sure-fire "yes," yet in China, doing business is far more complicated.

No matter where you went in China in those years, my face and logo were inescapable – appearing at stores, in airport terminals, on the streets, and on television. Such notoriety –

stemming from my television era – was simply a part of my life, a normalcy I accepted with as much grace and appreciation as possible. I wasn't a rock star, Madonna, or a Beatle, but I was proud to have established a loyal, courteous and respectful fan base nationwide. Of course, there are times even now when it would be nice to fly under the radar, to look my absolute worst in the middle of seclusion and not be asked for a photograph, however, I am grateful for everyone who followed and valued my work. I would not have had the opportunities that I have had without them.

A picture of me in black and white with plenteous red lips became one of China's most famous and recognizable images. People persistently asked if the photograph was the work of legendary artist Andy Warhol. It was my photo but Andy suggested using this as a logo. He did not sign his name to it, so I can't claim it's an Andy Warhol. I met Andy some time earlier through my German friend Hubert Burda, whose parents were collectors of Warhol's works. Hubert and I used to spend a lot of time with Andy in New York City, and I treasured the artistic yet intellectual energy he exuded, an ability to see subjects in illumination and vivacity that made me him the star he was, in addition to just being a solid and dependable friend. Andy even came to an exhibition of my father's paintings at the Hammer Gallery and didn't hold back in sharing his love for Dad's work.

On the day of the Pudong, Shanghai factory opening in the summer of 1998, we could not invite any high-level Chinese leaders to cut the ribbon as there was a new regulation prohibiting leaders from attending commercial events.

However, I asked the Vice Mayor of Shanghai, Gong Xueping, who agreed to attend as a friend but not as an official, to recognize what I had done for the city. I was incredibly grateful. The emcee of the opening was the famous TV personality and talk show host Yang Lan (杨澜), who said she came because I had introduced her to her husband, media entrepreneur Bruno Wu Zheng (吴征).

Tears streamed down my face the first time I saw the finished factory with the name "Yue-Sai-Coty" on the top. I was so proud. The grounds were beautiful and featured a traditional Chinese pavilion adorned with a carving of a couplet referencing one of the four great beauties of Chinese history. The couplet risked being over the top and lost in translation:

Comparing Yue-Sai to Xi Shi (西施), Yue-Sai is beautiful no matter how much or how little makeup is applied.

I worked hard. If this is what they thought, I'd let it stand.

The new factory was as mint as it was and efficient, and it allowed us, for the first time, to have the whole team in one place. There was one building for the factory, another for the office, and even more space for a bountiful warehouse to house large volumes of raw materials and newfangled electric trolleys with long robotic arms to reach items off the highest shelves. Our competent and agile Sam managed all the logistics and operations. We arranged for buses to transport our staff to and from work, and I took whatever means necessary to ensure a comfortable working environment for my staff.

Naturally, problems did arise throughout our working relationship, but I did my best to work through each one and ensure none of them blew into bigger issues than they needed to be. Still, I was disappointed by many decisions. For one, I recommended that Coty buy the land next to the factory because it was still relatively cheap. They decided not to, and years later, when L'Oreal finally bought Yue-Sai Cosmetics and needed more land, they had to pay a fortune for it, proving my mother's wisdom right again. Being the real estate investment wizard she was, Mom constantly told me I should buy the land or apartment next to me if it became available. I have also personally made good on such advice. I did this with my Shanghai apartment that I purchased in 2004 and after buying my New York residence. Each time, it proved a solid money-making strategy.

Nevertheless, in 2003, Proctor & Gamble joined the queue of big names expressing interest in Yue-Sai Cosmetics and offered to buy it outright. Then L'Oréal got wind of the discussions and said they, too, wanted to purchase the company. The time was finally right to dig down on these negotiations, sensing that a new life chapter awaited me. So, we decided to do an auction, and the final four bidders were Avon, Shiseido, P&G, and L'Oréal.

I didn't think Avon was a good fit because, in my opinion, they had never been very good at managing brands other than their own. Moreover, Shiseido – a Japanese cosmetic company founded in Tokyo in 1872 – was a major company with a stellar reputation but foreign to me. However, their level of efficiency was impressive. When the top management came to Shanghai to meet with me, they said the meeting would start at 9 a.m. and finish at noon, and to the minute, that is what happened.

Their team was a rather large group of only men. The only woman with Shiseido was their translator.

On my side, we were two women, my accountant and myself, and strongly that women needed to be front and center of such critical conversations. I also knew that some of the Japanese executives spoke English very well, and yet the entire meeting was conducted in Japanese and then translated into English. It was a rather odd experience that reinforced that Shiseido wasn't suitable to take over the company I had erected to empower and bolster Chinese women.

Then, P&G is, of course, an extraordinary company, and I appreciated the straightforward way they conducted their business meetings. To show their earnestness, the brilliant Susan Arnold, then Vice Chairman of Procter and Gamble, visited me in New York twice. Furthermore, was L'Oréal, headed by Jean-Paul Agon, an industry giant.

On the day of the auction, gripped by emotion, nostalgia and immense lethargy born out of the humdrum of business dealings that felt very personal to me, I configured that the foremost checkbox was that I wanted to sell to a place with the prowess to disseminate my products all over the world. I wanted a company to take Yue-Sai Cosmetics global, beyond China's borders. And only a major international conglomerate like L'Oreal could fulfill such a dream and do it much faster than I ever could. It was the most prominent beauty company in the world back then and remains so today.

L'Oréal called to put in a preemptive bid and request for two months to do due diligence. The number offered was reasonable, so we gave them two months. Still, negotiating with L'Oréal was tough, not because of the people but because of the locations involved. I lived between Shanghai and New York City, Coty was in NYC and L'Oréal was in Paris. The time differences made discussions exceedingly difficult. I did not sleep for a couple of months during the last part of our talks. Finally, the contract was signed. I followed my gut, and that was the best I could do.

I immediately arranged to go to Chiva-Som, my favorite five-star spa and resort in Thailand, for a much-needed rest with one of my best friends, Mayenne Carmona, a well-known society columnist in Manila. I had given everything I had to offer and needed to escape to tend to my mind and body's depletion.

As I walked towards the airplane, L'Oréal's PR department called asking for my approval for the press release on the transaction due to go out that day. I approved the release, holding back a flood of emotion, and off I went. I was exhausted in a way that I could not enunciate, as if my soul were ripped from my body and replaced by a guttural emptiness. When I got into my hotel room, I fell sleep and didn't emerge for two days.

When I finally surfaced from the cocoon of soft sheets, ensconced in the luxury of Southern Thailand's Hua Hin District, Vidal Sassoon's advice echoed in my mind: "If you are going to think that the company you have sold is still yours, then don't sell. Because it is no longer yours."

When you've sold your baby, you cannot look back. As Vidal Sassoon predicted, it very quickly became apparent that there were many things I did not like, including imperfect products with my name attached. L'Oréal, a company run by the industry's best professionals, is terrific with skincare, and their research and development are among the absolute best in the business. Thus, I hoped they would apply the same innovation to makeup and take on such endeavors as keeping the color momentum going while adding new skincare products, which they did best. From my lens, that would have made Yue-Sai Cosmetics unbeatable.

Yue-Sai Cosmetics had grown from three counters in Shanghai in 1992 to 800 counters across China when I sold it to L'Oréal in 2004. I also sold them three factories and 24 provincial companies. The products still have my name, and I am interested in the brand continuing to do well. I wish for its longevity and hope it will fulfill my dream of becoming a Chinese brand that makes it prominent internationally. It isn't a global product, which was my dream, but I haven't lost sight of the notion that someday it might reach such an echelon.

Over the past few years, the company has come back to me for advice about new launches and programs. While it is no longer my company and I don't have say over what will happen, but I want to see it thrive.

Yet now, I can only watch and observe from afar – as if standing behind a frosted glass window at the child that once was mine, all grown up and estranged. I had no choice but to let go. I had to accept that there would no doubt be times when the new owner would do things I was not really happy with, where I felt as though they were ruining the DNA of the lifeblood I had worked so hard to create. But once you have signed that dotted line and consented to walk away, you lose your right to complain. Yue-Sai Cosmetics may still bear my name, yet it was no longer mine. I learned to keep this in mind at all times.

Another lesson I learned from selling my company is the importance of selling to a company with a great culture. In that sphere, L'Oréal was very gentle and generous with everyone who worked for Yue-Sai Cosmetics and seemed to me a very "human" company. They treated everyone fairly, and I was impressed by their thoughtfulness, which gave me great peace of mind in signing on the dotted line. I may have been fortunate in such a regard, but this is not always the case. Just because a company is large, wealthy, and multinational does not mean it will understand your brand and corporate culture. Should you ever be in a position to sell a company, you would do well to find a person in your buyer's upper management who will truly understand you and listen to you as you educate them about your brand.

Another lesson, especially as a woman in business, is that lawyers can be beneficial, but sometimes you can make decisions better than they can. Your knowledge, your gut instinct, far surpasses any sanitized legal verbiage.

In the late eighties, amid my "One World" fame before I started my own company, Revlon requested I become a spokesperson for their fragrances. I asked my lawyer what my fee should be. He quoted me such a pitiful rate that I rejected it and instead took it upon myself to request an outrageous amount, and guess what? They paid me what I asked for. You know what you are worth better than anyone else.

Life is never perfect, but it can also come remarkably close to extraordinary. The money I received from the sale of Yue-Sai Cosmetics still felt unfathomable to me as I drifted back to those days as an immigrant in the impoverished streets of Hong Kong. Yet, that rather significant payday gave me the freedom to do everything I wanted to do – and there was so much left in my mind and on my horizon.

IN THE WORDS OF JACKIE DU (杜谭明) AND MONICA XU (徐吉英)

Yue-Sai always looks good. Her favorite color is a shade of red most of China – where we work as her assistants – knows as "Yue-Sai Red." She likes to wear bright colors: orange, fuchsia, and white. When she wears black, she makes sure to accessorize with colorful jewelry. She loves to color-coordinate jewelry pieces and scarves with her outfits.

Yue-Sai speaks Chinese in a unique way, and sometimes it's very funny. She often uses phrases that are directly translated from English. For example, she tells people to "turn off" their eyes when applying eyeliner or to "turn on" their mouth when applying lip liner. She is talented at picking up languages and can speak English, Cantonese, Mandarin, and Spanish.

Yue-Sai is a highly confident person. Self-doubt is not in her vocabulary. Her self-confidence comes from her world travel and years of practice engaging with people of many cultures. Yue-Sai has a keen sense of humor and often jokes about herself. She thinks fast and can handle tricky interview questions with ease. Impromptu speeches? No sweat. Yue-Sai is brave and eager to try new things. She is straightforward and always speaks her mind. She will shower you with praise when she thinks you deserve it, but never to ingratiate herself. She is compassionate and likes to help others in any way she can. Her selfless philanthropy knows no bounds. She is courteous and always says "thank you." She is decisive. When she makes a decision, she acts on it immediately. No hesitation.

Yue-Sai takes her work seriously and works hard. She does not splurge on luxuries. While disciplined in spending on herself, she is generous with others. She is punctual, reliable, and always keeps her promises. She is always eager to learn, constantly pursues new knowledge and is never satisfied. She is full of curiosity. She has infinite creativity and endless imagination.

Yue-Sai is down-to-earth and very approachable. From Presidents to house staff, she treats everyone equally. She has a big heart, doesn't hold grudges, and doesn't take things personally. She is a skilled social animal. She maintains good relationships with most of her ex-boyfriends.

She practices the traditional Chinese virtue of filial piety, taking good care of her entire family. She thinks it is never too late to chase one's dreams.

Yue-Sai's working style is to view time as her enemy. She always wants feedback and results instantaneously. She is a perfectionist, wants everything around her to be beautiful, and is picky about appearances. Even her driver's pen needs to be a beautiful pen. She has an unusual sleep pattern and often emails and WeChats people in the wee hours of the morning.

Yue-Sai has a vast network of friends and acquaintances. Her friends come from many circles—political leaders, businesspeople, royal families, and fashion celebrities. She chairs various international charities, cultural exchange organizations, and international film festivals. She is deeply respected and loved by many people. Many women in China often reminisce about their first encounter with makeup: a Yue-Sai lipstick.

From zero, Yue-Sai Kan built her cosmetics line into the number one brand, and for a number of years, it was voted the most favourite cosmetics brand voted by the Chinese consumers. Scan the QR code to access Yue-Sai's YouTube channel and view special moments from her life as an Emmy-winning television producer, best-selling author, entrepreneur and humanitarian.

Vice Premier Tian Jiyun, me, and James
McManus

New York makeup artist Donna Fumoso
was the first trainer for our beauty
consultants

With "little Yue-Sai," as Yue-Sai beauty
consultants were called by our customers

With Yue-Sai cosmetics staff

The first store window and the first group
of products

The biggest billboard in Inner Mongolia
extended over a whole city block

When I visited Da Qing oil field, the entire
city came out to welcome me

My cosmetic counters are always stormed
by customers for my products and books

Wherever I went, I was always surrounded by the police, the press, and fans

To popularize the use of cosmetics, I gave packed beauty lectures all over the country

The first lipstick most Chinese woman ever bought was a Yue-Sai lipstick

I have written 10 bestselling books in Chinese. This is a scene at a book signing.

The day we signed the contract with my new partner Peter Harf and Coty

Inauguration ceremony of Yue-Sai - Coty cosmetics factory in Pudong Shanghai, 1998

L' Oreal' s Jean-Paul Agon bought Yue-Sai Cosmetics. With Cyril Chapuy, and Natalia Noguera

April 2023 in Shanghai with LAN Zhenzhen and L' Oreal Yue-Sai China key team members

YUE-SAI

IT AIN'T ALL ABOUT
THE MONEY:
FINDING MEANING
IN EVERYTHING
I DO

Having established myself on television and then built and sold an incredibly successful and influential company in the then most populous nation in the world, I could have relaxed. However, a life of leisure did not interest me. More than anything, I wanted to continue down a path of giving back. This is ingrained in my DNA: an insatiable want to work.

While I have clocked up several triumphs in my life, none of them ever came easy, and nothing was ever handed to me. Every accomplishment emanated from vigorous work, a will to slough through hardships and tremendous sacrifice. Sometimes luck does fall into your lap, and like with the start of my television career, I so happened to be in the right place at the right time. But luck dissipates pretty quickly if you aren't willing to go above and beyond in the pursuit of a vision.

The new millennium dawned, and in a rare moment of respite, I asked myself, "What gift can I give my Chinese friends now?" I had no immediate answers, but I had dinner with China's Minister of Culture, Sun Jiazheng (孙家正), to explore the idea further. At that time, we discussed how Chinese people were doing pretty well in hardware terms – the economy and employment were accelerating. For the first time, many Chinese people had elevated themselves from impoverished shacks with little to eat and into lovely homes with bountiful meals. However, the software in their lives still needed much improvement. Generally speaking, the Chinese people had little idea about Western mannerisms, yet they continued to open up the country to visitors from the West.

"How about a book about etiquette? I'd call it 'A Guide to Modern Etiquette'?" I mused.

"You can't use such a boring title," Minister Sun replied with a laugh. "Tell me, what do you want to achieve with this book?"

"I want the Chinese to be a nation of people with charisma (有魅力的人民)!" I exclaimed.

"Then call it 'How to be Charismatic,'" Sun suggested. ("魅力何来!")

Over the years, I noticed that many Chinese officials, not to mention ordinary citizens, had yet to learn what was expected of them when dealing with Westerners. Some told me that they didn't even know how to use forks and knives given that their whole lives, they had eaten Chinese food, which is often served in bite-sized morsels and eaten solely with chopsticks. When facing new friends at a Western meal, a big piece of meat would be placed in front of them, and they had no idea how to cut it up. This made many feel very insecure. It was that insecurity which I wanted to address in my next book, and in doing so instill newfound confidence, just as I had done with the makeup line.

Before I sent the publisher my manuscript, which I entitled "Etiquette for the Modern Chinese" in the end, I sent it to Minister Sun, who offered editing suggestions and added a couple of stories of his own. I was touched by his serious approach to ensuring it was the best it possibly could be. The book contained sections on etiquette, manners, appearance, attitude, posture, table manners and correspondence.

Published in 2000, "Etiquette for the Modern Chinese" hit the bestseller list and stayed there for several years. The Beijing Municipal Government serialized it in the capital's leading state-controlled newspapers. Shortly after publication, pirated versions of the book appeared on the market using my name but different titles, causing me to call a press conference to try to end the fraud.

Despite such hiccups, this was the biggest-selling book on etiquette China had ever seen. It came to light at a time when the western floodgates had opened, and the population was in awe of this worldly influx but had not yet developed an understanding of the cultural differences. I sought to bridge this divide. For example, in a Chinese restaurant in China, it was very typical for a patron to take the warm towel served and wipe their face with it. However, by Western standards, this isn't appropriate – and if China was going to continue its progression into the wider world, it was paramount for such practices to be addressed.

Soon after its release, in February 2001, The Globe, then the bi-weekly magazine of China's state-run Xinhua News Agency, named me one of the 20 Most Influential Women in the World, based on a six-month reader survey that classed me together with former British Prime Minister Margaret Thatcher, former U.S. Secretaries of State Madeleine Albright and Hillary Clinton and actress Sophia Loren. I felt honored to be in their company, in readers' minds anyway.

And a year after my etiquette book was published, on July 13, 2001, Beijing was granted the rights to host the 2008 Summer Olympics, and that December, China acceded to the World Trade Organization. Where my TV show and cosmetics brand had offered a broad look at the outside world and a chance to improve one's surface appearance, my book emerged as a practice manual for millions of Chinese whose lives were changing and internationalizing rapidly.

"What do you mean you cannot barge into the front of the line at a bus stop?"

"Why do you need to help women with their coats if they're not in our family?"

"How come we shouldn't slurp or chew with our mouths open while eating?"

"Why use napkins?"

"Why should we open a door for women, and why do we need to hold the door for the next person?"

These were just a handful of questions I tackled. Learning the basics of modern, urban Western civility was quite a surprise for a nation of people just one generation off the farm. I once gave a lecture to the staff of the Chinese Consulate in New York City, during which the Consul General specifically asked me two questions.

"You said that when men wear suits, they should wear socks that reach the upper calf. Are you sure?"

It was a reasonable query. In those days, long men's socks were not found anywhere in China, only socks that barely rose above the ankle. I asked the Ambassador if he had ever seen a Western diplomat showing his bare calf when he crossed his legs.

"Never," he responded, nodding in acknowledgment, moving on to his second question. "Why do you say we must say 'I'm sorry' when we turn our back to someone?"

"Because turning your back on someone is rude," I replied promptly.

It was a concept foreign to most Chinese, a practice that did not originate from rudeness but simply from tradition. These and many other points in the book were alien to China in the early 2000s. Simple table manners associated with Western dining were strange but a growing curiosity.

"Why can't you cut a steak into pieces before you eat it?" was the second question that arose. I explained that that would be somewhat childlike, and the protocol is to slice as you go. Moreover, putting your napkin on your lap upon sitting at the table was confusing because the concept of a napkin itself was bizarre to most Chinese people.

However, my book helped familiarize the Chinese population with Western etiquette in all areas, helping the country join the ranks of advanced nations whose businesses could compete with the best of the rest and the best of the West.

By 2002, "Etiquette for the Modern Chinese" had become so commonplace in almost every household across the country that the official China Post asked if they could put my face on a postage stamp. At that time, you had to be dead in America to have your face on a stamp, so my immediate answer was, "Yes!" It was an incredible form of recognition. I provided two photographs, thinking they would choose one of them, but they printed both. I bought a pack of 300 stamps and amusedly sent them out on postcards to my friends worldwide.

A few years later, in 2005, I changed my hairstyle from a bob cut to a shorter style, setting off another cataclysmic trend across the country. China Post then printed a third stamp featuring my new hairdo. It was still surreal to see my face emblazoned on a stamp and think, I'm actually still alive!

WHY I CREATED A CHINA DOLL

In 2001, a neighbor of mine in New York, Sandra, asked me to bring a Chinese doll back from Shanghai (上海) for her daughter.

"Of course! No problem," I said. Piece of cake, I thought. However, I looked all over Shanghai – to no avail – and asked all of my offices to check the department stores nationwide. To my surprise, there were no Chinese-looking dolls available anywhere. All the dolls on sale were blue-eyed with blonde hair, like the Matel classic Barbie.

From my lens, this was an absolute shame. If China were to join the world of international commerce, it was pivotal to have modern Chinese dolls for Chinese children to play with and act out the newly worldly lives of the Chinese grown-ups around them. The lack of such a doll was another opportunity for me to tap into an untouched market and ensure that China's inherent beauty was known to its people and the big wide world. A Chinese standard was needed for the younger citizens to develop a sense of self-worth.

Sandra's request had triggered my next quest to create a prized, modern doll that looked Asian – a doll for Chinese kids to enjoy and feel close to, and one that reflected their looks, not some alien depiction of beauty.

First, I researched who could help me create such a thing. I then scoured southern China for the best doll-making factories. For six months, I tumbled down the rabbit hole, fixated on creating this Yue-Sai Wa-Wa (羽西娃娃) – the eponymous Yue-Sai Doll – with Wa-Wa meaning doll.

The Wa-Wa was to be ethnically Chinese, but her clothes could be both Western and Chinese. We would have one Chinese bride doll wearing a traditional red Chinese wedding embroidered gown and another wearing a Western white wedding gown with a long train. Again, bringing these two philosophies together was significant in interlacing these often-contrasting worlds. I also imagined a Chinese doctor, complete with an herbal Chinese medicine chest, cradling a small patient and a Chinese adventure girl we'd call "The Panda Protector."

I spent weeks at the factory, often until the wee hours of the morning, learning how to create these fragile, mini humans. What also invigorated me was seeing how hard manufacturers in China work, often with very minute profit margins, and under all kinds of constraints put in place by Chinese authorities as well as foreign companies who demanded low costs while simultaneously insisting on specific working codes, overtime mandates and requirements that take even more from the pockets of the struggling to survive workers. The excessive competition for such work in China exacerbates these difficulties. I have great sympathy for manufacturers, who are among the most hard-working and conscientious humans I have encountered. (I remember the owner said to me, "Tell me, how can I produce products at the price point the clients give me, yet I'm told we cannot work over time or under all kinds of other constraints?")

It was challenging to understand and learn the intricate mechanics of bringing these delicate dolls into being, but soon, I had created the first truly authentic Chinese doll in the world, replete with black hair, black eyes, and an Asian complexion.

And then, the strangest thing happened to me with the doll's debut in late 2001. I started losing my hair, just like many women do in the postpartum period after giving birth to live human babies. I was scared and confused and finally plucked up the courage to visit several Western doctors who had nothing to offer except oily hair regrowth products. Finally, I shuffled over to the Huashan Hospital (华山医院) in Shanghai. The dermatologist there prescribed me a Chinese medicine made of an herb called shou wu (首乌), known for promoting hair growth, longevity, and virility. Within a week, and much to my relief, my hair was back to normal. This is yet another successful outcome that came at a time when no Western medicine could compare the age-old remedies of Chinese medicine.

The dolls sold incredibly well in China, and the buyers at the Home Shopping Network (HSN) in the United States soon reached out, wanting to sell them on American TV. Even FAO Schwarz, the largest individual toy store in America, issued a request to stock the Wa-Wa collection. I invited four beautiful Chinese models to come to New York to help promote the dolls. I had replica dolls' outfits made to fit the models' tall, lean figures and put on a fashion show at the FAO Schwarz store, right across the street from The Plaza Hotel on the famed Fifth

Avenue. The show was glamorous and very well received.

Afterward, I flew the models to the Home Shopping Network headquarters in St. Petersburg, Florida, to do precisely the same thing, this time for a television audience. Each model emerged on the screen, holding a doll donning a beautiful, matching outfit in its original box. In one hour, we sold more than $1 million in Yue-Sai Wa-Wa products, a record for HSN at the time.

Interestingly, the biggest buyers of the Yue-Sai dolls were predominantly white parents who had adopted Chinese children and wished for them to feel connected to their Chinese heritage. That struck quite an internal chord for me.

In China, in addition to the dolls, we also launched a series of weekly comics called "Yue-Sai Adventures." I hired Yumiko Igarashi, Japan's most well-known comic book artist and illustrator of the super-famous manga "Kyandi Kyandi" (known as 'Xiao Tian-Tian 小甜甜' in Chinese). I sent Yumiko storylines about the comic book character Yue-Sai, and she made them come to life in full color. In one, the young adventurer Yue-Sai takes a trip to Egypt to visit exotic sights such as the Pyramids and the Sphinx at Giza. In another, Yue-Sai is chased by an elephant while on an African safari. The idea was to show young Chinese that they, too, could get out and see the world and be a part of this prominent place they knew so little about.

Yumiko's stunning drawings and my exploit-laden stories combined into a comic strip that was published in China's official Youth Daily newspaper. Decades later, people (probably my young readers now grown up) still approach me with excitement and feedback, sharing how the visuals inspired them to take a far-flung vacation or experience a new adventure far from the comforts of home.

Despite the joy I derived from the creation of the dolls and the comics, they were infinitely demanding to bring to life and to continue marketing. The per-unit cost per doll was expensive because we couldn't produce more than five hundred at once based on our sales volume. With Barbie, Mattel makes hundreds of thousands, all in the same style, so the unit cost for each is extremely low. Although our sales through Home Shopping Network started well, maintaining staff throughout the year to handle the promotion on TV was expensive.

After some time, I felt the ping that it was time to walk away. Leaving a project, no matter how much it had wedged into the fabric of my being, was not a difficult concept for me. I always felt that there were many acts to my life and places I needed to be.

Thus, I sold the doll company in 2005 to an agent who, regretfully, didn't do a particularly good job growing it. Nevertheless, I wouldn't take that venture back for anything. Creating the Wa-Wa collection was a wonderful and meaningful expedition that helped pave the way for the appearance, later on, of more ethnic dolls in the market. Amid the 2023 hoopla of the Barbie movie, someone in China actually brought me a Wa-wa doll for my autograph.

Today, collectible Yue-Sai Wa-Wa dolls can be found on eBay and Chinese e-commerce giant Taobao (淘宝). I am immensely proud of the self-confidence these dolls instilled in

Chinese girls and women who needed something to preserve – something to call their own.

IN THE WORDS OF JENNY CHEN (陈涓玲)__

I worked as Yue-Sai's personal assistant from 1999-2007. In my mind, she is the messenger of beauty who stands at the intersection of Eastern and Western culture. Yue-Sai helped bring Chinese people out of the gray world of the early 1990s into a colorful world and also brought that world into China. What I learned the most from those days around her was her spirit and values. I saw an interview with her not long ago, and one of the questions asked was what she would want to say to herself thirty years ago.

"Try harder, try harder, although I know I have already tried hard!" she stressed. It inspires me even now.

In the early 2000s, I mostly lived in Shanghai amid a Chinese real estate market boom. After buying a house or apartment, the idea was to give the abode an intensive facelift, but few Chinese understood proper interior design. For most Chinese in those days, interior design merely meant that after securing an apartment, you go out and pick up a television, and then you put two couches next to it. That was it. End of story.

While I am not a professional interior designer, I thoroughly enjoyed furbishing and embellishing my homes with beauty and comfort. In the same way that I love cosmetics, clothes, and shoes, I love getting my living space in order. Home should be your most relaxing place and a space to work, entertain guests and throw a party. The walls that encompass you should be an extension of your personality – revealing your taste, style, fashion sense – and even your attitude towards life.

Once more, I had unearthed a hole in the marketplace – and one that I felt I could fill, bringing my Chinese sisters closer to the outside world of the finer things in life. Throughout the years, I met many esteemed interior designers in various pockets of the planet. I relished sharing my tastes and then asking them to tailor the furniture's style, color, and function for my home. Over time, I created what was, in effect, my home brand. I decided to take this to the Chinese market in 2007, naming it "House of Yue-Sai (羽西之家)." I wanted to inspire a new generation of Chinese designers and fill the absence of high-quality design that had not yet made its mark in the blossoming country.

House of Yue-Sai included fine furnishings for the bedroom, kitchen and living room, decorative lamps, soft interior decoration, accessories, and thousands of products such as artworks, gifts, food, and wine. 70 percent of these wares were designed independently or exclusively for the House of Yue-Sai. The other 30 percent I curated from Italy, France, the United States, India, Thailand, Indonesia, Vietnam, and the Czech Republic.

Most Chinese knew little about beautiful design at this time and had minimal choices when decorating their homes. Much like the clothes they wore, most people still purchased the same colors and styles of dull furniture; a relic of economic tough times and having such few choices for so long. I longed to encourage people to think about style and the benefits of an elegant environment, even down to something as simple as recognizing that a bowl doesn't just have to be a clump of plastic to serve food, but an ornate accessory that brings a family together and exudes a different sort of attitude to life.

House of Yue-Sai employed Yue-Sai Red on a peony as its theme color and logo, embossed with the words, "Taste, Elegance, Inspiration," a motto that I hoped would guide design concepts rooted in Eastern aesthetics to fuse with leading international ideas and capture the imagination of a growing wealthy class of Chinese urbanites.

Furthermore, I wanted to sell porcelain and ceramic tableware, and an acquaintance suggested that I visit Tangshan (唐山市) in Hebei Province (河北省). This coastal, industrial city was wiped out by a magnitude 7.6 earthquake in 1976. Although skeptical, I inspected an impressive factory making quality home-related products anyway. The manager explained that the factory had recovered quickly with the assistance of an investment by the state-owned China Travel Service (CTS) based in Hong Kong. At that time, CTS was cash-rich from the rising number of bookings by overseas travelers arriving in China. In the government's mode of thought, it was a perfect match: CTS, a travel agency, would help with a ceramics operation that was distinctly cash poor. That was typical of Central Government planning in those days.

Incidentally, in September 2023 I visited Wen Chuan (汶川) county in Sichuan province where a devastating earthquake struck in 2008, claiming the lives of 75,000 people. In the aftermath, the same Central Government of mode of thinking was put into place. Guangdong province was subsequently asked to help to rebuild this county. They did such a great job that the rebuilding lifted the living standard of the people by 20 years. It seems that the thinking can often be very helpful. As another example, I also visited Nanning of Guangxi province that same month for the Asian Summit. My first visit to Nanning was in 1997. At that time, it was one of the slowest growing in the nation. The government decided that because the picturesque coastal Guangdong province is so wealthy, they should start investing in Nanning. Because of that attention and investment, the Nanning of today is incredibly modern, beautiful and a drawcard for many visitors.

The flagship House of Yue-Sai boutique opened in Shanghai in late 2007 on Beijing Road (北京路). Beyond home furnishings, we also sold a successful line of branded jewelry, a selection of fine wines and high-grade teas grown in the highlands of Taiwan (台湾) – classy, curated components to make up a beautiful home and a high-end lifestyle. I didn't want the House of Yue-Sai to sell traditional Chinese furniture, but instead offer an East-meets-West product line, signaling my whole attitude toward life. I hoped that the House of Yue-Sai would lead Chinese people to discover that decorating a home can be poetic.

In addition to our exquisite local and imported homewares and our ceramics from Tangshan, we offered exclusive interior design services. From my purview, this was the most critical part of the House of Yue-Sai. The design component was staffed by a young English designer, Karen Wilson, and the young American Luke Van Dyun, who had just graduated from design school in the U.S. at age 19 and gutsily ventured to Shanghai to work. Immediately upon meeting them both, I sensed their brilliance and innovative eye. Today, Luke is an independent designer working with some of China's richest tech billionaires, and we remain very close.

However, the average Chinese consumer then spent little on home decor. Most of what sold was in the "economy" and "affordable" categories, often represented by outlets such as IKEA, which first opened in China in 1998. The luxury life concept offered by the House of Yue-Sai proved ahead of its time. It would be another decade before Chinese people could contemplate purchasing bespoke tables and chairs and designer dishware.

Sometimes, you can give every sense of your artistic vision to a project, but if the timing isn't right and the customer base is not ready, that is how it is. I still reminisce on the products and personally use a lot of them. I am deeply proud of their beauty, however, all the elements required for a massive hit were not ready to converge.

House of Yue-Sai lasted for just under two years, suffering product development, marketing challenges and terrible mismanagement – all with my name on it. Perhaps the most prominent blotch, even more so than the struggle to bring a mass market into the luxury furniture fold, was that the managers I needed to count on let me down, such that I ended up serving as both the face of the company and its back-of-house. I could not keep up with giving interviews all day and then running to the warehouse after hours to check on the inventory. The stress mounted day after day and my health was drastically impacted. I constantly contracted the flu and other immunity-gnashing illnesses. Once, I even fainted on the floor, overcome with a kind of tiredness that seeped into every bone.

This is a lesson every entrepreneur must learn. No matter how much you try, you can't do everything. Staffing is key. Sadly, I faced many problems in this regard, from a General Manager with a great resume but experienced in already-established conglomerates rather than in the start-up space, to a dishonest purchasing department that buys things more expensively than the ones I see sold on the street along.

That is why so many entrepreneurs start their companies with trusted partners; even then, it may or may not work out.

Alibaba, for one, China's biggest e-commerce platform, had 18 founders who later became billionaires. But if you don't have solid partners, you must hire competent, trustworthy staff to run your company's various departments. The man I recruited away from a large home furnishing chain was just the wrong hire. He treated my little start-up like a big corporation and built a disastrous surplus inventory. Speaking from an experience I wish I had not had, one must be especially mindful of hiring in finance and purchasing, as those department heads can rob you blind if you're not careful. Unfortunately, our offerings were ten years ahead. The macro environment at that time was not ready, but if it launched today, it would be a very different story.

A Chinese astrologer warned me that my body would give out if I continued to run the business and cautioned that the following year would be worse. I was scared. Nothing is more important than one's health, and I felt as though I was standing on the most fragile footing of my life. We had built a compelling reputation, and our products sold, even in a market unfamiliar with such luxury. Several large-scale real estate companies also wanted us to decorate their mammoth developments, the commissions were large, which helped sustain the business for some time. However, nearly two years in, I made the decision to shut the company down to prevent my body from breaking down. Once again, the universe had signaled me to move on. I did not want to stubbornly cling to the past, and risk missing the opportunities that awaited my future. I was well aware of the risks of my ventures, and I chose to take them anyway. After all, we regret the things we do not do much more than the ones we tried.

From the inception of House of Yue-Sai, I felt compelled to author another book, this time to explain interior design for the Chinese, many of whom, at that time, felt that all that was needed to complete the home was a television and two couches. I worked on the book for two years, and in 2009, I published the very first coffee table book on the subject in the Chinese language published for the Chinese market. Under the title "Exquisite Spaces: 25 Top Interior Designers of the World (魅力之家)," the book included my interviews with the best of the best globally, from Peter Marino and Geoffrey Bradfield to Mario Buatta and Bunny Williams.

Despite the passage of time since the House of Yue-Sai's closure, people sometimes reach out, requesting an interior design consultation or more information about opening a

House of Yue-Sai franchise. Each time, this reminds me that even projects that could be deemed closer to the side of failure are still triumphs that have made a significant impact. With the continued boom in wealth in China's ever more cosmopolitan big cities, I often wish someone would guide the Chinese toward a refined sense of taste and away from the impulse to furnish their homes exclusively with famous designer brands that break the bank. Money is different from taste. But China, like many developing nations, remains a work in progress.

In the early 2000s, sweeping changes were taking place. China was knocking down its old city centers, filled with ugly buildings left over from when concrete, Soviet-style architecture was in fashion, furiously replacing them with gleaming glass-and-steel high-rises. Construction cranes littered every corner. People's living standards were on the rise, too. At the start of the new millennium, the entire country was preparing for the 2008 Beijing Olympic Games. Even Beijing taxi drivers were learning English and spouting words like "globalization" and phrases like "global village." I wondered once again what I could do for China to strengthen its integration into the world and prepare it for the Olympics' "coming out" party when much of the world would see inside the modernized nation for the first time. I was perpetually searching for something meaningful to do.

A friend suggested I create another TV show, this time introducing Chinese viewers to the lives of celebrities worldwide, shining a light on their achievements, comparing and contrasting Chinese and foreign cultures, and finding the charm and lessons in each other's strengths.

To be a TV producer and host again, to record and share profound human stories on camera, requires time, energy, perseverance and a lot of confidence – and I could not wait to dive back in headfirst. In 2005, I launched "Yue-Sai's World" (羽西看世界) early on Sunday evening on Shanghai TV, with two repeats during the week. The audience response and the press reviews were so impressive that starting in January 2006, the show was moved to a better, later time slot, airing Sunday nights at 10:30 p.m. with three repeats during the week. The series quickly went national, airing on 30 provincial and city stations to a potential audience of 500 million people. With this coverage, it was one of the best-syndicated shows of its kind in China and probably in the world.

In April 2006, the state-owned satellite TV network CETV, covering 85 percent of China, started carrying the series, giving "Yue-Sai's World" a dizzying potential audience of 800 million viewers every week. We shot 52 half-hour episodes in Mandarin, filmed worldwide, and produced them in the United States. Due to its international content and the high production quality, my audience was a lovely group – upwardly mobile, international-leaning, educated and relatively wealthy. The main sponsors of the series were Audi and China Merchants Bank, and advertisers included L'Oréal, United Airlines and Chinese state-controlled telecom giant China Unicom.

My goal was, and has always been, to aid the Chinese people to broaden their horizons and ascertain a richer understanding of the world. By introducing them to the lifestyles of influential people, Chinese people could take inspiration and begin to grow their lives in ways that I had when I first traveled. Returning to the full screen not only felt familiar but was a lot of fun, too.

I wedged myself in some interesting situations in the interest of this greater understanding. I became part of a trick shot pulled off by the world's top-rated billiards player; I was nuzzled and licked by photographer William Wegman's famous Weimaraner dogs; and I sang a duet with Julio Iglesias. I always endeavored to go the extra mile, and my guests appreciated it. Josh Groban, Paul Anka and Wynton Marsalis all performed for the show. Naomi Campbell, Queen Noor and Catherine Deneuve offered rare insights into their private lives.

"Yue-Sai's World" was a cosmos of excitement, adventure, style, and culture. I took the audience behind the scenes to meet the world's most famous people, giving them an unprecedented glimpse of the glamorous life. From the incitement and tension of the Miss Universe pageant, the heavenly music of violinist Itzhak Perlman and the stunning images of Canadian nature photographer Gregory Colbert to an intimate dialogue with actress Andie MacDowell, the urban melodies of R&B superstar Usher and the magical charm of Adrien Brody – the youngest-ever Best Actor Oscar-winner – I brought it all to life for my viewers with poise, personality and charm.

I ADORE QUINCY JONES, MY BROTHER FROM ANOTHER MOTHER

In 2007, supermodel Naomi Campbell introduced me to Quincy Jones, letting me know her legendary American record producer friend, whom she called pops, might need a hand. Quincy was due to go to Beijing as a Beijing Olympic Organizing Committee consultant. Yet, eight days before the ceremony, he could not get final confirmation of his air ticket and hotel room and could not put his life on hold forever. Happy to help, I called officials, and everything was quickly put in order.

From that day on, Quincy and I became close friends, and he remains a big brother to me today. Always thoughtful, I receive Valentine's Day cards and Christmas gifts from him every year. Of course, it isn't just me who admires him, but the world. Quincy has an aura everyone wants to be around. He created sounds that never existed before and makes everyone in his presence feel wanted and special.

Quincy owns a gorgeous, sprawling residence at the top of the exclusive Los Angeles community of Bel Air, where he often invited me to stay in his home's "Oprah Suite." Being with him is always a blast. Quincy doesn't sleep until at least 6 a.m. and doesn't rise until around noon unless he absolutely must.

I met a lot of people through this legend of a man, each one more special than the last – from U2 frontman Bono, pianist Herbie Hancock, Jerry Inzerillo, Miky Lee of C.J.

Entertainment, Badr Jafr of Dubai, and Raymond Chambers, to director Lee Daniels, Ted Sarandos and his wife Ambassador Nicole Avant (the former ambassador to the Bahamas) the Black Godfather Clarence Avant, to actor/director/diplomat Sidney Poitier. Many of these remarkable individuals became close and dear friends. Quincy just has an uncanny knack for picking good people and is always surrounded by the most talented, successful and interesting humans, yet remains humble. I have never heard him boast about himself or the company that he keeps. Quincy discovered the actor Will Smith and found Oprah Winfrey when she was working at a small Chicago TV station. He is constantly introducing people to each other, incredibly generous with forging connections and bringing everyone he knows and loves into a singular orbit.

In 2007, Quincy hosted a lavish dinner for me at his home. Guests included actor Denzel Washington and his wife, the actress Pauletta Pearson, the award-winning movie producers Arnold and Anne Kopelson, actress Suzanne Sommers and her husband Alan Hamel, the Canadian television host. Alfredo Rodriquez, Quincy's protégé pianist, played for us that memorable evening.

Two years later, I invited Quincy to the Shanghai Film Festival to be honored with a Lifetime Achievement Award in the hope that by bringing over one of the world's top composers for films, I would play a part in inspiring China's moviemakers. Unfortunately, all but one of the films Quincy scored over his extensive career were released during a dark time in China's modern history when imported films were banned. Very few

Chinese at the SIFF would likely have seen the films he scored unless they were the most devoted cinephiles seeking out pirated DVDs of late 1960s classics such as "In Cold Blood" and "The Italian Job."

Ironically, the 1985 film "The Color Purple," which Quincy both scored and co-produced with director Steven Spielberg (who he convinced to cast Oprah), came out in a brighter period for China but was never released there theatrically as its depiction of brutal sex would have been too much for China's censors. However, Quincy was unfazed by the prospect of meeting an audience largely unaware of his work and accepted the festival's invitation. Boy, did we have a ball. I took him to all the best jazz clubs and discos Shanghai offered, provoking a highly complementary observation about club life in China.

"Whether you are in Monaco or Shanghai," he commented. "The drinks, the music and the noise, it's all the same."

Introducing Quincy at the Shanghai International Film Festival in 2009 proved a milestone in the event's history and a marker of just how far the festival had come since its inception year in 1993, an outgrowth of the Shanghai TV Festival, where I was that event's inaugural host, back in 1986.

The one laugh I always have with my dear friend is over his inability to be on time for anything. That included when I hosted a dinner at my home in Shanghai ahead of the Film Festival. Naturally, Quincy arrived an hour late. Why? He had gotten wrapped up ordering twenty bespoke suits for himself from a Chinese tailor in the silk market. That was Quincy, ever the style icon.

In recent years, Quincy would tell me mournfully that one by one his best friends had passed away. However, there was one thing all of us close to Quincy understood: he does not go to funerals. He did not even attend the funeral of his brother. But at the virtual grave side of his beloved sister-in-law who was living and working with him for years after his brother died, Quincy surprised us when he did call in.

Moreover, Quincy is very proud of his 7 children. They are all really beautiful and successful and he loves to brag about them all the time. There is Jolie, Rachel, and then his only son Quincy Delight Jones, followed by Kidada and the amazing actress, director/writer Rashida Jones. She created a documentary about her father called Quincy in 2018. If you have not seen it, you should.

But there are a couple of things Quincy told me that I will never forget. For one, he said that when you want to go to a country, especially one that you have never been to before, you don't need to know a lot of people – you only need to know ONLY one, the one that can open all doors for you, a notion that I have found to be remarkably true. Second, I once asked Quincy why some very talented musicians never make it despite their abilities being far superior to ones that are famous. His answer was only one word: personality.

In 2010, when Quincy heard I wanted to go to the Oscars but couldn't get tickets, he exclaimed, "I'll take you!" His amazingly capable, long-time assistant, Deborah Elaine Foreman, told me that Qunicy hadn't been to the Oscars in many years, but he made an exception to take me. Going to the Oscars with Hollywood royalty felt like a far-reaching dream coming to fruition. I met everyone who was anyone, including the dashing George Clooney, who ran over to greet Quincy. We all walked the VIP red carpet, surrounded by fans screaming "Quincy! Quincy! Quincy!" The cameras fell upon us, and almost immediately, my mobile flooded with texts from friends around the world excitedly sharing that they'd seen me on TV at the Oscars in my floor-length, vivid pink dress designed by John Anthony. Mayor Antonio Villaraigosa's post-awards celebratory dinner also drew the A-List crowd, and there I was, with Quincy, feeling most glamorous.

Soon after, when dear Qunicy discovered that, like the Oscars, I had never been to the Grammys, he took me along to that extravaganza, too. As one of the Grammys' founders, there wasn't a single musician in the house who didn't show him respect. Alongside Quincy, I met legendary musicians at the acclaimed awards show, from Usher and U2 to Stevie Wonder to Jennifer Hudson. Even in his eighties, ever-dashing Quincy was still a chick magnet. It was hilarious to watch how women flocked to his presence. And yet, he was always gracious, taking the time to engage with everyone who approached him sincerely. However, if a male or female musician came and asked him to listen to their music, Quincy would politely respond, "Don't ask me to listen to your music until you have written 500 songs."

The most amazing part about the Grammys week was the star-studded dinner given the night before music's big event by the legendary record producer and agent Clive Davis in the ballroom at the Beverly Hilton. It almost felt more impressive than the Grammys itself. The Clive Davis Grammy Party is the hottest ticket in town and is even more exclusive and jam-packed with music industry creme-de-la-crème than the awards showdown.

Not long after my whirlwind with Quincy at the Oscars and the Grammys, Mr. Hu Jingjun (胡劲军), one of the organizers of the World Expo 2010 in Shanghai, reached out to see if I could persuade Quincy to write a theme song for the upcoming event in Shanghai. Quincy not only accepted, but he also warmly wrote the song "Better City, Better Life" at no cost. The Expo only paid for time at the Westlake Recording Studios. Quincy spent two nights recording in the same famous Los Angeles studio where he produced Michael Jackson's "Thriller," the best-selling album of all time, with 70 million records sold. Watching this icon at work was remarkable, starting at midnight and finishing at 6 a.m., directing each musician and singer with meticulous care and attention to detail. In the middle of the night is when Quincy seems to come most to life. I'm proud that he calls me his Chinese sister. He has been an inspiration to me and a good, ever-dependable friend.

Quincy, forever thoughtful, believed I would enjoy meeting Oprah Winfrey. Once, while a guest at his palatial Los Angeles home, he invited Oprah over. I was thrilled at the chance to sit with one of my idols. Oprah's intimate, confessional interviewing style and her ability to bring a highly polished show to air day after day had been a guiding light for me professionally. My adoration of her was amplified by the notion that she also happened to build a media empire, become the wealthiest Black woman on the planet and remains an incredibly devout philanthropist. This spoke volumes to me as a minority in America whose greatest gratification comes from storytelling and giving back.

I met Oprah along with her best friend, Gayle King. The meeting couldn't have been more pleasant. It was 2011, and she'd just announced she would wind down the renowned "Oprah Winfrey Show," the highest-rated television program of its kind for a quarter century. Oprah shared that she was thinking about international shows next.

"You'll have so much fun," I enthused. "But, please, take your time to enjoy the places where you'll shoot. When I traveled the globe doing 'One World' for CCTV, I was rushed and always on deadline. It wasn't until I revisited the places where I produced shows that I got to enjoy them."

I'll forever be grateful to Quincy for his kind consideration in bringing me together with Oprah. While she and I haven't kept up, Gayle King and I stayed in touch. When her only son, William Bumpus, whom she calls her "favorite son," visited China, he came to stay with me in Shanghai.

In August 2018, at the age of 86, Quincy released a new album, and in 2022, he published the self-development book "12 Notes: On Life and Creativity." (He said he wrote it for musicians). He still brings concerts, movies, and books to life. For him, age is truly just a meaningless set of digits. He agreed to be the executive producer of the music for my next story-telling endeavor, "Trending China." I love that man. Quincy inspires me to do more with myself and for humanity. What a great human being.

In early 2023, beloved Quincy became really sick and was hospitalized for months. By July, he was home but was not able to walk or receive any guests. Nonetheless, that same month, on July 28 and 29, the Hollywood Bowl presented two sold out concerts in honor of Quincy's 90th birthday. His illustrious body of music was on full display with some of the best-selling songs of all time performed by some of the greatest musicians of all time, including Jennifer Hudson, Siedah Garrett, Patti Hudson, Stevie Wonder and John Legend. I am grateful that such a tribute was performed while he was able to see it for himself, on television at least.

As of this writing, Quincy is still recuperating.

AN INTERNATIONAL TV FESTIVAL WHEN WE BARELY HAD TV

Fresh off the success of "One World" in the late 1980s, then-Director of Shanghai TV Gong Xueping (龚学平) telephoned my home in New York and offered to fly me to Shanghai for two days just for the Shanghai TV Festival's two-hour opening ceremony. Although "One World" was a hit in China, making me Letterman-famous in the country of my birth, I was somewhat skeptical about China's broader television industry, which is still very much in its post-Cultural Revolution infancy. A television festival assumed an understanding of the intricacies of buying and selling filmed content and the existence of an established and regulated commercial marketplace for advertising.

Nevertheless, like almost everything in China, the Shanghai TV Festival had to start somewhere, and I was happy to be on the ground floor, doing what I could to link the Chinese industry to the rest of the world. While there may have been a lack of content, the festival didn't start entirely empty-handed. After all, there was the festival leaders' vision for the future and how to get there: a quality of foresight coupled with fearlessness, patience and diligence, a combination I've always admired in Chinese leaders.

Scores of people from around the world, curious and eager to visit China and explore the country's potentially massive money-making market, arrived at the Shanghai TV Festival. At the opening dinner, the hosts served hairy crab, a delicacy the Shanghainese only available in season, much adored but often problematic for diners with no experience eating around the fiddly shells. Then there was karaoke with a live band, but the foreign guests quickly – with much disappointment – discovered that the local musicians didn't know any internationally famous songs. From 1949 to the 1980s, China was plunged into a sort of a time warp, riding first a physical war, then devastating famine, pursued by the Cultural Revolution – isolating it from the broader world. Nothing came into China from the outside during those years, so the band could not play the most popular songs from the West. Instead, we were all relegated to singing songs like "Santa Lucia" and "Auld Lang Syne," international hits popular in China in the pre-revolutionary times.

After the TV festival concluded, the Shanghai International Film Festival (SIFF) started. It's a miracle that today, the annual event, which begins each year on the immediate heels of the TV Festival and marks its 38th year in 2024, is considered one of the top 15 film festivals recognized by the International Film Producers Association. The film festival's true ascension into the Hollywood elite began in earnest when the new executive secretary, Ms. Tang Lijun (唐丽君), called me.

"Yue-Sai, we need your help," Sugar, as we who love her know her, said pleadingly. "We have a budget and want to invite international filmmakers, but we don't know how to approach them."

Imagine a so-called international film festival, then eight years old, still waiting for international contacts. Sugar asked me to be an Ambassador of the Shanghai International Film Festival to bolster its prestige by inviting overseas filmmakers and celebrities to promote the festival globally. I accepted, understanding that it would be a long-term volunteer job.

I had attended the festival each year since its start and knew that many of the team members running it needed to learn how an international festival ought to work. For SIFF to grow and take hold, it was imperative that the team learn how to invite and receive important guests. In 2004, for instance, when Hollywood actress Meryl Streep arrived in Shanghai with her family right after winning the American Film Association Lifetime Achievement Award, the Chinese festival organizers did little to acknowledge her status as one of the industry's leading talents. All they asked her to do is to walk on stage to present an award with little other fanfare. I was so embarrassed. Two years later, when I took on the role of Ambassador to help invite influential filmmakers from overseas, I managed to attract the likes of Catherine Deneuve, Andie MacDowell, Natasha Richardson, Sigourney Weaver,

Liam Neeson, and Hugh Jackman to join us on the red carpet at a time when China's box office was becoming increasingly tantalizing to Hollywood studios. From then on, the SIFF strove yearly to align with international standards and make a mark on a much broader scale.

Over the next few years, I invited at least 70 producers, writers, directors, actors, musicians, singers, photographers and designers. Many of the A-listers I invited accepted with great curiosity about China and loved their time in Shanghai. My guests were Halle Berry, Adrien Brody, Matt Dillon, Ralph Fiennes, Hugh Grant, Taylor Hackford, Sophie Marceau, Helen Mirren, Hugh Jackman, Susan Sarandon, and Sigourney Weaver.

Initially, it was challenging to convince big-name stars to come to Shanghai. I spent days emailing and calling, negotiating to cover some, if not all, of their travel expenses. I made over 50 international calls and sent over 100 emails before French great Catherine Deneuve finally decided to come.

Most international celebrities command a hefty appearance fee, but the celebrities I invited all attended the SIFF for free, saving organizers tens of millions. As the guests were attending without charge, as a favor to me, some – such as Russell Crowe and Sylvester Stallone – felt it meant they could back out at the last minute, foiling countless hours of meticulous and personalized arrangements. This was incredibly frustrating and disheartening, however, I had to learn to dust myself off pretty quickly. It would be their loss.

But those who did show up as they promised enjoyed

a personalized itinerary I'd designed for them to make the trip to Shanghai worthwhile. For example, Catherine Deneuve loves the sleek, high collar Chinese dresses known as cheongsams, so I took her to the best tailor I know and had six of the dresses, especially for her lovely frame. I always took all of SIFF's jet-setting stars on a river cruise and introduced them to China's top directors, writers and actors over delicious meals at high-end restaurants.

IN THE WORDS OF STEPHANIE JACOBS _____

Anyone who knows Yue-Sai knows she knows how to party! Not only is the food good, but the company is also gorgeous and interesting, and each spot she chooses to entertain in is a beautiful environment. In all the time I worked as her assistant, each evening ended with a sense that Yue-Sai made everyone feel comfortable and important! Everyone has fun. She always treats everyone as if they are the only people there, showering each with attention.

AMBASSADOR TO THE SHANGHAI INTERNATIONAL FILM FESTIVAL _____

The Shanghai International Film Festival had never held an official reception/welcome dinner. While the Chinese are predominantly the most amazing hosts who always treat their guests with the utmost candor, the lack of such a formality in this case was mainly due to the festival organizers' general inexperience with glamor.

I like a good party, and I've been to classy film festival soirees worldwide. As Ambassador, I took it upon myself to welcome old friends and new arriving at the festival from around the world into my home – in style. The hope was that the gatherings would spark the kind of film industry cooperation the organizers needed to establish their brand as sustainable.

Andie MacDowell was one of my first overseas guests as Ambassador at the Shanghai International Film Festival in 2006, and the actress best known for her roles in "Groundhog Day," "Green Card" and "Four Weddings and a Funeral," returned to SIFF as a judge in 2009. In my role as Ambassador, nothing was more exciting than watching relationships such as these flourish. That year, Oscar-winning producer Arnold Kopelson and actress Suzanne Sommers joined us for the opening ceremony, and French screen goddess Catherine Deneuve attended the closing ceremony.

2009 was a particularly memorable year at the SIFF in other ways, too. "Close My Eyes" star Clive Owen strolled into my living room at 11 p.m., drawing squeals from my female guests. Soon after, the gents gathered in my home all gasped when Halle Berry, Caterina Murino and Maria Grazia Cucinotta, three stunning Bond Girls, all strode in together. Moreover, everyone was thrilled to meet our guest Danny Boyle, the Englishman who'd just won the Best Directing Oscar for his Best Picture-winning drama "Slumdog Millionaire." My friend Quincy Jones had such a wonderful time he didn't roll out for his hotel until 4 a.m.

In 2014, as Asian films made more of an international splash, led mainly by those from South Korea, my opening night welcome party was absolutely off the hook when K-Pop star and actor Rain and the model and actor Song Seung-Heon made appearances in my home. The guests were so excited their screams nearly brought down the roof. Word got out via social media, and the lobby of my building was mobbed. The two modest and dashing Korean men hid in my bedroom until veteran Chinese actress Gong Li (巩俐) arrived, drawing attention. By then, the superstar guests from Seoul had calmed down, joined the party and took a selfie with the stunningly beautiful Gong, the festival's chief competition judge that year. Days later, backstage at the festival, superstar Song told me he was thrilled to have met Gong around my table. Building bridges is often just that much fun.

I worked at the Shanghai International Film Festival for twelve years and was never paid a dime, but I spent a lot of my own money and mobilized all my contacts around the world and my staff, both in China and the U.S., to work on the event for months at a time. Why? Because I love the movies and regard the festival as an important part of international cultural exchange. China possesses the largest film and television market in the universe, and I was proud to have played an interlocutor in bringing Tinseltown inside.

The year 2018 marked the 40th anniversary of the market reforms put in place by Deng Xiaoping (邓小平) to open China to the outside in a way not seen for decades. That year, the producers of the Chinese language documentary film "Modern

China: How We Made It" interviewed me as a witness to and participant in the reform – someone whose life work has been related to cultural exchange between East and West.

I also ushered the documentary film crew backstage at the Shanghai International Film Festival to ensure that viewers of the film, set to release in 2019 on the 70th anniversary of the founding of the People's Republic, could see for themselves the significant changes that have taken place in China as measured by the progress in and opening up of its film industry.

Along with the rest of China's construction boom and rise in its citizens' expendable income, the country's movie screens exploded from roughly 3,500 in 2007 to more than 80,000 in 2021, ranking first globally. Fittingly, as Shanghai was the movie capital of China before the communist takeover, its international film festival boomed leaps and bounds, with festival attendance soaring to more than 6,000 people in 2021, up from only 1,000 in 2008. In 2021, the SIFF received a record-high 4,443 submissions from 113 countries and regions, indicating growing faith among global filmmakers in the importance of China's movie market.

Several cooperations grew from my work to bring overseas talents to the SIFF. After I invited American director Barry Levinson and French director Jean-Jacques Annaud to participate in the Shanghai International Film Festival, they worked with Chinese film companies. Jean, who'd been blacklisted in China for years for his work on the film "Seven Years in Tibet," which addressed the sensitive issue of the controversial spiritual leader the Dalai Lama, went on to make the hit film "Wolf Totem," based on a bestselling Chinese novel.

However, compared with other international film festivals, such as the Venice Film Festival and the Cannes Film Festival, the Shanghai International Film Festival still needed to broaden its international appeal and recognition. My biggest concern was that the VIP reception would only partially meet the expectations of the global stars arriving as guests. In 2014, Oliver Stone, a director who has won three Oscars, was almost lost in the bustling city because festival organizers failed to arrange a car to escort him to my home for the opening night dinner. He found a taxi but couldn't communicate with the driver and was thrown out on the street. My assistant had to rescue him. Oliver was tolerant and didn't complain, but his experience dampened my mood for the entire evening as it should not have happened.

To continue to grow, the Shanghai International Film Festival should look to the European film festivals, whose vibrancy and excitement draws celebrities from fashion, music, art, literature, and even politics who want to celebrate the movies. Each European film festival features opening ceremonies and many sponsored social activities that unite everyone and simultaneously do wonders to promote luxury brands, films and worthy causes. At Cannes, for example, the jeweler Chopard organizes parties for stars to show off its diamond-studded wares, and actors such as Leonardo DiCaprio attend fundraisers for the global fight against AIDS.

For a time, the Shanghai International Film Festival was progressing in living up to its name. However, beginning in

2015, SIFF began to take a more conservative and downward turn, a puzzling move when China as a whole is trying to engage the rest of the world through programs like Beijing's much-touted Belt and Road initiatives to help the developing world.

It strikes me that China's film industry is in danger of going the route of Bollywood, producing hundreds of films a year that speak primarily to Chinese audiences worldwide and do little to cross over into universal appeal. While Chinese television series have made modest progress globally, following in the footsteps of fabulously popular dramas from South Korea, there are to date only two Chinese language feature films that have ever made any real box office success outside of China — Director Ang Lee's (李安) "Crouching Tiger, Hidden Dragon," and Zhang Yimou's (张艺谋) "Hero."

In 2018, I suggested that SIFF give actor Al Pacino a much-deserved Lifetime Achievement Award. Organizers immediately declined and hinted that no foreigner would be given an award going forward. They also rejected Ben Kingsley and Julie Andrews, whose performances helped shape many Western classic movies. I was particularly disappointed that Julie Andrews was not invited. Festival organizers shrugged and lamented that she was too old. Her "Sound of Music" was a perennial favorite of the Chinese, being the only Hollywood movie played in China for many years during the Cultural Revolution.

Organizers in Shanghai, once happy to be counted among the true international film festival leaders, nowadays appear to me to be inward-looking and content with a locals-only flavor, with nothing international about it at all. The time had come for me to hang up my festival hat.

GOD'S GIFT OF BEAUTY MUST BE USED FOR GOOD _____

There is little denying that those who possess an aesthetic beauty command a certain presence and attention, no matter the situation they find themselves in. I feel that if you're born with such physical goods – a pure gift that you didn't work hard to get – you have an obligation for life to use this gift to do something good for the world. I know some people do not think much of beauty pageants. However, I have twice been a judge at the Miss Universe International Pageant, and I have a favorable opinion of pageantry as an institution despite some dark facts that came out about what was going on behind the scenes at Miss Universe when Donald Trump was the owner of the prominent pageant from 1996 to 2015. His behavior, from walking into changing rooms while contestants were undressed and then boasting about it on talk radio and joking that, as the owner, he had the right to sleep with them – was deplorable and tarnished the brand. Trump also eliminated some contestants he deemed "too ethnic." His horrific demeanor dishonored the excellent work of the pageant's real organizers.

Miss Universe, historically, is different from any other beauty pageant. It is the most esteemed and, before Trump, was the world's most professionally run beauty contest.

Debuting in 1952, the pageant is recognized as the Olympics of beauty pageants. Each year, outstanding ladies from about 90 countries come together to be judged for their poise, looks – in both swimsuit and evening gowns – and their ability to express themselves. The training and the competition prove that nothing is simple about a pageant of this scale. The final Miss Universe competition is broadcast yearly in over 190 countries worldwide to an audience of over 500 million people.

My history with the event started pre-Trump in 1987, in Singapore, where I flew to be a judge of the Miss Universe final. Of course, all my male friends begged me to take them along as my escort, or even pleaded to be snuck in via my luggage. In judging, I learned that Miss Universe was run fairly and with the highest level of professionalism. Each judge at the final was an attractive, accomplished professional. The year I was a judge, I joined a group composed partly of actors Isabel Sanford of "The Jeffersons," Peter Graves of "Mission Impossible," Nancy Dussault of "Too Close for Comfort," and the great Italian American flamenco dancer Jose Greco. I befriended a few of the judges in Singapore, including the late, great movie producer Arnold Kopelson, who had just then won the Oscar for best picture for "Platoon" and would become a lifelong and close friend. We all volunteered our time to participate in exchange for what was, essentially, a luxury working vacation at a nice hotel with all meals and drinks comped. One guest, Paramount Studio executive David Niven Jr., made so much use of the complimentary booze that we joked he drank Canada Dry.

That year, the stunning beauty Cecilia Bolocco of Chile won

– her thick brown hair, bountiful red lips and long, lanky legs and vivacious personality bowling us all over. It was such a colossal honor to nab the Miss Universe title that the President of Chile, General Augusto Pinochet, announced a large-scale parade through the capital to mark the momentous occasion when Cecilia returned.

She went on to become a very well-known actress and television host on CNN and Telemundo, and later married the 44th President of Argentina, Carlos Menem, and showed all Miss Universe aspirants in the subsequent years that the title and its powerful platform can enhance life and help fulfill lofty dreams. It's a pity that few Miss Universe winners have leveraged their title as she did and used the accolade to set themselves up for life.

I was fortunate enough to judge the Miss Universe final a second time, in 2002, in Puerto Rico. Miss Russia Oksana Fedorova won that year, signifying the first time the Russian Federation cinched the lauded title. However, she reigned for only 119 days and became the first Miss Universe to be dethroned. The reason? She didn't show up for appointments, a big no-no for whoever wears the crown and draws a salary for a year from the Miss Universe Organization in exchange for traveling the world and promoting the brand and its partners and charities. First runner-up, Miss Panama, Justine Pasek, an enthusiastic, dark-eyed and natural beauty, then assumed the Miss Universe crown and got to work.

Having had my wonderful experience with the Miss Narcissus beauty pageant as a student in Hawaii in the early 1960s, I related to the Miss Universe contestants and the highs and lows of competition. I was, I think, a good judge and a huge fan. In 2010, I received a call from Paula Shugart, the President of the Miss Universe Organization, inviting me to serve as the national director of the pageant for China. I was delighted but full of apprehension in taking on another great responsibility.

Paula was named President of the Miss Universe Organization (MUO) in 1997 when Trump owned the pageant. She told me that she felt her job could be in jeopardy from one minute to the next because of her boss's unpredictable and mercurial behavior. Nevertheless, Paula outlasted her former boss, who was forced out in 2015 when MUO's broadcaster NBC dropped out after Trump made racist remarks about Mexicans during his campaign for the White House.

Paula cautioned that the challenge was especially concentrated in China, as the country had never before produced a viable Miss Universe contestant. I informed her that the reputation of Miss Universe in China was messy because many people claimed to be the license owner.

"If you want me to take over," I responded. "You need to come to Beijing and hold a big press conference and announce that I am now the only National Director."

So, Paula came to China with that year's Miss Universe, the glamorous Ximena Navarrete of Mexico, whose job, I quickly learned, was far more challenging than it might appear from the outset. When Paula and Ximena arrived in Beijing at 3 p.m., Ximena had a cold, and the airline had lost her luggage. But by 5:30 p.m., there she was, smiling at a reception for 300 people hosted by Mexico's Ambassador to China, Jorge

Eugenio Guajardo-Gonzalez. Not three hours off of a 12-hour flight, Ximena looked fresh and vibrant, dutifully shook hands with all who approached her and posed for hundreds of pictures.

The next day, after the press conference announcing my new role, Ximena was right back to the airport and on to Europe for another appointment – not a moment of downtime to recover. This was a typical day in the life of Miss Universe. After winning the crown, they immediately fly to New York City to a Trump Towers apartment provided by the organization. They then embark on a year of service wholeheartedly devoted to charity events, commercial events with sponsors, press conferences, TV appearances and preparation for the next pageant. It's no secret that each Miss Universe winner works extremely hard during her reign, and, honestly, she is thrilled when it ends, and she can resume her everyday life and pursue the greater goals on her agenda.

Afterward, the service pays dividends for a lifetime. Everything ever written about a winner from that point on will include "Miss Universe" as her title. She is given everything from jewelry to clothes to shoes and gets to travel the world and meet fascinating, influential people. Miss Universe is good for the girls because they learn a lot and are empowered by their participation. The pageant is a fantastic platform for young women, many of whom come from very modest backgrounds, to jump-start their lives. Many become extraordinary and accomplished ladies, working as entrepreneurs, philanthropists and actresses.

In 2022, the Miss Universe Organization was sold again,

this time to Anne Jakkapong Jakrajutatip, the CEO of the JKN Global Group, and the first woman to own the Miss Universe Organization. She is a Thai businesswoman and television host. Being transgender, she is definitely making changes to the institution. Jakkapong surely will be a transgender advocate and will allow married ladies to join the contest. I had the pleasure of having dinner with her in Thailand in August 2023. I can't help but smile when I think that the 70-year-old MUO is now for the first time, own and run by a woman!

I took over the Miss Universe China Pageant in 2011 and began training the contestants from all over the country to put their best foot forward. It was important in China to emphasize that Miss Universe is primarily a charity, complete with a gala dinner whose proceeds are donated to projects run by the non-profit Smile Train, repairing cleft lips in children and offering them recovery treatment. Miss Universe China allows unfortunate children to change their fate and make them smile, literally. I also encouraged the Miss Universe Chinese contestants to actively participate in publicizing the Smile Train projects wherever they went to raise more awareness and money. The hopefuls told me it was truly meaningful to use the gift of their beauty for a greater cause.

The first year, we only had one major event, no regional contests or finals. We hosted the crowning ceremony in Beijing's Mastercard Stadium and ended up with 32 contestants and an audience of eight thousand people. I trained the girls over three weeks at the luxurious Pine Valley Golf Club outside Beijing, owned by Yan Bin (严彬), the Chinese-Thai distributor of the Red Bull energy drink and chairman of the privately held industrial conglomerate Reignwood Group, owner of the Fairmont Hotel in Beijing, the Four Seasons in London, and England's prestigious Wentworth Golf Club, home to many a PGA competition.

In addition to golf, Pine Valley, roughly a 90-minute drive from the capital's center, exposed the Miss Universe China contestants to horseback riding and a health clinic. During the three weeks at the club, the contestants, the trainers, our TV crew, and Yan invited me to mingle with celebrity VIPs, interactions designed to build the girls' confidence.

I had selected the 32 contestants from all over the country, treating each one equally. Some girls came in with greater sophistication, while others were practically straight off the farm. To our surprise, some in the latter category began to stand out during the training, proving that everyone has an equal chance in a pageant.

"Fate brought all of you together for a reason," I told the young woman. "All of you are here training with so many outstanding girls from all over China. Together, you will pass through one of the most exceptional times of your life, learning things you would not have learned otherwise. Yes, you are competing in the final, but only for three hours. The rest of the time, before and after, you have the potential to become very good friends."

The contestants resided two-to-a-room, and naturally, problems arose, notably when some revealed their petty jealousy. One contestant told us that her roommate had $250,000 cash in the room's safe deposit box. When we confronted the contestant, and she couldn't explain why she was holding on to so many funds, we suspected foul play or at least lousy intent, and let her go.

Another girl came to me crying two nights before the final showdown to declare that she could not participate because others told her she had no chance of winning. I told her the real prize was simply participating.

And then there were the parents. Some didn't care much, but others were determined to see their daughter win, no matter the cost. The night before the final, during the final rehearsal at almost midnight, one of the girls sprained her ankle. It swelled up to such a degree that we were intensely alarmed and sent her to the hospital. An X-ray showed that she had torn a muscle and was given a cast to wear. Sadly, I informed the young woman that she should not compete the following day because it could not risk worsening the injury. She cried and said she had to compete as her whole family was coming to see her, and it would be a significant loss of face for her family if she failed to get on stage.

At 2 a.m., the girl's mother called in extreme panic and stress and insisted that her daughter must compete. At 4 a.m., the father called to echo the sentiment that his daughter must continue with the competition. After discussing the matter with our lawyer, we drafted a letter for the contestant to sign, saying we bore no responsibility for any mishap if she insisted on taking the stage. She signed.

The next day, the injured contestant removed the cast, went to the hospital for a shot of a heavy-duty painkiller and, to our amazement, went through with the whole competition. She didn't win, but she put on a good show. This girl wouldn't give up. She had learned a part of the Miss Universe ethos of determination.

The pressure on each contestant was great enough that, in year two, we learned to bring a psychiatrist along. What I wanted more than anything was for these women to understand that while life itself is a competition, irrespective of the industry one is in, we are always competing – but it can be executed with kindness and decorum. I was determined to create an environment where the girls viewed one another as sisters. Just as my parents had instilled in me the importance of always loving and having a good relationship with my siblings, I aspired for the contestants to really wrap their heads around what an opportunity this was and the beauty of having other souls to share it with. I did not want to hear of one more instance of a girl destroying another's evening costume backstage or sabotaging their swimwear so they could not take to the stage.

Having a trained psychiatrist impart these pearls of wisdom year after year was a tremendous leg up. Her skills and knowledge in navigating this arena helped us close out that year with the girls hugging each other – a welcome change in their attitude toward competition. Some of them did indeed form friendships that last to this day, and I view that as a colossal success. The girls' internal transformation was often so arresting by the end of the competition that their parents would tell me they no longer recognized their daughter but were so proud that she had turned over a new life leaf.

In 2011, Roseline Luo (罗紫琳) was the outstanding contestant. She towered at 6'3" without shoes, possessed a beautiful body, and her English was passable. The only problem was that Roseline was trained as a model, and models were taught not to smile. As a Miss Universe contestant, one must learn to smile and exude personality. Smiling is an art. Sierra Lu, a famous pageant trainer we hired for each year's event, explained it succinctly to the girls.

"There are three kinds of smile depending on your mouth, teeth and the structure of your face," she noted. "Some people show off great teeth if they smile broadly; some can only have a half-smile, and some just a small smile. Once you have learned which smile is the best for you, you must practice in front of the mirror and make it part of your life."

During a practice session, Roseline again failed to smile and was still working on her more approachable, less runway-ready walk.

"What is the matter with you, Roseline?" I lamented. "It has been two weeks already, and you still cannot smile!"

Roseline disappeared into the bathroom and sobbed hard. Sometimes, I confess, I was too tough on the girls. But then again, beautiful girls – so often spoiled – need to learn to work hard, too, like everyone, as things will not always come so easily for them.

"When you walk on the stage to become Miss China, how do you wave your hand?" the etiquette teacher asked the trainees.

All the girls waved at different heights.

"All wrong!" she declared. "You must wave your hand really high. From now on, you must learn how to wave and practice every day."

Furthermore, tough-as-nails speech teacher Miss Gao instructed the women to lower their voices and breathe deeply from their diaphragm.

"And change the level and timbre of your voice," she instructed. "You need to learn to speak with substance in your speech."

To drum down on the importance of impeccable table manners, we set up the Pine Valley dining room elegantly for a Western-style meal, complete with multiple forks, spoons, knives and various glasses of water and wines. We taught the girls how to eat properly with silverware, something they had never learned before. If one of them were to win and go to the final pageant, she would have to know how to eat elegantly, with internationally accepted good table manners. Most Chinese girls in their late teens and early twenties still have only used chopsticks and a spoon.

Of course, for my part, I taught the girls all about makeup, issuing them a standard Yue-Sai Cosmetics primer on the three basic color groups – orange, pink, and neutral – and how to match lipstick with clothes.

"Choose an orange lipstick for an orange dress, not a pink lipstick," I told them. "For blush, put it on the apple of your cheek, not on the rim of your eyes or the rim of your nose."

Mascara, I told them, was key for beautiful eyes, especially in photographs. The girls were required to learn how to put on fake eyelashes fast and appropriately use the brown shade where they wanted to recess their faces and the white shade to highlight their features.

In the 2011 competition, the long-limbed head turner

Roseline won and went on to the finals of Miss Universe in Brazil, where she came as the fourth runner-up. We were crazily happy, waving our Chinese flags. It was a pity she did not win the title because, in my opinion, she was the most breathtaking of all the young women on stage.

A little while after that, Naomi Campbell called.

"Yue-Sai," she said in her distinct British accent. "I am going to start a new reality show called 'The Face.' Would you be able to recommend a Chinese girl?"

I recommended Roseline, and she did very well, becoming one of the finalists. Naomi was generous with her time and was a wonderful mentor, but what Roseline did next stung. She began dating Vlad Dronin, Naomi's longtime boyfriend, from whom she'd recently separated. Vlad was a handsome and wealthy Russian businessman, international real estate developer and owner of the Aman Resorts. Although Roseline insisted to me that by the time they got together, Naomi and Vlad were over, Naomi was furious at what she considered an act of fierce betrayal. The scandal became hot fodder for international gossip within the pageant and fashion world, and Naomi, with her powerful connections, essentially halted Roseline's modeling career in the West.

In all my efforts to help China join the world, to build bridges between the country of my birth and the world I discovered, it is very disappointing that there has yet to be a winner from China in nearly 70 years of the Miss Universe pageant. I wanted desperately to shatter this losing streak, and Roseline Luo's fourth runner-up place in 2011 was as close as we came.

I've often asked myself why China's women haven't risen to the top of the pageant world. I've landed at this answer: China is a country where most people don't think physical beauty is that important, or certainly not as important as intelligence. In many other countries, girls learn beauty from their mothers early. But generally speaking, I've found many Chinese girls have little understanding of beauty because their mothers were never all that interested in physical beauty. If I wanted to find girls who could represent Chinese brains, beauty and womanhood, I needed to push the pageant culture.

Each year, I racked my brains about how to present a spectacular beauty contest for the audience, spending thousands of dollars hiring the best events companies to produce an unbeatable finals party. I invited famous performers and celebrity judges to our events, including Paris Hilton, the 2012 Miss Universe Olivia Culpo, Japan's Miss Universe Riyo Mori, supermodels Petra Nemcova, Lv Yan (吕燕) and Ma Yanli (马艳丽), the president of leading independent Chinese film studio Huayi Brothers Media Corp. (华谊兄弟传媒股份有限公司) Wang Zhonglei (王中磊), Hong Kong movie stars Lui Leung-wai (吕良伟) and Cecilia Cheung Pak-chi (张柏芝, famous hosts Chen Luyu (陈鲁豫) and Cao Qitai (曹启泰), comedian Jiang Kun (姜昆), and designer Guo Pei (郭培). I brought in famous performers such as French singing legend Charles Aznavour, Emmy-winning violinist Miri Ben Ari, "The Voice" champion Tessanne Chin, magician David Blaine, and "Chinese Idol" singers Jane Zhang (张靓颖) and Ai Fei (艾菲).

In the 6 years I ran the pageant, the Miss Universe China Finals became China's largest and most influential fashion event. After the inaugural year in 2011, when, at the last minute, the government censors told our partner, Guangxi Satellite TV (广西卫视), to stop the live broadcast, we learned to recast the event as a charity, something the government could get behind, even if they remained nervous about the beauty pageant part.

The following year, at the 2012 event, the Shanghai Youth Channel (上海星尚频道) broadcast our final ceremony, and Paris Hilton, as one of the judges, stole the show. In 2013, I combined the pageant with a charity fundraiser for Smile Train. We sold 600 seats in an instant. Then, in 2014 and 2015, with raising more charity money in mind, we added designer Zhang Lili's (张丽莉) traditional Chinese-style lingerie pieces for each contestant. With a stunning stage design and performance, the finals seethed with excitement, topping any show ever put on by Victoria's Secret. The contestants aimed to gain honor and praise for their accomplishments and beauty and strove to be charity models for millions of ordinary Chinese women. I insisted that each contestant take an active role in philanthropy and work to benefit the people of China and the world.

The most crucial mission of Miss Universe is charity. A year of philanthropic activities is compulsory for every Miss Universe, and the public welfare aspect is deeply ingrained in each contestant's heart. I wanted each of them to show the natural beauty and charm of Chinese women through love and wisdom. That should be the Chinese-style Miss Universe.

We filmed a series of short documentaries for each annual contest, recording behind the scenes at the pageant and the girls' transformation. I invited Jonathan Finnigan, an award-winning British producer, to head up "Finding Miss China." The six episodes of the first year's documentary were broadcast on the leading Chinese web video platform iQIYI (爱奇艺) and attracted tens of millions of views. Fashion brands flocked to offer sponsorship that funded the expansion in years two and three to 13, much more robust episodes.

I wrote another book, "Life is a Competition," and published it in 2013 in Chinese as 《人生就是一场海选》, with my Miss Universe girls in mind. The book taught the reader my firm belief that it wasn't luck that allowed me to create and build Yue-Sai Cosmetics; it was hard work, dedication and thinking in new ways. I wanted to impress this upon young Chinese women of all walks and stripes – you will be competing for the vast majority of your life, and you can do this in a way that benefits both yourself and the world.

During the filming in 2014, I was particularly impressed by a contestant from a family so poor that she dropped out of high school to work instead and earn money to send her brother to grade school. When she first entered the Miss Universe training camp, she was very self-conscious because other contestants included a few excellent A-grade university students, overseas students, and many girls from wealthy families. I noticed that the girl from the low-income family was honest and had an incredible physique, so we waived her training expenses and admitted her to the camp. She was very humble. I learned her family was so poor they lived on a boat with a wood-burning stove.

"Miss Universe is not simply a beauty contest, but an

all-around test for everyone from the inside out," I told the contestants. "It's also a place where people can be reborn."

Imagine the shock of the girl raised on a rickety boat eating at a candlelit table with forks and knives. I told her that while she couldn't change where she came from, she could transform herself in all other ways. Our camera recorded her growth after entering the camp, and even though she still couldn't speak English at the end, she won the Best Body award in the China finals.

A few years later, I was saddened to hear she married a man without an education or a decent job. After all the training, I had expected, or perhaps secretly wanted, more from her. But this did serve as an important reminder that each person makes life choices and becomes what they choose to be. Life is your choice, and I could not impose my personal will on my girls, however much they meant to me.

In 2014, the First Lady of Sri Lanka, Madam Shiranthi Wickremesinghe Rajapaksa, invited China's Miss Universe contestants to visit her homeland for a cultural exchange, a first for our program and a once-in-a-lifetime opportunity for our girls. As Goodwill Ambassadors, 15 of our most beautiful women, accompanied by our staff, a documentary team, and representatives of 10 Chinese state-run media organizations, all flew off to Sri Lanka for a week of exploration. We immersed ourselves in local culture and visited orphanages, bringing presents to the children, using the power of beauty for charity, fulfilling my original intention for the pageant.

The most memorable part of the trip was our meeting with the First Lady, who insisted I be present. We wondered why, until she revealed she had been a Miss Universe contestant. Madam Shiranthi wanted to meet me to share how the experience had changed her life. Each Chinese contestant shook Madam Shiranthi's hand and chatted; for many, this was their first trip outside China and, indeed, the first time they'd ever met such a distinguished person. It was a precious experience they would learn from and never forget.

To film the whole experience and ensure that the TV audience saw the real story of beauty pageant contestants taking their experience abroad, I insisted on funding and producing the documentary myself. Travel for cultural exchange is the best way to test a contestant, to see how they do out there in the real world, in life, teaching them that every experience is an audition for what's next. I wanted them to be seen learning and expanding at all times, and there is no better medium in China to reach a broad audience with this knowledge.

On a separate occasion, I took the Chinese Miss Universe contestants on a cruise to Japan. Many Japanese and tourists approached the girls to take photos, an experience they had not previously encountered. I wanted them to learn how to confront each situation with grace and dignity and how to communicate with others. Taking their pictures in swimsuits under the sun and getting them up at the crack of dawn to do yoga on the deck of the rocking ship were activities not just for the documentary, but tests of their ability to face difficulty with calm and how much they were willing to step outside their comfort zones and grow.

We arrived in Fukuoka and found in those days that it

was a boring place with nothing much to do and see. But we subsequently met a wonderful gentleman called Su Qing, who would later go on to dramatically change the dullness of the city. A very special man, he single-handedly changed the situation. Su Qing had lived in Japan for over 30 years but was still not a Japanese citizen due to the stringent Chinese immigration law that did not allow foreigners to become Japanese. But Su Qing adored Japanese culture and studied it in college. He built a gigantic complex featuring all types of Japanese cuisine and even conducts classes on how to make sushi. Furthermore, Su Qing launched the Meihodo International Youth Visual Media Festival, encouraging young people to enter the competition and celebrate the power of digital art and the immersive cosmos of emerging technologies. Su Qing asked me to be the Honorary Chair, and soon prominent figureheads including Michelle Yeoh, Maggie Q, Michael Douglas, Maestro Tan Dun and Juliette Binoche became Ambassadors, overseeing the thousands of annual entries.

Su Qing boasts the biggest collection of Japanese bento boxes in the country, and also went on to be something of a real estate maven. He launched a Samurai Complex set out in the sprawling Aso countryside, immersed in nature, which accommodates residents and serves as a learning center for numerous traditional samurai arts from karate, Iaidō, and archery to tea ceremonies and meditation.

During a visit to Thailand in 2016, the Tourism Bureau of Thailand invited the Deputy Prime Minister of Thailand to make an appearance to support Miss Universe China. I had visited Thailand many times, and I deeply love the Thai people and their culture, which values respect, self-control, and a non-confrontational demeanor. It was a delight to bring our girls to experience Thai customs and to utilize the Miss Universe platform to strengthen the bond of friendship between China and Thailand.

A highlight of the trip was our 15 contestants visiting the Grand Palace to pay their respects to King Bhumibol. Each of the beauties especially learned Thai genuflection etiquette – various forms of kneeling and bow – to ensure a proper expression of respect.

What we achieved in Thailand and elsewhere in a post-2010 world, at first, felt unimaginable to me. Back in the 1980s, when I was hosting television shows, I had no choice but to run around with vast and heavy piles of camera equipment. Cut to decades later, and each contestant had her own mobile livestream channel and could anchor her commentary wherever she was. Practicing addressing their smartphones taught the girls how to present themselves on camera on the go and developed their eloquence.

I constantly stressed the importance of learning English and urged the contestants to use their mobile phones and iPads to study as often as possible. During the training camp, I often gave them one-on-one sessions to correct their pronunciation, reminding them that, for now, it's impossible to bring China to the world without speaking good English.

All the major Chinese state media outlets reported on our activities and the pageant itself each year, and we cooperated with the web video platforms iQiyi and Leshi (乐视) to livestream the finals, getting over one million viewers online. Typical of many charity events, we also had an auction component. People were very generous with us, not only with donations but with some serious buying. The most amazing gift to me was from Prince Robert of Luxembourg, owner of the great French vineyard of Chateau Haut-Brion. His Highness gave me a set of two wine cabinets designed and made by David, Earl of Snowdon, well known as Great Britain's Royal Carpenter. In each cabinet were nine bottles of the finest white and red wines in the vineyard's history. We raised $1 million with them. Today, wines of that caliber would bring at least twice as much at the auction block.

The audience clamored for the moment we chose the winner, but what I cared about most was what each of the girls had accomplished along the way: to make people pay more attention to women and beauty. As the event evolved, we moved the Miss Universe finals into ballrooms at fancy hotels whose owners competed to host us. We raised about $1.5 million each year for our primary charity partner, Smile Train.

Beyond the charity work, I am thrilled to have had such a chance to turn a young woman's life around and pass on my hard-earned wisdom to a new generation. I remain close to many of the contestants today, and I love hearing of their adventures and how they have been able to chart a new journey that would never have been imaginable before.

CHARITY AS A DRIVING FORCE

Over the years of developing the Miss Universe China contest, I observed the upper end of wealthy Chinese begin to donate heavily to charities, sometimes to the tune of billions. Since I find my charitable work to be the most rewarding part, I was happy to see this trend in a country that was so poor and closed off for so long. To me, it's not about how much money you give; it's about doing it consistently and doing it to the best of your ability.

In 1995, my New York City neighbor, Mrs. Leah Boutros-Ghali, whose husband was then Secretary-General of the United Nations, invited me to her house for tea. She and her husband were preparing to leave for China to host the Fourth United Nations World Conference on Women. To make this first visit to China as successful as possible, she wanted my thoughts on what role I may want to play in the event.

"The conference will push forward the women's agenda in the world," Mrs. Boutros-Ghali noted, oozing with excitement. "Besides, I really want to see you in China."

I was determined to be involved and quickly called on Sherry, my cosmetics company's head of marketing and sales, whose background, as I have written, was in the Ministry of Foreign Affairs.

"Please find out what we can do," I asked her. "The world's most important women are coming to China to discuss women's issues. We are in the business of women. We must be involved."

Sherry returned to me quickly and remarked that the Chinese Women's Federation was looking for corporate donations.

"How much?" I asked.

"How much can we give?" she replied.

There would be no donations from Chinese companies. Donating money to such events was not customary in those days.

"Let's be the first Chinese company to donate to a United Nations charity event," I enthused. "How much did we make this first year in business in China?"

"RMB 1.5 million," Shen told me.

"Then we donate RMB 1.5 million," I said.

Sherry was hesitant, emphasizing that it was a lot of money for a new company that was only one year old. But I was adamant.

"We have to do it," I continued, defiant. "What is the purpose of doing a women's business in China if we're not supporting the issues of women?"

On the day of the event, we walked into the Great Hall of the People in Beijing, and as we sat down, we found a shocking surprise waiting for us on our seats: a small gift package from a competing cosmetics brand. We stared at each other in disbelief. Yue-Sai Cosmetics was supposed to be the exclusive cosmetics sponsor. This was a time before China's market understood the notion of offering branding exclusivity in exchange for a substantial donation. It was also advantageous to be reminded that no good deed goes unpunished and that giving to charity should not lead to expectations of a return.

Mrs. Boutros-Ghali was by my side throughout the conference, and I met all the First Ladies in Beijing. I was especially delighted to meet Mrs. Chirac of France, Mrs. Mubarak of Egypt, Queen Noor of Jordan, First Lady Hillary Clinton, and other celebrities such as the American actress and feminist activist Jane Fonda. A few days after the event, there was another surprise. A very dejected Sherry came into my office and proclaimed in distress, "You won't believe it. The Tax Bureau wants to tax us for the money we donated."

"Are you sure? In the United States, there is no tax on charitable donations," I responded, trying to remain calm. "We donated everything we earned this past year."

"Right!" she replied. "Charity is very new in China. There is still no charitable tax deduction. I'm sorry, Yue-Sai."

Soon after the United Nations Women's Conference, I strengthened my commitment to undertaking charity initiatives along with business within Yue-Sai Cosmetics. At one of our company meetings in 1996, I declared that as we were in the business of women, it made sense as a part of our commitment to women to give scholarships to brilliant female students from low-income families.

"Which school should we donate to?" I asked our board.

Sherry recommended Peking University (北京大学), the most prestigious university in China, so I requested that she set up a meeting with the school's leaders. Dr. Min Wei-Fang (闵维方), Peking University Communist Party Secretary from 2002-2011, thanked us for establishing a scholarship for outstanding female students.

"Your idea is great. We don't have many corporations that

set up university scholarships," Dr. Min said.

"We will start this year," I announced. "We will award the top students from 12 provinces who need financial assistance. Is that too few?"

"Oh my, Yue-Sai," Dr. Min replied, his eyes widening. "We appreciate your generosity so much! With this scholarship, students will definitely want to come to Peking University even if they have been accepted at other universities. So, we can get all the best students."

I asked him to start the process and assured him that I would not issue any opinion on the candidates nor try to influence their selection. To present the scholarships, the university organized an event.

"Today, we have chosen to award 12 students from 12 provinces who have achieved an excellent grade point average," Dr. Min told the audience. "Congratulations. And thank you, Yue-Sai Cosmetics."

The founding principle of Yue-Sai Cosmetics was never simply to sell lipstick, I then explained on the podium.

"The idea was always to empower women so they could have the confidence to achieve more in their lives," I continued. "The scholarships are given in the same spirit. Please accept our gift to fulfill your dreams for the future. Enjoy your studies at Peking University! Congratulations!"

Virtuous deeds are best disseminated when they are done without expectation of reward. When I practice selfless giving, however, I often receive rewards in unexpected ways. I once attended an exquisite corporate party in New York City thrown by the high-end stereo equipment manufacturer

Harman Kardon. A young woman rushed over to me to say hello, extremely excited.

"I am so overwhelmed to meet you, Yue-Sai; thank you for coming to our event," she said excitedly. "I am a senior manager of this company, but I want you to know that I was a recipient of a scholarship you donated to Peking University. My family was impoverished, from Liaoning Province (辽宁省), and without the scholarship, I could never have attended this prestigious university. Thank you!"

It wasn't until twenty-one years after my first large donation to the UN, in 2016, that China began to give tax deductions for charity. First, 3 percent, then 4.6 percent; now, a company in China can deduct 12 percent of its profit as charitable donations. This means if your company has a profit, you can deduct 12 percent in proportion to your profit.

The pace of change dawned on me when I recently bumped into Jack Ma, the co-founder of the multinational technology conglomerate, the Alibaba Group. I asked him how he was doing now that he had earned more money than God – well, some $26 billion, according to Forbes Magazine.

"Giving away money is such hard work," he sighed.

I was momentarily speechless. I could not imagine that anyone would utter such a thing three decades ago when I started working in China. Indeed, it is more challenging than it might seem from the surface to give away money meaningfully. But philanthropy has become such an exciting topic in China. Like everything else in the ever-evolving country, it has changed so much and so quickly in a meager thirty years. Under communism, the government is supposed to take care of all citizens in every aspect of their lives, from food, clothing and housing to medical and even burial after death. Charity began to spread across society, and individuals began to give money to various causes, which embarrassed the Chinese government, and officials actively discouraged it.

As recently as 2015, China ranked as one of the least generous nations in the world, coming in at around 144 on global charts. A prominent cause of that was because setting up a foundation was a messy and complicated process that required Ministry of Civil Affairs approval and navigating a lot of red tape. But in 2016, the government enacted the China Charity Law, which provides a framework for aspiring charities and makes it much easier for individuals and businesses to establish non-profit organizations. The following year paved the way for the never-before-seen China Global Philanthropy Institute – a school dedicated to teaching and educating the next generation of philanthropists, set up by five incredible givers from China and the United States, including Bill Gates and famed investor Ray Dalio.

In 2023, the government launched a "shared prosperity" program to narrow the gap between the very rich and the poor, encouraging the wealthy to give to those less fortunate. And so many – especially those in the high-tech sector – are doing all they can to give back and give right. Ma's Alibaba has pledged to invest almost one-fifth of its assets by 2025. Tencent – the technology conglomerate and owner of popular messaging service WeChat – which made a $12 billion USD profit this past year, still managed to give away more than $13.5 to charity in the first four months of the year alone.

There are more than 10,000 registered and recognized charitable organizations in China, in addition to thirty web-based public fundraising platforms designated by the Ministry of Civil Affairs, which have raised almost USD 9 billion annually. Large donations have become the norm, to the tune of billions, and donation records are constantly made and broken and then made again, only to be abruptly shattered. Fulfilling social responsibilities has become the conscious pursuit of many Chinese enterprises and entrepreneurs.

The Chinese have expanded from donating money and materials to giving away stock shares and real estate to support initiatives near and dear to their hearts. Volunteerism, too, has grown significantly, with the number of registered volunteers soaring from 2.92 million in 2012 to 217 million in 2021, equivalent to 15.4 percent of the population. China is also significantly vested in e-commerce, with live streaming now the hottest sales model in the country. Famed figures sell agricultural products virtually to help others accumulate funds, especially in rural areas. TikTok launched a massive initiative working with local governments to connect consumers to regional goods they can sell. Farm-centered entrepreneurs can also receive professional training through this outreach campaign and go on to sell their regional items throughout the whole of China via the live streaming platform.

In addition, China also hosts a nationwide "Charity Day," which takes place on September 9 each year, encouraging citizens to participate in public welfare. In 2023, a mind-blowing 69 million people participated, raising almost USD 5 billion. It is not far from my memory that as recently as 2012,

I could not sell a charity ticket for more than $25. In 2021, my charity event sold tickets at more than $5,000 each – and we sold every available ticket in less than two months. The growth of the philanthropy sector in China is incredibly magnificent, and I cannot wait to see what the future holds.

PAYING IT FORWARD

Giving was first taught to me by my parents. They were kind to everyone around them, often taking in people who needed a place to stay and treating them as family members.

Then, I joined the Mormon Church as a teenager, where we were encouraged to tithe 10 percent of everything we earned and to volunteer regularly and in diverse ways to help others. For someone like me who made so little money back then, 10 percent seemed like a lot to give away. However, I noticed that I never lost too much by giving. Somehow, I always got a lot in return, more than I had given.

Early on, I established charity as a part of my life. If there is one thing I learned from Americans, it is to be involved in helping others. For as long as it has been recorded, the United States has been ranked as the most generous nation in charitable giving. In the United States, giving to those in need is a way of life. These days, Americans donate some $500 billion to charity annually. Over the years, I've donated time or money to set up many U.S. scholarships or work with various kinds of charities in the United States. To give two examples, I've supported ORBIS, which sends doctors to provide free eye operations to patients living in remote places worldwide, and was on the board of City Meals on Wheels. This nationwide organization delivers food on weekends and holidays to elderly people without relatives or money to take care of themselves.

I hosted a popular and successful fund-raising campaign while serving on the City Meals on Wheels board. I asked New York City's finest restaurants, serving everything from pizza to Peking duck, to set up booths at the event venue. In the academic arena, from 2000-2007, I offered scholarships to immigrants from China to attend The International English Language Institute at Hunter College (IELI), one of the oldest and most well-respected ESL institutes in New York City. This work was particularly gratifying to me as somebody who learned, back in the 1960s when I first arrived in New York, that Chinese immigrants who didn't speak English as well as I did were relegated to live in Chinatown, a parcel of the city where they were forever deemed outsiders.

I also established a perpetual scholarship at Brigham Young University in Hawaii because of my strong belief in empowering young people with quality education. The Yue-Sai Kan-Endowed IWORK Scholarship Fund supports students from Mainland China to go to school at BYUH. It allows them to receive an education through a work scholarship, just as I had. I spent my college years at Brigham Young University Hawaii and greatly valued my working experience there.

Many of the gifts I've given over the years were money, but many also were gifts of time and attention paid. These latter forms of giving are, I find, the most gratifying. If I get involved, I feel the magic of giving working on me and my sense of well-being in much more profound ways than merely writing a check. One focus of my giving has been on children and their education. As a small girl in Hong Kong, I greatly benefited from the strong emphasis my loving family placed on education.

In 2001, the Soong Ching-Ling Foundation (宋庆龄基金会), a public welfare foundation established in 1986 with a particular focus on implementing programs to support maternal and child health care and children's education and culture across the country, illuminated my charity work in Chinese society by establishing the China Beauty Fund (中国美基). I was appointed its Ambassador and Executive Chairman. Together, we created the Safety for Mothers and Infants Project to help poverty-stricken areas of Western China establish maternity and child-care centers. In my eyes, the Soong Ching-Ling Foundation is the most important charity in China. There is no more noble cause than bolstering the backbone of our society – mothers – and the most innocent and vulnerable among us: the young.

In the years since, we have raised tens of millions of dollars by selling tables at gala charity dinners and auctions whose proceeds go toward buying basic medical equipment, training medical and nursing personnel, and promoting scientific reproductive methods, all of which have significantly helped reduce the mortality rate of pregnant women and newborns in Western China. China's infant mortality rate in 1950 was approximately 195 deaths per thousand births for children under one year of age. Almost one out of five babies born in 1950 did not live to see their first birthday. Since then, China's infant mortality rate has decreased gradually to just ten deaths per thousand births today.

In 2002, I was named Ambassador of the UNESCO Children's Fund and promptly made a broad call for healthy, peaceful, and beautiful living environments for children. This was a program called "Say Yes to Children." I attended conferences, filmed public charity videos to spread the word, and sent "Promise to Children" brochures, calling for individual donations at more than one thousand Yue-Sai Cosmetics counters across China. (I believe I was really the first Chinese UN ambassador).

Not far from where I was born in Guangxi Province (广西省), I found out that the local Guidong Primary School (桂东小学), built in 1985 as a mud tile structure, had fallen into severe disrepair. I could not sit by and idly do nothing. In 2004, I donated enough money to support a total reconstruction of the school, prompting the local government to rename it in my honor the Jin Yuxi Primary School (靳羽西小学).

The following year, in 2005, I established a Jin Yuxi scholarship at the Ai Guo School (爱国学校) next to my Shanghai apartment. Founded in 1901 by the famous educator Mr. Cai Yuanpe (蔡元培), the Ai Guo School Jin Yuxi scholarship encouraged students to participate in more social activities and international exchanges in the hope that their learning through greater exposure to the world would repay Chinese society in the future.

In keeping with my desire to have China engage the rest of the world, in April 2018, I was honored to be named Ambassador to the French maritime research ship TARA, whose crew works to safeguard marine environments and promote Sino-

French ocean research and science. My Ambassadorship coincided with the first time the ship came to China. Its crew was focused on measuring the impact of climate change and the harm of plastic waste on marine ecologies, especially coral reefs. My task was to help raise awareness of this critical work to Chinese youth, and I invited five thousand mesmerized children onboard the vessel.

The following year, in 2019, in conjunction with the prestigious Chinese institution Tongji University (同济大学) and the charitable Zeng Ai Foundation (增爱基金会), both headquartered in Shanghai, I sponsored a program to encourage the creation of businesses that hire disadvantaged college students, thus protecting one of China's most revered sources of "intangible cultural heritage" – kids who might not otherwise get a chance to shine.

No matter how much philanthropic work I do, it can never be enough. At any given moment, countless people, causes and heart-wrenching stories require others to chime in with a helping hand. If I can help, I will. What is the purpose of life if we acquire our riches and wealth only to keep it all to ourselves?

Further bolstering my work to empower Chinese in America, decades ago, I joined The Committee of 100 (C100). The non-partisan leadership organization of prominent Chinese Americans in business, government, academia, and the arts was established in 1990 when veteran diplomat Henry Kissinger suggested to the late great architect I.M. Pei (贝聿铭) that they team up with the most successful and distinguished Chinese Americans from the arts, business, academia, public service, and the sciences to serve the interests of American citizens of Chinese ancestry. Membership, by invitation only, is composed of pioneers in their respective fields, including master cellist Yo-Yo Ma, Blackberry CEO John Chen, architect Maya Lin, Ambassador Gary Locke, the first Asian American woman to serve as a U.S. Attorney Debra Wong Yang, the CEO of Morgan Stanley Asia Wei Sun Christianson, scholar and director of the Brookings Institute John L. Thornton China Center, Cheng Li, President of Baidu.com Ya-Qin Zhang, Chairman of East-West Bank Dominic Ng, famed pioneer HIV researcher Dr. David Ho, "Crazy Rich Asians" film director Jon Chu, actors Joan Chen, Maggie Q, Lucy Liu and Awkwafina, along with Olympic Gold Medalist skier Eileen Gu, journalist Lisa Ling, fashion designer Vivienne Tam, writers Amy Tan and Maxine Hong Kingston, owner of the Los Angeles Times Patrick Soon-Shiong, politicians Andrew Yang, Elaine Chao and Grace Meng, musician Wang Ju-Jia, philanthropist couple Chen Tian Giao and Chrissy Luo, and renowned restauranters and chefs Martin Yan and Ming Tsai.

And that is merely the tip of the iceberg.

Currently, the C100 boasts over 150 members whose mission is to promote the full participation of all Chinese Americans in American society and to act as a public policy resource for the Chinese American community.

Another way I have purported to bring visibility to China's contributions to America is through "The Pandas are Coming to New York," a non-profit project I helped spearhead with Carolyn Maloney, my Democratic Congresswoman, beginning in 2016. From our purview, Central Pak Zoo in the middle of the most fantastic city on earth deserved to have a pair of China's giant pandas – iconic creatures believed to bring good luck and happiness. American International Group (AIG) Chairman Hank Greenberg and civic leader and philanthropist John Catsimatidis served as co-chairs of this project. They helped in our mission to raise U.S.-China mutual respect and awareness. Though the project never came to fruition, we did give it a great try. One thing I learned from this experience is how hard to get anything done in this big city. The last meeting on this subject was with five different city government agencies. Going through this meeting was a nightmare. Five agencies had the ability to come up with fifty reasons to object to any change.

To support another defining part of New York City, I am honored to serve as a member of the board of the Ellis Island Medals of Honor Committee, which honors immigrants whose accomplishments have contributed significantly to American society. The winners' roster reads like a Who's Who of American society. Both Houses of Congress have called the Ellis Island Medal one of our nation's most prestigious awards, memorializing winners in the Congressional Record. I am a thrilled recipient of the 2014 Medal and also a board member of the organization.

In the same way I embrace immigrants, I also enjoy spending time with philanthropists. Each year, The Prince Albert II of Monaco Foundation gathers a dozen of the world's most outstanding altruists over a couple of days to exchange ideas and discuss ways to achieve progress toward big-picture goals. I was one of the founding members of this invitation-only round table, and I am privileged to meet and pay tribute to some of the most interesting people in this giving back sphere, who leave me inspired and with the will to do more. While meeting the philanthropists is a joy, the part I treasure the most is spending time with Prince Albert, the son of the late Princess and Hollywood superstar Gracy Kelly. The Prince is a charming and easy-going individual who treats everyone he encounters with sincere respect and kindness. While he takes his work very seriously, especially his devotion to cleaning up our oceans, he doesn't take himself too seriously and is the first to put on a smile on the faces of those around him. Prince Albert and I have spent countless hours discussing our deep and mutual interest in Chinese culture and the arts, and he hosted President Xi Jinping when he visited Monaco in the late winter of 2022.

In addition, in 2013, I set up my own foundation entitled the China Beauty Charity Fund, to further work to support my belief in the power of beauty to accomplish good. As the first order of business, the foundation hosted the China Fashion Gala in New York as a platform to recognize the remarkable talent of emerging Chinese designers who carry Chinese aesthetics and inspiration to the world.

Since then, I have hosted the China Fashion Gala in New York every year, highlighting outstanding Chinese designers and bringing them recognition on a global scale. The 2013 Gala introduced designer Guo Pei to a world audience and led her to be selected by the Metropolitan Museum's most popular exhibit, "China: Through the Looking Glass." Pop star Rihanna wore a Guo Pei gown at the Met Gala to kick off the exhibition, making Guo the most talked-about designer of the year.

Today Guo is undeniably the Queen of Couture in China and the best known around the world. When I presented her in New York City that first time, we brought in some of her most iconic clothes some made with actual gold threads. We ensured the clothing collection for $1.5 million USD. The evening was truly a dazzling spectacle. The audience was truly spellbound by Guo's creations. When she finally came on stage to say thank you, she was sobbing uncontrollably.

Other Chinese fashion designers showcased by the Gala include designers Lan Yu (兰玉), Grace Chen (陈野槐), Heavenly Gaia (盖娅传说), and Jason Wu (吴季刚). The China Fashion Gala has also honored top-notch professionals in the fashion industry to celebrate their achievements and contributions, including the world's most famous shoe designer, Christian Louboutin, fashion photographers Chen Man (陈漫) and artist Sun Jun (孙郡), the legendary model Carmen Dell'Orefice, and the renowned Chinese American designer Vivienne Tam (谭燕玉).

China Fashion Gala is the most prominent platform for displaying China's rich cultural heritage and modern creativity. The last few years, I joined hands with the China Institute to host the highly anticipated gala. Funds raised benefit various fashion and beauty-related initiatives, such as the Fashion Design Competition Award and a scholarship program for Chinese design students at the Fashion Institute of Technology (FIT). Another China Beauty Charity Fund program at FIT is "Education in Sustainable Fashion" for Chinese fashion and textile executives. China faces a vast sustainability challenge as the world's largest textile manufacturing country. In 2015, over 30 million tons of used apparel were discarded, and only 10 percent could be recycled.

Meanwhile, hundreds of new fashion and lifestyle brands have been created in the past few years. As it stands, the fashion industry in China is estimated to be the largest contributor to the overall market revenue – and, sadly, one of the biggest polluters.

The "Executive Education in Sustainable Fashion" program aims to inspire and push for progress in sustainability growth in fashion and lifestyle industries in China. I must continue to educate the nation's industry figures to understand what sustainability means, how to secure materials for their products that will better serve the environment, and how to properly discard what isn't used so that it doesn't end up saturating our landfills and precious oceans.

THE CHINA INSTITUTE: PROMOTING CULTURAL EXCHANGE FOR 97 YEARS

The most overarching of my charitable activities is my co-chairmanship at The China Institute (CI) in New York, whose objective is to create a deeper understanding of China through programs in education, culture, art, and business.

The China Institute is the go-to resource on China, from ancient art to today's business landscape and rapidly shifting culture. Our programs, school and gallery exhibitions bring

China's depth, complexity, and dynamism to life. Founded in 1926 by the highly respected Chinese reformers, educators, and scholars Hu Shi (胡适) and K.P. Wen along with John Dewey, it is the oldest bi-cultural, non-profit organization in America focusing exclusively on China.

I co-chaired the China Institute's annual Blue Cloud Awards Gala for two consecutive years in 2016 and 2017, raising several million dollars. In addition, I personally secured the commitment to attend the gala of honorees Bob Chapek, then Walt Disney Parks and Resorts Chairman; Richard Gelfond, the IMAX CEO: business tycoon Howard Milstein; Dame Jillian Sackler; and the designers Vera Wang (王薇薇) and Guo Pei. The featured performances at the 2016 and 2017 Galas were by the modern Shine Peking Opera Troupe and the Snow Lotus Sisters (雪莲三姐妹), representing quintessential rural culture. Each received rave reviews.

Since 2018, I have also served as co-chairman of the China Institute (华美协进社) together with Chinese American architect Chien Chung Pei (贝建中), son of architect I.M. Pei. I have brought in additional trustees and contributors to the campaign to move CI downtown and into a bigger and more modern space in line with its forward-looking mission.

My devotion to the China Institute is the culmination of my life's work, centered on truly connecting Chinese culture to the world, far removed from politics and social stigmas. Government and administrative policies come and go, but the China Institute does illuminate a history dating back thousands of years, steeped in a vibrant reminiscence of music, art, language, and costume.

Did you know China was the earliest country to create and use musical chimes? The Bianzhong, 编钟 a group of 64 beautiful flute-like bronze bells of varying sizes excavated near Wuhan dating back 2000 to 3600 years old. Today, an original set is displayed in the Hubei Provincial Museum in Wuhan, and it still can be played after 2500 years! From my purview, the Bianzhong is the world's earliest piano except these bells are hung in a wooden frame and played with wooden mallets. They disprove the common misconception that Chinese music consists of only five tones. They play 12 tones. Each bell produces several tones, depending on what is used to strike it. The China Institute owns a set of 20 duplicated bells. If you wish to see them come visit us at China Institute at 40 Rector street, New York City. At a time when adverse politics seems to dominate hearts and minds, I believe in continuing to elucidate Chinese heritage. It is remarkable, and we have every reason to be proud of it and promote it globally. No matter how much hatred may cascade from news channels, social media, or talking heads and pundits, we will always be united by shared love and knowledge.

Scan the QR code to access Yue-Sai Kan's YouTube channel and join her on a very personal journey through a China you haven't seen before.

I'm on the Board of Ellis Island honor society, where we honor some great Americans on Ellis Island every year

With Anla Cheng, Senator Mazie Hirono

2023 Blue Cloud Gala, Princess Reema bint Bandar Al Saud of Saudi Arabia presented me the Award

China Institute Blue Cloud Galas

Monaco with Prince Albert and the board of Philanthropy Roundtable

My China Fashion Galas

Outstanding Asian American Women Who Dared Awards

NAVIGATING TOUGH TIMES

MARRIAGE, LOVE AND BUSINESS ARE ALL BASED ON TRUST

For years, Mortimer Levitt, my eighty-year-old millionaire friend, and his wife, Mimi, were trying desperately to marry me off. To them, matrimony and lifelong companionship was an ideal they considered very sacred.

However, in my whirlwind existence, marriage was never a big deal nor prominent in my mind. First of all, it is tough to be married while immersed in a globe-trotting television career. I was perpetually in and out of the country, never staying long and rarely around for a second date. My relationships lasted only a short time, mostly because I was never available. Nonetheless, I did meet and date and have incredible lightning love affairs with some amazing, accomplished and exciting men over my younger years. It was an education of sorts, as my exes hailed from various disciplines and were often at the top of their respective fields. Whether musical composers, businessmen or writers, I learned so much personally and professionally from each of them. I never considered being single a detrimental notion and spent most of my life without one abiding partner by my side – and I wouldn't trade that freedom for anything.

Still, Mortimer and Mimi each month invited me to their beautiful New York City home to have dinner with them and a potential suitor. On October 12, 1988, James McManus and I met in their dining room on a blind date. I was immediately impressed. James was comfortable in his skin – six-foot-three, thick red hair, polite, well-spoken, and around eighteen years my senior. He was not necessarily handsome in a conventional sense but engaging, intelligent with a striking appeal. After his wife passed away from cancer several years earlier, James was left to raise their four grown children on his own. I was intrigued.

James was raised in a poor family in Wisconsin, so poor that his mother was unable to even afford to buy him a Boy Scout uniform. But from nothingness, he single-handedly built an enormous ownership empire across advertising and marketing, aviation and automobiles, hotels, restaurants, and real estate. James had worked incredibly hard, and by the time I met him, he – like Mortimer – was a remarkably wealthy man. James' Marketing Corporation of America had the largest office in Westport, Connecticut, and the company was the city's biggest employer and its biggest taxpayer. James embodied every sense of being a real entrepreneur, unafraid to take calculated risks that inevitably paid off.

The weekend after we met, I prepared to deliver a speech about my work in China at the Greenbrier Country Club in Virginia. The distance from New York to Chesapeake, Virginia, was only about 370 miles, but the travel was inconvenient with indirect flights and infrequent trains.

"You have to change planes to get there," James commented over the phone. "Why don't I just send you a Cheyenne to take you there in comfort?"

I wasn't so moved by his offer to use a private Piper PA-42 plane as by his warm and thoughtful tone. A strong but gentle, attractive male voice is one of life's pleasures. Not long after that, James formally asked me out. The age gap made me hesitate, although not for long.

James was a man of great attentiveness and consideration. Whenever I arrived home at the airport, he was always there to pick me up. While some of my powerful – albeit past – boyfriends complained, "You are so busy, why don't you have any time for me?" James instead asked, "What can I do to help you?" How could I not fall in love with someone like that? But on other occasions, he was admittedly a little bolder.

"Yue-Sai, if you marry me, you'll never fly commercial again," he routinely exclaimed.

James immediately grasped how to court my family, sensing their importance to me. He would take my mom, dad, sisters, niece, and nephews on vacations on mega yachts along the New England coast, to the south of France for long and luxurious summers, and once we sailed on a super sailboat along the idyllic Turkish coast. In 1992, James took us to the Olympics in Barcelona, Spain. We all adored him. James knew how much family meant to me, and he was extremely gentle and sweet to my parents and very reverential to my sisters and my little niece and nephews. They still speak of him with great affection.

Moreover, James owned several homes, including one in Westport, Connecticut – complete with a dock and a boat – a winter home in Key Biscayne, and, for twenty years, he owned the National Landmark Hotel Jerome in Aspen, a historic and beautifully lit lodge in the heart of the city. The hotel was where the wealthy scions of business hobnobbed with an array of artists and writers, from The Eagles to Bill Murray to

Hunter S. Thompson. It was a real treat being able to explore different pockets of America with him.

James and I always traveled in grand style, flying private from Paris to Dijon, sometimes just to enjoy lunch at a three-star Michelin restaurant before turning homeward bound again. It was a marvelous, whirlwind time in my life. We once flew to São Paulo to inspect Embraer planes that James wanted to buy for his company, Business Express Airlines. A retired U.S. Army Reserve Captain, James was also a skilled pilot and occasionally got a kick out of arranging to fly a fighter jet.

A few months after we met at Mortimer and Mimi's, James suddenly pulled me close and kissed me out in the open, right in the middle of the bustling and vibrantly lit Times Square, smiling with satisfaction and whispering how much he had desired to do that. James often joked that the real reason he loved me was that I was always on time, which he said was quite different from his late wife, who was notoriously unpunctual.

I was so deluged with happiness during this season of my life. With someone as wonderful as James loving me, I felt so protected and blessed beyond measure. Soon, he bought what he called my "starter home," a beauteous red brick Georgian townhouse on Sutton Square, halfway up the East River from the Battery – just a stone's throw north of the United Nations. James also gave me a credit card to spend on anything I wished and was shocked that I didn't use it for a year, not until I needed to spend money on decorating our new house.

Furthermore, James wanted to gift me a car. But to his confusion, I requested a large van rather than a fancy sports car. I explained that, after all, I couldn't take my whole family to Chinatown for dim sum (点心) on Sundays in a two-seater Porsche. Such a vehicle would have been of no use. While James was incredibly doting and generous, material objects did not mean that much to me. What I wanted, more than anything else, was to learn, grow, and work hard so I could soak up the sights and experiences that this life had to offer, and give back to so many around me in need.

One long weekend not long after James bought the house on Sutton Square, we were enjoying a relaxing dinner at a neighborhood restaurant when James produced a six-carat diamond from Tiffany and asked me to marry him. My jaw dropped to the floor. We had been dating for around nine months, but we had never even discussed being in an exclusive relationship, and I was still casually seeing other men. In my mind, I was still free from the snares of commitment.

I paused, taking in that perhaps I was ready, and that my nonchalant existence really was about to change. I replied with an excited "yes." Although it hadn't really crossed my mind before, I did want to marry James – and for all the right reasons. Sure, he was wealthy and witty, but I was in love with this kind, good-hearted and honorable man. As I fell asleep each night, I thanked God that James had entered my life.

After our engagement, he asked if I wanted children. I responded that I had never thought it was necessary and never carried that instinct that many women perceived as the focal point of their lives and the reason they were placed on the earth.

James exhaled a loud sigh of relief, as if removing the world's weight from his shoulders. He already had four grown children and was more than happy with that. My fiancé then did something that was the ultimate act of a true gentleman: he invited his children, Melissa, Stuart, Mitchell, and Robert – all in their late teens and early twenties – over to the house for a family meeting.

"Kids," he told them gently. "You are my children. I will always love and be there for you, but Yue-Sai is now the most important woman in my life. She will be my wife. Please remember this."

James's words ensured I felt safe with his children and in doing so, reinforced to me, and to them, that I belonged. His children never once questioned our relationship, and they all fell in line, extremely happy for us both. As they were already quite grown, I never needed to embody the stepmother role, and we never became incredibly close as they lived a distance away. While they were never my children, I so appreciated how much they had accepted me without a flinch and how much vitality they gave to their very smitten father.

On February 11, 1990, James and I married in lavish style, surrounded by one thousand guests – the crème de la crème of New York society – who had all gathered on a Sunday night to celebrate the occasion beneath the five hundred glittering lanterns hung from the ceiling of Chinatown's then famous Kam Moon Restaurant. To host a fancy wedding in Chinatown back then seemed like an oxymoron, as the neighborhood was not exactly known for its affluent taste and extravagance. However, we oozed out an extravagance the district had never seen before.

I wore a traditional red Chinese gown embroidered with

a red dragon-and-phoenix pattern and promised my friends that I would wear a white gown when we renewed our vows in five years. From my slightly biased eye, ours was the wedding of the year. The dining room was festooned with 50,000 flowers arranged by the celebrity florist Remy, and we hired three orchestras. The first was a traditional Chinese orchestra to welcome all guests, followed by a trio of singers to serenade us during the ceremony, and lastly, a dance band to prompt all attendees to party and shake off the twelve-course Chinese banquet meal and the most delicious cake – a five-layer, delicately sculpted Chinese pagoda baked and built by the famed wedding cake designer, Silvia Weinstock. Friends continue to remind me about that cake to this day.

Well past midnight, when the music wound down and the guests – many who came from foreign lands like Hong Kong and Canada for the occasion – steadily streamed out, exhausted from the dance floor, found limousines waiting outside to take them home safely, courtesy of the ever-thoughtful James. Ours was a party no attendee could forget.

But my fondest memory of the evening was the glimmer of absolute delight on my parents' faces. I think they had given up on my ever getting married. Although my mother was still terribly ill from her stroke and couldn't talk and barely walk, I saw in her eyes how pleased she was that I had finally found a gentleman to have and to hold.

As starry-eyed newlyweds, we settled in at Sutton Square – one of fourteen houses, each more than a century old, arranged around a lush private garden along a stretch of the East River between 57th and 58th streets, looking out toward the southern tip of Roosevelt Island. Invisible from the street, the block-long private riverfront garden is a unique haven in all of New York City, an oasis in the middle of the mayhem. I loved the way the morning light cascaded through the large windows and sent delicate pools of luminance across the dark wooden floor.

I slowly began to decorate our new abode with the precious things I had collected from my travels. The garden patio is edged by a low wall made of a sandstone panel modeled after a bas-relief of dancing girls I saw at a Buddhist temple in Cambodia. Inside, I placed beautiful and serene Buddhas of gold, stone, and clay wood I brought back from Cambodia, Myanmar, Japan and Thailand. I also commissioned a highly sought-after decorative Dutch artist, Heather Jeltes, to paint the library ceiling with the most spectacular gilt – a swooping Dragon, and extraordinarily glowing Phoenix.

I replaced the townhouse's staid front door with a teak door covered with an intricate carving from Bali and two panther-like Barongs to protect our space. My door was indeed the only one of its kind in all of Manhattan. I often joked that I'd have acquired an extra million dollars if I earned a dollar for every person who stopped to take a picture of this special door.

James gave me the creative freedom to breathe new life into the old house. Renovations were costly, and we had to navigate excessive city red tape to obtain permits and licenses. Our home, however, became a sleek and storied place to entertain family and friends. And most importantly, it was our unique, serene space to thrive as a couple.

Our new neighbors included the world-renowned architect

I.M. Pei and, a few doors over, Javier Pérez de Cuéllar, Secretary-General of the United Nations, who lived in an official residence donated by lauded philanthropist Ann Morgan and reserved for whoever occupies that post. Over the coming years, in our common garden, always lush with color and the sensations of solitude, I would run into and get to know Pérez de Cuéllar's successors from Egyptian Boutros Boutros-Ghali, Ghanian Kofi Annan, South Korean Ban Ki-moon and Portuguese António Guterres.

James was a wonderful husband, and he boasted to everyone that I was a great wife because I was no longer Yue-Sai Kan the moment he walked into the house after work. I instantly transformed into Mrs. McManus. I never viewed this as a negative and was thrilled to love and support my husband in any way that I could, just as he did for me. James appreciated my old-school wifely dedication, even if it didn't include cooking or laundry, two things that I told him were off the table from the get-go. He often joked to others that I was the only Chinese he knew who didn't do laundry or cook but that it wasn't a problem because he was happy to hire housekeepers, cooks, and drivers for me.

James paid careful attention to nutrition and enjoyed healthy, hardy breakfasts and in the evenings, he never ate meat – always fresh fish. He took care of himself, running miles daily, and always smelled fresh and masculine. Furthermore, James's closet resembled a high-end department store and was perpetually neat and tidy, with all clothes folded or hung after he wore them. He wiped everything clean after using the bathroom sink and always put the toilet seat down. Intricate details matter, and James was ahead of the curve. In addition to being extremely polite, he always helped me put on my coat, opened doors for me and insisted on carrying my bag, even when it wasn't cumbersome. Every day, these little things added up and made our marriage stronger.

When I decided to start Yue-Sai Cosmetics, James was most supportive. He valued that I was a young woman who did not want to stand still, knowing full well that time and opportunity do not always pass our way again. Thus, James assiduously raised the startup funds, assigned his accountant to set up the books for the company, and dutifully trained our General Manager, Sam. It was wonderful to talk to my husband about the pitfalls of a startup, even if most of the problems we encountered were unique to China. James was new to understanding my country of birth, but he understood business more than anyone I had ever known, and his partnership was inestimable.

With all our trekking back and forth to China, some strange moments cropped up – although James handled them with consummate coolness. At one point, a man from the Federal Bureau of Investigation (FBI) called, declaring that he wanted to meet James; however, he didn't seem interested in me. We invited him over, and it turned out the FBI agent wanted to know if my husband had anything interesting to report about the trips he took to China, where his wife was a celebrity and where we met influential people in the Chinese Communist Party. I was surprised by this direct approach by the federal government and glad James had zero interest in speaking with the agent at length. Besides, we didn't have anything useful to share with the FBI, as neither of us was engaged in Chinese politics. Naturally, we met some of the leaders in Beijing (北京) but since I was never explicitly political or interested in inter-governmental affairs, nobody we encountered ever shared political information and our conversations were relegated to business and the arts and cultural appreciation.

James was a very disciplined individual. He told me he used to smoke three packs of cigarettes a day, then one day decided to quit cold turkey and never touched a cigarette again. His level of self-control was astounding. But the incident that most struck a love chord with me happened on an airplane from China to New York. For two days before the flight, James suffered from an extraordinary swelling rash that itched unbearably. He knew he shouldn't scratch it because it might bleed. He feared that if he arrived in the United States bleeding, he might be detained at the airport by Customs and Immigration. I was extremely impressed that James never once touched this horrible rash throughout the seventeen-and-a-half-hour flight. He marched straight from the airport to the emergency room when we landed.

James's discipline was a great complement to his creative mind. When my company faced challenges, he always produced intelligent solutions, drawing on his tertiary studies in marketing and accounting. James understood money and numbers, but they did not rule his judgment. Instead, he made money work for him in innovative ways. For instance, I once asked why he habitually left such large tips.

"People rely heavily on tipping because their base salary is very low," James said, explaining that if he ever stayed at a friend's home, he tipped their staff well. "I want the servants to feel good that their boss has generous friends."

He relished the positive energy his generosity created. Once, we went to his alma mater, Northwestern University, where he was on the board of trustees and donated an entire newfangled sports stadium in addition to The McManus Living and Learning Center, a seven-story apartment complex designed to suit the needs of Kellogg students, their partners, and families. James wanted to show me around the facility, but we were stopped by a security guard asking us for identification.

"But this is Mr. James McManus, the donor of this building!" I protested.

"Oh, so sorry. I thought Mr. McManus was already dead," the guard responded, prompting belly laughs from us all.

James constantly espoused that it was good to be charitable while alive and to enjoy what your donation brings to people. Among the other major recipients of my husband's philanthropy was Carnegie Hall, New York's musical juggernaut located steps from Central Park. The three-auditorium hub was a frequent destination for us while we were married, and we savored every opportunity to experience the best of the best classical musicians that the world had to offer.

James and I worked well together and had fun for a few years, but soon, neither of us could deny that some ominous factors had started to creep in between us. First was our age difference. At eighteen years my senior, James was etching close to retirement and was looking forward to golfing in

Florida, skiing in Aspen, and traveling the world to enjoy the fruits of his labor. However, I was in my prime and craved learning new things, and wanted above all, to fulfill my wildest vocational dreams. I had seen many young women marry older men and felt that it was mainly for the money, nothing else. But I spent my life sculpting my own path to the moon, and I wasn't about to rest on my laurels.

And regardless of love or money, age eventually matters. Perhaps when your man is about fifty, and you are in your thirties, you don't notice the gap. Wait until you're sixty and he is eighty, and then you will really feel it.

There were also cultural differences. I had lived in the United States since I was 16 years old and was now fully immersed in American culture, speaking excellent English. But for James to marry me, a woman of Chinese descent, knowing nothing of my cultural background, and making no effort to learn my mother tongue nor showing any interest in Chinese history and culture, meant that he could not adjust to and accept me for who I was. James and I also had different hobbies. He golfed and skied, but I didn't, mostly because I'm not too fond of the sun. Moreover, I wasn't a fan of how time-consuming each sport was, and taking to the slopes triggered my fear of heights.

I know that being married to me was not easy for James. I traveled to China so often on business. At first, we said we wouldn't be apart for more than two weeks at a time, and he agreed to go to China with me. I soon realized he was bored to tears in my homeland. There were few people around with whom he could speak English. My very capable general manager, Sam, was his only companion, and they played a lot of golf together. Every other activity centered around me. It was hard for an American businessman with an empire of his own to stomach playing the role of Mr. Kan. All over China, photographers and fans rushed me, pushing James aside. He could only watch me signing autographs and talking to people in the crowd. He didn't understand what was being said and must have felt terribly excluded.

James soon started to complain that I wasn't with him in New York often enough. I remember him sounding so belligerent and unhappy over the phone that I would often jump on a plane and fly all the way home to calm him down. This happened many times. He had never done business in China, so he had little comprehension of how incredibly complicated it could be, and the importance of my being there to make sure impediments were addressed and overcome. As Yue-Sai Cosmetics grew, I had an obligation to be with my staff. I had no choice, which became a monumental cause of conflict between us. Traveling back and forth, dividing my attention, I lived in a state of constant jet lag. I was torn.

Six years into our marriage, and I was very aware that many women were interested in James for assorted reasons. Wendi Deng (邓文迪), who would go on to marry Australian media mogul Rupert Murdoch, found out James was on the Kellogg School of Management board at Northwestern University and invited him to lunch, supposedly seeking advice about studying at Kellogg. But I knew Wendi, and I knew how clever and conniving she could be when it came to relationships and getting ahead. When I found this out, I did not hesitate to call her.

"Hi, Wendi, if you want to see my husband, please let me know," I stated flatly.

But the real blade to the abdomen came when I found out about the mistress – the woman who was more than a coffee date. Betty was James's office manager, took golf lessons from him and learned how to ski purely to keep him company. This woman chased James, and she got him.

I learned about the affair quite unexpectedly when an American friend arriving in Beijing to pick up her adopted Chinese baby innocently mentioned that she had just seen James with a woman at the airport in Fort Lauderdale. When I asked my friend to describe the other individual, I comprehended instantly who she was and what was transpiring in my absence. While I had not necessarily suspected anything until that conversation, reality immediately dawned. Women are highly intelligent, and we are very in tune and sensitive to the idea of our significant other straying. My husband had wandered, and it took all my strength to pull my shoulders back and hold myself together in such an epiphanic moment. Yet I could only hold myself together so much. This was all happening while I was in the process of selling part of my company to Coty, and I was so nervous that my entire body broke out into hives, and it wouldn't be long before I developed a twitch.

That day, I was in Beijing hosting the first International Band Festival and had no alternative but to put on my bravest face. After the night's event, I telephoned James and calmly told him I was returning to New York the next day. As usual, he met me at JFK, and I dove in for the confrontation kill. A look of fear immediately glazed James's eyes. He started by denying it, but I had done my own investigative work and had managed to confirm that he was indeed having an affair with his employee.

To try to save our marriage, we went to a famous therapist. But this was little help as I am one of the few people I know who doesn't believe in therapy. From my purview, rehashing events only causes more pain and makes things worse, a fixation on the past that prevents people from moving forward.

One afternoon, I called James at his office, and he wasn't there. His secretary said he had left the office at 1 p.m. He arrived home at seven o'clock. Of course, I knew where he had been. We went to dinner that night at an Indian restaurant close to home, and I told him bluntly that the life we were living was not a marriage.

"Would you consider changing the way you live?" I asked him.

"No," he eventually replied.

"Then we should divorce," I said.

"Yes," he agreed, almost too readily.

Our divorce was simple and straightforward but emotionally taxing. James said I could keep the house, but he asked to be paid for his work with Yue-Sai Cosmetics and a commission for the seed money he had raised from investors to start the company. In the end, I gave him everything he requested and bought him out of the Sutton Square house, too. I wanted a clean break.

"Don't tell anyone I'm your lawyer," my famous divorce attorney, Robert Cohen, said in exasperation. "You're giving away everything."

I didn't want to fight. For what? It was only money. I could always make it back. I didn't need his money. Above all, I needed to protect my heart and head from further hurt. I know my attitude was right, but still, it was hard to see my dream of lifelong nuptials die. While the notion that love doesn't always work out is as tried and true as time itself, no one goes into a marriage with the idea of divorce, least of all someone like me who waited so long to tie-the-knot in the first place. Some people say that nothing is more painful than the loss of a loved one to death, yet I say that divorce is a contender for the cause of the worst pain because it shatters the dream you thought you were building with a partner. On paper, the legal justification for our divorce was "abandonment." To me, divorce was the death of all fantasies, more than only the loss of a loved one.

James told me he was moving from our house into the home of an old friend, but, in reality, I found out he had moved directly to his mistress's house. That stung. On Valentine's Day 1996, we signed our divorce papers. I wasn't there to sign in person, instead burying the pain with business dealings on the other side of the world.

On that day, James wrote me a letter:

February 14, 1996

Ms. Yue-Sai Kan
6 Sutton Square
New York, NTY 10022

Dear Yue-Sai,

This note of friendship and love is being written to you while I sit in the all-day closing session for our marital separation, the transfer to you of the Sutton Square houses and the restructuring of our mutual YSK business interests.

My feelings at this moment are of an appreciation of your love and tenderness since our meeting on October 12, 1988, your partnership support over 6+ years of marriage, the honesty and energy you brought to our relationship, and a sense of wonderment and confusion as to how we ended up at this point-of-no-return.

I wish to restate my great admiration for you, my hopes for your continued growth as an exceptional person who brings good things to others' lives, my desire to help you achieve your business objectives and my hope that you take great care to pace yourself in the interest of preserving your spirit and good health.

There are many other feelings and ideas that I might express at this time, but a historical or philosophical recitation of our personal connection is not my purpose here. I simply want to say I care about you and want only the best for you.

I hope we might have lunch or coffee when you return to New York from China later this month so that, among other things, we can determine the basis upon which we will be able to maintain and advance our friendship in the months and years ahead. I will await your call.

Happy Chinese New Year and take good care of yourself.

James R. McManus
Chairman and CEO

After it was all done and dusted, I wanted only to continue numbing myself with work. There is no universal formula for managing grief, and we never know how we will respond until we fall right into its lair. Some may laugh, others will cry – and for me, at least at first, I needed to distance myself from the pain.

I flew directly to France to attend a large cosmetics industry business meeting, where Coty, the company that had purchased a portion of Yue-Sai Cosmetics, introduced me to its senior staff. Before leaving China for Nice, I arranged to rent a small house near Saint-Jean-Cap-Ferrat. I knew no one there. When the meeting was over, I moved into an anonymous cottage in the south of France for two weeks, all on my own.

Standing in the sunlight, surrounded by the seaside every day while listening to the sweeping sound of the tide, I cried my heart out – mourning an unparalleled kind of loss I had never experienced before. Being alone in the stillness, in the bosom of such a beautiful setting, is equally as distressing as it is divine. I promised myself that I could weep as much as I needed to now and let my mind dip into those dark crevices of mourning. However, I set a deadline for my mourning period. After two weeks, I would wipe my eyes and turn a new page.

Upon returning to New York, I went to Tiffany's with my assistant Stephanie Jacobs. With her by my side, I exchanged my engagement ring – now a symbol of unhappiness – for a beautiful yellow diamond ring.

The majority of divorces I have seen are acrimonious. In the end, mine was not. Today, I even say that my divorce was a success. One of the reasons it was relatively uncomplicated for James and me is that we did not have children together; thus, we could settle our finances without dispute. This made it easy for us to stay connected loosely through the years, especially for the first decade after we parted. James married his mistress Betty a couple of years after we divorced, but he and I still had lunch every year on his birthday at his request. Two years after our divorce, James sent me a BMW 7 series sedan with a bow on top for Christmas.

I am unsure if he was still hanging on to something that no longer existed, however I was absolutely certain that the love I once felt for him had dissipated entirely, and my heart and mind had moved on. I am not the sort of person who clings to the past or dwells in what could and should have been, personally or professionally. When it is over, it is over. Wounds do heal.

In August 2017, I heard James was extremely sick with prostate cancer, so my sister Brenda, Vickie and I paid him a visit. When my eyes fell upon the man I had once cherished so dearly, I almost gasped. James had changed entirely. His thick red hair was gone, replaced by sparse, gray strands. Age spots coated his entire skin, and his spine was bent over, no longer the strapping six-foot-four man I married. He appeared drained of energy and could not sit for long. James's wife, Betty the mistress, was his caregiver. I appreciated this, but in my heart, I thought that I would never have allowed him to deteriorate so badly.

James and his new spouse drank a fair amount of alcohol, something I would have discouraged as I don't drink at all. My belief in alternative medicine could have led him to treatments to ease him through his cancer. I would have led him to live the healthier lifestyle he seemed to relinquish when our marriage broke down.

Even long after the severing of our nuptials, the astrologist I have turned to over the years to guide my decisions assured me that our marriage was meant to be – that we were both meant to walk through those years together, collecting lessons along the way. These days, with the benefit of accumulated wisdom, I don't so much believe in formal marriage. Why get married unless you want children who have the benefit of both parents perpetually present? Looking at how my friends suffer and work so hard for their children, I have come to the admittedly cynical conclusion that, in many cases, as a wise old friend once joked, "children are punishment for sins committed in a previous incarnation."

I am, perhaps, too selfish to have kids of my own. I can love my niece and nephew as much as I do because, at the end of the day, they go home to their parents, and I go about my own life and passions. I advise young friends only to have children if they really want them and understand the hardship they must endure to raise a new generation. Most importantly, I caution that they must have the money and the time to spend with their kids. The Chinese philosopher of Confucianism, Xun Kuang, once highlighted that the person attempting to travel two roads at once will go nowhere, and I felt strongly that my arms were destined to aid other children in need rather than have my own.

In my day, I have seen many couples living together happily whose problems began when they decided to get married. Thus, I will never get married again in my life. I don't see the reason for it. And divorce? It's awful at first, but over time, it turns out, the silver linings emerge. James and I were happier after we split. Life, it turns out, goes on.

Don't fear the future, and don't pine for the past. James passed away in January 2018. May he rest in peace and be happy in heaven. Every once in a while, I still speak to his wife Betty. She is doing well, and I harbor no ill feelings toward her. I have been able to forget everything. One character trait I am grateful to possess is that I am able to forget, to move through the discomfort and move on.

James's daughter, Melissa, still calls me from time to time and it is always lovely to hear her voice. Sadly, James's son Robert passed away from a heart attack and another son, Mitchell, is struggling with brain cancer. Although I was never really a stepmother figure, I still treasure his children with all my heart.

DOING BUSINESS IN CHINA AIN'T EASY_____

In several respects, marriage and running a business are incredibly similar endeavors. Both require passion and conviction and are rife with highs and lows, hunger, and heartache. You don't know what you are in for until you are in the middle of the magnificence and the madness. But ultimately, trust and transparency must exist at the core of both. A marriage and a business can only thrive with these essential ingredients.

In dedicating almost all my adult life to work in China, I am frequently reminded how far my mothership has come – and how far it has to go.

When Xi Jinping (习近平) came to power in 2012, he announced that unless corruption were eradicated, the Communist Party would lose its credibility and be in danger of being overthrown. I was elated to see the subsequent crackdown on malfeasance that unfolded, starting in 2013. Today, doing business in China is far easier for those currently in favor than it used to be – more transparent and less unethical. If, however, by some accident, one crosses the often-difficult-to-discern lines drawn by the ever-shifting rules and regulations set by the Party and falls out of favor, then business in China can be as tricky as ever.

A special department deals exclusively with government issues at many foreign companies in China, including L'Oréal, to which I sold my cosmetics company in 2004. Without the passion and business brilliance of Lan Zhenzhen (兰珍珍), the

Vice President of L'Oréal China, I doubt very much if L'Oréal could be as successful as it is.

Furthermore, I have served on the board of IMAX China since 2015, alongside executives such as Chen Jiande (陈建德), who truly understand China and have all of the right government connections to help the company navigate the bureaucracy – were vital in propelling the company in the complex process to go public in Hong Kong in October 2015.

For Yue-Sai Cosmetics, I was most grateful to have Sam, Sherry, and several other key figures who were savvy enough to guide and guard me every step of the way, so I didn't make big mistakes. Persistent and loyal people are at a premium in China. Without them, slicing through the beadledom can be confusing, frustrating, and ultimately soul-crushing.

To do business in China, it's vital to learn the language or at least master the basics. Knowing even a little Mandarin will unlock many aspects of the culture that will aid you in your dealings. While I was born in China, I only spoke Cantonese when I was young, not China's official language, Mandarin. I was initially unable to communicate directly with Chinese decision-makers, and everything spoken had to be translated both ways. A lot of communication is body language, and while I got many of the nuances that way, I desperately needed to learn to speak the best Mandarin I could. For example, I discovered that the Chinese find it hard to say "No" outright.

It took me several years to become fully fluent in Mandarin, and dedicating time and resources to this mission proved to be the most valuable gift I could ever have given myself.

Foreign business aspirants must learn the culture and

adjust. Any outsider striving to work in the Chinese market should have a local by their side, someone who can clue them into the particulars of Chinese culture, ranging from the unfamiliar to the shocking. In Chinese communications, there is almost always a subtext. The brilliant Hank Greenberg of the U.S. insurance giant AIG was fortunate to have Rick Niu (钮小鹏), his interpreter in language, culture, and political nuances, as his sidekick.

Ultimately, China is a very complicated country with a complex history and ruled very much by the nature of relationships. Foreigners purporting to do business are prone to make mistakes; thus, having a trusted local by your side – I call them gurus or rabbis – is priceless. For me, my assistants in China are vital. They can pick up the cues and nuances in conversations, and as an added bonus, officials or people in places of authority will often divulge things to the locals they won't to an outsider. However, these basic principles apply in any country. In any foreign land, you must conduct business locally. Globalization is localization. Do everything you can to learn about and adjust to new surroundings. You will never know what is happening around you unless you do, and you'll never succeed in the business realm.

Next up, get connected. Every foreigner who works in China learns at least one Chinese word: guanxi (关系). Guanxi means relationships. Personal relationships are far more critical in China than in the West. For example, one never makes "cold calls" in China. In most cases, it's who you know that helps to resolve problems or establish your position. In this regard, foreigners are in a poor position when breaking into doing business in China. The Chinese turn to their parents, uncles, cousins, or former schoolmates to help when in doubt or trouble. This cultural concept is why MBA programs are so popular in China today – it's not the studies that are so important as the guanxi one can cultivate when attending these prestigious schools. You need to spend a great deal of time and effort developing interpersonal relationships in China, understanding that there will be a quid pro quo. You scratch my back, and I'll scratch yours.

Those who complain about the difficulty of doing business in China today don't know how hard it was when I started doing business there in the early 1990s. I was a household name, but I still encountered many problems. The business environment was just being established, and officials threw an array of mandates into the melting pot with no resources to succeed. Government legislation mandated that companies fund all kinds of employee insurance policies, from endowment, medical and maternity to employment injury to unemployment. While often noble, the expectations make it incredibly hard for businesses to grow and thrive.

Further, there were no logistics companies; banks offered few services, and laws and regulations needed to be more mature, particularly not business laws. We found ourselves negotiating with the government all the time. We were making retail products, but there were no chain stores. In the United States, if I sold to Saks Fifth Avenue and did well, my products would instantly have been in 45 beautiful stores whose business rules were the same nationwide. In China, Yue-Sai Cosmetics products were on sale in 800 stores nationwide, but we had to haggle and mediate with them individually. Each had its own archaic rules and regulations.

Traveling around China was also onerous. Planes were old, trains were worse, hotels were dirty and old, and the food was horrific. People stole with abandon and infringed my trademarks all the time. At one time, sanitary napkins and medicinal wines were on the market, hawked in my name. China at that time had very few experienced and English-speaking business or technical managers. I had to bring in many Americans to kick-start the industry and train the local staff. A lawyer, let alone a good one, was non-existent.

I admire anyone who succeeded in doing business in China, especially in those budding days when superhuman patience was required, along with tremendous resourcefulness, hard work, and fearlessness. Those who started back then, in the 1980s, and stuck it out were rewarded. The government wanted to open up, and despite all the words of warning laid out here, things have gotten better year after year over the last 20 years.

Today, it is easier to hire bilingual, experienced staff, and the initial protocols are much smoother. It now takes only nine days to set up a company. In 2019, the government implemented several reforms to make it easier to do business in China, such as lowering the Value Added Tax for some companies and implementing the country's first Foreign Investment Law to clarify the governance of business capital from outside China.

According to the World Bank's 2023 "Ease of Doing Business" ranking comparing 190 economies worldwide,

China rose to number 31, a massive improvement from 91 in 2006. This by no means says that it's now easy to do business in China, but things are improving.

Still, for Western company executives used to relative transparency and the power of business journalism to explain what's really going on in their industry, undertaking business in China can be supremely frustrating. One of the most challenging components to fathom in Chinese business is a general inability to determine why certain things are done the way they are. It's hard to adjust one's business strategy without that discovery ability. I sit on the board of IMAX China. The brilliant IMAX Corporation CEO Richard Gelfond repeatedly stresses that he can't understand why China's censors bar certain movies from entry. For example, in 2022, the latest Spider-Man movie, a box-office smash hit everywhere else in the world, was not allowed to screen in China. Nobody was able to tell Gelfond why.

I sometimes reflect on the ceaseless stream of stumbling blocks and wonder how I maintained my patience and perseverance. But when you have a sincere and unwavering goal, you wade through the murky waters and push against the current for dear life. And that was all I knew to do. Although perhaps in a much less visible way, millions upon millions of Chinese from my generation and before swam against an overwhelming time, intent on seeing what lay on the other side, too. And they found it: an existence teeming with lights, cameras, and prosperity. The China I remember in the 1980s is not even a skeleton of what exists today. Physically, there is no comparison as the cities are each filled with neon illumination, six-lane highways, and endless towering hotels – each more majestic than the next. Indeed, this is a considerable change from the days of having to bring my own cleaning products to tend to the bathroom!

CHINA'S MEDIA MAZE

Having worked primarily in the media industry, there are many stringent rules and regulations, the purpose of which I still do not quite understand.

The mid-1980s, when I was producing "One World" for CCTV, was the most open time for the media in China, an era when the country was finding its feet on a global map. When the gates were unlocked, euphoria flooded in – there was so much to do and share, and CCTV had a lot of freedom to tackle many topics.

In the 104 fifteen-minute segments we produced, censors only questioned two episodes – the Pope and Mother Teresa – and were upset over a feature about me prior to the show even graced the airwaves. The week before the series started airing, the all-powerful weekly TV Guide CCTV published a full-page profile about me. It was understandable that the CCTV audience would be inquisitive about this U.S.-based woman whose 104 shows would be broadcast at least once a week for the next two years. However, the editors and writers were subsequently scolded because, as a foreigner, I was not supposed to be featured, let alone on the front page.

And when I launched my Chinese language biography "Be a Pioneer" several years ago, it took the censors an entire year to approve the publication. This was my tenth book, and the nine others all took around three months for the final greenlight. This most recent time, for no specific reason, the censors questioned me on so many passages and mandated redactions on so many anecdotes and aspects, and insisted I remove the names of leaders – dead and alive – that I started to think the book would never see the light of day. Finally, after much back and forth, it was considered passable.

In 2019, I was approached by a prominent Chinese state TV network to make a 36-episode series on my life. Everyone on the network was extremely excited about the possibility of working with me to create the biographical series. After six months of vigorous discussion and twelve departments within the network signing off on the long and tedious contract, executives sent the final paperwork to the top guy and – surprise – he refused to sign. We were all shocked. The reason was that I was considered a "politically sensitive person" because, after reviewing my bio, he learned that Yue-Sai Kan was a Chinese American raised in Hong Kong.

It just happened that during that negotiation period, just after then-U.S. President Donald Trump ignited a trade war with China in 2018, causing significant diplomatic tensions between Beijing and Washington, massive pro-democracy demonstrations erupted in Hong Kong. It didn't help my cause that I was associated with Hong Kong.

In hindsight, I thank God that we did not go ahead and produce the shows. We may have spent vast amounts of time and money, and due to the climate and the timing, the censors may have canceled the series before they even went to air. All films and TV shows that wish to be screened or broadcast in China must be approved by government censors throughout their production process. First, scripts must be green lit before shooting can even start. If you apply to produce a 36-episode series, you must finish making all 36 before the censors review them and, hopefully, offer their final approval to air your work. This approach means considerable risk and puts enormous power in the hands of the censors. After making 36 episodes of anything, what producer wants to tell their backing sponsors that they are walking away from the work because the censors who control the keys to the airwaves are simply wrong?

In the U.S., we can produce a couple of episodes first and see how the audience reacts. Visiting the Shanghai International Film Festival as my guest, the Oscar-winning director Oliver Stone once told the audience that the Chinese movie industry will never be genuinely vibrant unless authorities lift this restriction. Making everything political definitely stifles creativity, and truth-telling is necessary for great productions.

Given all that I have shared about doing business in China, especially the media business, it may seem that the negatives outweigh the positives. Indeed, there are days when it can feel that way. However, China is a fantastic place filled with incredibly kind people and landscapes that amount to an unprecedented visual feast – and all that has happened there in the last four decades is nothing short of a miracle. It is important to remember the big picture in China: Over the last

40 years, 600 million Chinese have moved out of rural poverty and into cities, transforming them and the whole country in the most dynamic way.

And from my lens, the freedom of the press the United States once held in great esteem has also withered into a bleak hole of fake news controlled by politics and personal agendas.

As the relationship between China and the West hits its lowest point in decades, rife with misunderstanding in both directions, I would like once again to use the medium I know so well – written and visual communications – to help Western viewers see beyond politics and to witness instead all the changes happening in China. After all, what happens to one in every five humans on the planet affects us all.

The best way to understand a country better is to go there and see it for yourself. Yet most people can't simply pick up and travel to China, especially since the outbreak of the COVID-19 pandemic when the country closed its borders to outsiders. Thus, I intend to soon film a new 10-part series tentatively titled "Trending China" – with Quincy Jones at the music helm – made up of episodes taking international viewers on a fun, fast-paced tour of China's ten most exciting cities, focusing on people, culture, lifestyle, history, and the latest trends. Perhaps one part will illuminate a hip new vegetarian restaurant in China, in another the audience will learn about the almost extinct Golden Monkey or have the chance to "hang out" with me inside the quaint Xiamen University.

I have worked in China for some 40 years, coinciding with China's historic opening up. I witnessed and contributed to China's remarkable changes, many of which happened at breakneck speed. And that time for understanding and cultural exchange has arisen again. But this time, I want to leverage the power of social media and streaming to share these segments, entirely unconstrained from the conventions of television and what producers and marketers dictate to be the best approach. I am no longer willing to bring content to life with restriction. The beauty of this day and age is that we no longer must follow such a legacy model.

The revered Chinese saying, "One year, small change. Three years, big change," is more accurate now than ever. I hope this series will further understand China and the rest of the world and make it a better place.

EDUCATION IN A CHANGING CHINA

A recent international study comparing the status of teachers in 21 countries found that teachers in China have the highest level of public respect. There is even an official Teachers' Day, which amplifies the strong Chinese emphasis on the importance of growth and education. The compulsory nine-year, free-of-charge education covers over 85 percent of the population.

I have personally funded the building of libraries and schools and actively support charities that send teachers to rural areas of China. In China, every high school student dreads the Gao Kao, the National college entrance examination, which students must take in their last year of senior high school. Depending on the result of this crucial test, the students will find out if they can go to the Chinese equivalent of an Ivy League college, such as Tsinghua University or Peking University. My driver's wife rented a hotel room with her son during this period, so he was not distracted by any of the customs of daily life. Sadly, the importance placed on this exam and the subsequent stress has led to some student suicides.

In rural China, there is a lack of schools, and most of the ones that do exist are in poor shape. The school I built in LiPu in Guangxi province is in a very remote area where there was not even a paved access road to the school. The few buildings I saw when I first went there were constructed in the 1940s. During the rainy season, the roofs leaked, and the rooms were freezing cold in the winter. Some of them looked like they were in danger of falling. Some students who lived in nearby villages had to walk an hour and a half in the morning to attend school and another hour and a half in the evening to go home. Thus, I provided funds to the school to tear down the old buildings for new ones, and for the first time, the school had a dormitory that allowed the students to sleep in school from Monday morning to Friday afternoon. The shortage of teachers remains a problem, but there are gradually more charities that aim to fund qualified teachers to relocate to these very impoverished pockets of the country.

Besides a lack of teachers, there are a few glaring problems with the rigid education system in China. Chinese kids spend a lot more time in school than their Western counterparts. School starts at 7:30 a.m. and goes on till 4 p.m. After school, kids have to stay up very late to finish their homework. Even with that, there needs to be more time in a regular school day for teachers to cover all the material demanded by the Ministry of Education. Many students find it impossible to cope without the help of tutors. As a result, many Tutoring Schools have sprung up nationwide. Today, 60 percent of children aged 3 to 15 are being tutored outside of school, and parents spend an extra USD 1300 per year on their child to cope with this academic pressure. Unfortunately, if you can't afford it, you drop out. As children, we were told that we must study hard to make our parents proud. We are also told that you will find gold through books, aka intensive study. In other words, wealth, and fame.

However, the traditional learning method is to memorize information rather than acquire knowledge. In trying to combine Eastern and Western education, many International Schools have opened across China to establish this type of learning. Since the 2008 Summer Olympics, there has been a big push to learn English, the second language in China. With over 300 million Chinese learning English on an ongoing basis, a lot of English Schools, including online education platforms, have also opened in China, expanding to second and third-tier cities. China's First Lady Peng Liyuan is fluent in English and has given speeches in impressive English on her official visit to the USA. President Xi, however, used an interpreter.

Recently, Jack Ma, the founder of Alibaba, who used to be a teacher himself, said in a speech that he wanted to help change the archaic education system in China. He says the traditional way to gain knowledge through memorization is passive learning and unnecessary because the internet and AI machines will always be more intelligent than humans. From his perspective, students should not learn to be smart because intelligent people want only to win. We should want to teach kids to be human, to care about others and to aspire to become wise. But wisdom can never be learned from a classroom. It is through life and through experience that we garner true knowledge. Jack wants Chinese children, starting in kindergarten, to learn dancing, music, and painting because, in these curriculums, students learn to use their hearts. These are exciting and very on-target points. I hope Mr. Ma succeeds with this vision, and I look forward to seeing what he will do to the education system over the coming years.

Chinese parents, like my own, place a very high value on education and make great personal sacrifices to send their children to university. When I was growing up in Hong Kong, going abroad to university was a massive deal. Usually, this privilege was only reserved for rich kids, but my amazing parents managed to sell things and send all four of us to the United States for a college education. It was only in 1979 that the first two Chinese mainland students came to the USA to attend Columbia University. Since then, more than 3 million Chinese have studied in the United States. Today, Chinese parents send their children to school all over the world. The most popular destinations are the USA, the UK, Australia, Japan, and parts of Europe. In the USA alone, 400,000 plus Chinese students are here, and each year, they will spend about 30 billion dollars in America. Many Chinese students are accompanied by their mothers, which is a phenomenon rather unique to the Chinese culture. Many of these mothers have bought apartments and helped to furnish them for their children, and wealthy parents are major donors to many Ivy League universities. No other country contributes so much to the American economy and education. Many schools will suffer if these Chinese students are pushed out or deterred from studying here.

In recent years, due to the economic growth in China, most students who study outside of China return to China once their degrees are finished, unlike the old days when the goal was to remain and build a life under the storied guise of the American Dream. There are indeed many alluring and bountiful opportunities available in China now.

But beyond the traditional approach to education, China also emphasizes another kind of subject: Western Etiquette. Many Westerners who visit China often comment negatively about Chinese behaviors in public. They find much of the population rude, dirty, pushy, loud, inconsiderate, and worst of all, unforgivably, they also spit! However, this terrible trait is becoming less common every day.

Although I do not intend to defend the bad social behavior in Chinese society, it is essential to know what it was like before 1978, when the open-door policy came to light. China was primarily an agrarian society where 80 percent of the population lived in rural areas. If their children wanted to pee or poop, they would go outside and use the open field as their toilet. When it was time for the family working outdoors to come home for lunch, those in the home would scream from the top of their lungs to announce that the food was ready. In the countryside, people sit on stools rather than chairs to eat and do not have napkins. Chinese farmers, unlike American farmers, live closely in a village together. There is no public or private space; everywhere is considered communal. Therefore, everyone knows about everything about everyone. Etiquette instructors must teach the Chinese never to ask a lady about her age, salary, and how much she paid for this or that.

Such a lifestyle makes Western etiquette largely unnecessary on the home front. But although Chinese tourists bring large sums of money to spend wherever they go, the YouGov statistics show that Chinese tourists are vastly unpopular in the countries where they make up a large proportion of foreign visitors. Three-quarters of Singaporeans surveyed say the Chinese are the worst tourists. In Thailand, Malaysia, and Vietnam, around 40 percent of locals concurred. Among Australians in the survey, approximately 25 percent also fingered Chinese as their least favorite tourists. Horrifyingly, Chinese tourists have been known to destroy art installations while taking selfies, graffiti important buildings like the Temple of Luxor, or priceless statues with scribble like "Ding Jinhao was here." And who could forget the guy who threw coins into the aircraft's engine in 2019 when he was about to board, an act of self-sabotage rather than the offering to the God of Jet Engines he believed would make his journey safe. The flight was canceled, leaving hundreds of passengers stranded, and the 28-year-old was fined $17,200.

Further, the Chinese are particularly bad with public toilets, so much so that some tourist places do not allow Chinese to use their toilets. Outside the Louvre in Paris, a Mandarin sign tells visitors not to defecate in the surrounding grounds.

After many years of living in what I called "secluded abject poverty," the Chinese were beginning to emerge out of the cocoon but were not received well by the world. It became a huge embarrassment to the Chinese government. So, on June 1, 1995, the Shanghai Government issued a proclamation called "7 Don'ts" (七不规范):

1. No spitting
2. No littering
3. Don't damage public property
4. Don't damage public greenery
5. Don't cross the road indiscriminately
6. No smoking in public
7. No vulgar or obscene language

In addition, the tourist bureau issued travel guidelines for Chinese travelers. The "Guide to the Civilized Behavior of Chinese Citizens Traveling Abroad" informs Chinese travelers to pay attention to hygiene and care for the environment, to dress appropriately and to not be loud, to respect the elderly and remember ladies first, to be polite and modest and line up in an orderly manner. The guidelines further instruct one to eat quietly without waste, enjoy only healthy entertainment, refuse gambling and pornography, and respect other countries' customs and cultures. And by 2010, when Shanghai was the host of the Shanghai World Expo, some communities in Shanghai thought it was necessary to launch a campaign to dissuade citizens from going out in pajamas. A slogan circulated everywhere: "Be a civilized world expo host, don't wear PJ out of your home!" (睡衣睡裤不出门,做个世博文明人)

Chinese culture has its own etiquette, but it's different

from Western etiquette. Let me share with you the ten rules of thumb that I was taught as a small girl:

1. Let elderly people eat first, or when you hear an elder say, "Let's eat," you can start. When you're a guest at someone's home, allow the host to lift his chopsticks first before you touch yours.

2. Don't dig around the food in the serving plate with your chopsticks. Eat from the little area close to you.

3. Don't leave your chopsticks stuck vertically in food. (It is superstition. This custom is reserved for the ghosts.)

4. Don't bite your chopsticks when eating, and don't make chewing noises.

5. Fill the teacup only 3/4 full.

6. Don't leave the teapot spout pointing directly at someone, and don't pour water/alcohol with your backhand.

7. Don't shake your legs or cross your legs when seated.

8. Don't talk loudly.

9. Don't lie.

10. Do address seniority by honorific title.

Some Chinese who needed to deal with Western counterparts were in a challenging position because they had zero idea what was expected of them in terms of behavior and felt very insecure. So, in 2000, the best offering I could give the Chinese for the millennium was to publish a book about modern etiquette.

I have yet to find out how many copies were sold due to poor accounting on the part of the publishers. But I am sure it was millions because it was on the bestseller list since its publication from 2000 to 2002 and designated by the Beijing Municipal Government to be serialized in their newspapers. Shortly after that, some pirated versions of the book appeared on the market, with different book titles using my name. I had to call a press conference to clarify that I did not write them. The book's second edition was published in 2004, accompanied by a DVD. I created several videos to teach these etiquettes. It was the first book in China about modern etiquette and the first textbook with video teaching.

At 3 dollars a copy, I received less than 10 percent of the profits and made little money, but it felt like a calling to spread such wisdom to my Chinese counterparts. While there is a long way to go for Western etiquette to resonate with all parts of the population, each time I return, I see more and more how manners are morphing and changing across the country. As a result of the surging Chinese desire to go global, particularly parents who want to send their children abroad to study routinely enroll their offspring in etiquette or charm schools, hoping to give their children a leg up in this ultra-competitive world. Many such etiquette schools have sprung up nationwide, particularly in Beijing and Shanghai.

These elite academies can cost nearly $400 per child for a four-hour course. But these schools are not only for the young; they also attract wealthy ladies. The hefty price tag can be as high as 100,000 yuan (15,000 dollars) for a 12-day adult course.

Money cannot buy happiness, but in China, it can buy you manners and social status. Many women attend to learn how to host dinner parties, not only for their husbands' clients but also to expand their own social networks. Knowledge of

Western social etiquette has become a status symbol and a tool for gaining global social mobility.

WHAT ELSE YOU MIGHT NOT KNOW _____

Food

In the ever-evolving landscape of China, the nation's tastebuds, too, have drastically transformed with the country's opening.

Less than fifty years ago, the government needed to control one's consumption due to a shortage of food and resources. Chinese people are thus used to using coupons to buy everything from rice, cooking oil, and cigarettes to eggs and coal balls. (Coupons were also used to purchase other daily necessities such as sewing machines, bicycles, and clothes.) But people could afford to eat meat more than once a month. When I visited China in the early 1980s, I did not notice the use of coupons; however, the practice officially lasted until 1993.

Nonetheless, I noticed on that first trip to China how atrocious the food was everywhere I went. Even the rice I was forced to gulp down was soggy and smelly. And after 8 p.m., there was nothing open. The only place expats could congregate with other expats was the Beijing Hotel. The bar there functioned like an international club. Many of the leading China experts of today, such as the world-renowned Chinese law expert Jerry Cohen and his wife Joan, Steve Markscheid, a lifelong China businessman who opened the

Chase office in the 1980s, and Stephen Orlins, President of the National Committee on US-China Relations emerged from that tightknit group of bar socializers.

But thank the heavens for Chinese American architect Clement Chen, who, in 1982, built the Jianguo Hotel on Chang'an Street. For many years, that was the only hotel we stayed at and the only one where we could sit down to a decent meal after 8 p.m. In those days, hotels were the only places you could find decent food. That has changed, of course.

Chinese can now buy any food and eat anything they want. While my first taste of rice was foul and odorous, in the Chinese markets of today, you can buy rice from Vietnam, Laos, the USA, India, South Korea and all over China, including organic and non-organic varieties. Having many types of rice to choose from is also a human right, don't you think? My favorite is the wild rice grown in Huangshan, the fabled yellow mountain range in the southern Anhui Province of eastern China. And regarding the vast range of protein options, my cook will only purchase the black-bone chicken raised by farmers in the countryside. Such a niche option was unimaginable a handful of decades ago.

Moreover, you can now find great Chinese restaurants from the twelve major cuisines almost anywhere nationwide. Wealthy clients provide a renaissance of fine Chinese regional cuisine, and many have created marvelous new dishes in addition to the traditional favorites. The dining scene is vibrant and full of energy and innovation. Eating out in any Chinese city reminds me of an interview I did with the food guru James Beard. I asked him what the three most sumptuous cuisines in the world are.

"Chinese, Chinese, and Chinese," he responded without hesitation.

But that doesn't mean the dishes were all the run-of-the-mill varieties you find in most Chinese restaurants abroad. I have also enjoyed many opportunities to tantalize my taste buds with everything from water cicadas, silkworms, and camel hump to the rare bird, bears paw. However, my uncontested favorite is Shanghai Crab, in season just for October. I would plan a trip at this time just to relish this delicacy. It's a small crab and more complex to eat than blue or king crab. But the taste is super sweet. I first ate Shanghai crab in 1987 when it was only $1 per kilogram. But today, it is considered a luxury and thus is crazy expensive, averaging around $105 per kilogram. Furthermore, I love sea crab from Beidaihe, a popular beach resort and a district of the city of Qinhuangdao on China's Bohai Sea coast, as well as West Lake shrimps and eels cooked the Shanghai way, which is often braised in dark soy sauce or stir-fried, giving it a heavier taste and something more akin to homemade.

On that note, over the last few years, the new trend of "private home cuisine" (私房菜) has emerged, whereby talented chefs who used to work in large restaurants now cater to one or maybe two tables per day, generally only in the evenings. One top chef, in particular, sets a dining table in the couple's bedroom and serves a multi-course offering starting at $50 per person. The waiting list stands at more than one month.

Meanwhile, much-adored Western restaurants have popped

up, too. In Shanghai, a restaurant called "Ultraviolet by Paul Pairet" with 3 Michelin stars, is rated one of the world's 50 Best Restaurants. It's expensive and costs around $550 to $850 per person for 22 courses. There are also a few steak houses like Morton's and Wolfgang's that are doing very well in China, showing the changing taste buds of the Chinese. Traditionally, the Chinese did not eat meats in huge quantities, but today, steaks from Australia, New Zealand, the USA, and Japan are among the favorites. The most successful Western Chef in China is Jean-George. Jean-George at Three on the Bund was one of the first French restaurants in Shanghai. Subsequently, he opened another restaurant called Mercato, which is equally superb.

Many major cities in China also boast cuisines from other countries, such as Italian, Japanese, Indian, Korean, and Vietnamese. I once even had Peruvian food in Shanghai. Meanwhile, the Chinese have taken a shine to eating fast food. Fast food arrived in China in the 1980s, with Kentucky Fried Chicken (KFC) launching in 1987. I remember how much excitement there was at its opening! The first McDonald's was opened in Shenzhen in 1990, and the largest McDonalds in China opened in Beijing two years later with 700 seats and 29 cash registers. It served over 40,000 on its opening day.

But as of 2019, the pioneer – KFC – is by far the most popular fast food restaurant in China, with more than 5,000 restaurants in 1,100 cities compared to McDonalds, which has more than 3,000 locations. The growing popularity of Pizza Hut was a surprise to me because it was cheese-based. I thought the Chinese would not like cheese, a Western dairy staple not in the Eastern repertoire.

Yet, how wrong I was in underestimating the adaptability of the Chinese taste. There are over 2,200 Pizza Hut locations in China and a few other brands of pizza, too.

And what about coffee? In 1984, I was the one to put the very first coffee advertisement of Maxwell House Coffee in my TV series "One World" on CCTV. As you may recall, they were my first sponsor, and I was apprehensive about promoting such a drink to a country of devout tea drinkers. Maxwell House Coffee had prepared three months of supply, but it was sold out in three weeks. As it turned out, the Chinese loved coffee! Nowadays, although Starbucks is expensive, there are over 6000 company-operated stores in China. But the ever-quick Chinese entrepreneurs have now created a considerable number of coffee shop chains like Luckin, which has almost 10,000 locations nationwide.

The most interesting recent addition to China's food scene must be the entry of robot restaurants. Today, there are many restaurants where food is made and served by little computerized machines shuffling from the kitchen to your table. It is simply amazing. After all, food connects us in the way eyes do when they meet across the room or lock during an intense conversation – it is shared experience that can never quite be replicated twice.

Wines And Liquors

Once, I had lunch at an old friend's home. As I was leaving, he handed me a gift – a bottle of the high-end Chinese liquor, Maotai. I was just about to say, "Oh no, thank you, I don't drink," when my assistant stopped me and whispered, "You must accept this gift, not because it is so valuable, but because it must be real."

I paused. Due to the income growth and the Chinese love of alcohol, the problem of fake alcohol has become rampant. It is reported that 60 percent of Maotai on the Chinese market is fake. Expensive French white and red wines have also become targets of counterfeiters. Someone once told me that more so-called Lafite wine is sold each year in China than the vineyard can produce. KTVs, private karaoke clubs, carry the most fake wine, followed by nightclubs, bars and hotels. But fake wine can also be bought in branded stores and supermarkets. Counterfeiting methods and sales channels are complex, involving a well-heeled network of factories, distributors, and stores. It is difficult to stop it.

When we touch on traditional liquor in China, Maotai and Wuliangye (五粮液) are the most important and popular. Kweichow Moutai is high-end, selling at USD 350 a bottle and is the king in the stock market. It trades at USD 237.23, making its total market capitalization over 2 trillion dollars. However, the demand for liquor in the low-end market is greater for the domestic liquor market. As the saying goes, "Not everyone can afford Maotai and Wuliangye, but everyone can afford to drink Erguotou (二锅头, which costs only about 10 yuan (US 1.20) per bottle. The Niu Lanshan Erguotou (牛栏山二锅头) annual sales at 10 billion yuan (US 1.5 billion) are enormous!

While the Chinese are still the largest consumer group of traditional Chinese liquor, they are also the largest consumers of imported Western liquor. In 2019, China imported $820 million US dollars worth of beer and $2.9 billion US dollars in wines. There is also a growing demand for vodka, brandy, Japanese sake, whiskey, rum, and tequila.

As for those with money, the Chinese are now known to be the most prominent collectors of expensive wines. There are tens of thousands of bottles of wine in the wine pavilion of 55 by The Group (伯衡55). Lu Jinyuan (卢津源), the founder of The Group, is known as the "wine king of China" (中国酒皇) and has a very good relationship with the world-renowned wine critic Robert Parker. Lafite 1982, and Romanee-Conti are highly recognized and coveted among Chinese people due to Lu's appreciation and dissemination of the fine wine in the earlier years.

According to the Sunday Times, Hong Kong tycoon Joseph Lau (刘銮雄) owns a collection of 10,000 bottles of red wine and is an avid art collector. He has spent over USD 150 million to store his bountiful wine collection. Joseph bought a lot of good wine when he was young and when Lafite was only 100 US dollars. He has accumulated thousands of bottles of Lafitte. Yet Henry Tang (唐英年), the former Financial Secretary of Hong Kong (财政司司长), has probably the most extensive collection of wine in the world with a wide range. He once sold off part of his rare wine collection for over HK$48 million (US 6.19 million).

In recent years, Chinese vineyards have sprung up like bamboo shoots after a spring rain; wine quality and brewing technologies have made significant progress. The vineyards have become more and more beautiful.

AoYun, China's first luxury wine brand, is produced by a

joint venture between Moët Hennessy and Shangri-La Winery; the winery itself is considered "a bit of a start-up within LVMH." When AoYun was launched in 2013 with a price tag of around US$285, the market did not receive it well. Moreover, Ningxia Helan Qingxue Vineyard (宁夏贺兰晴雪酒庄) was founded in 2005. This winery has many types of wine, including Pinot Noir and Chardonnay, but the most representative is the "Jia Bei Lan 2009 Cabernet blend". 2011 Qingxue Vineyard won the International Trophy at the Decanter World Wine Awards (DWWA), making them the flagship of China's fine wine producers.

But the first Chinese winery to enter the European market was Château Changyu Moser XV (张裕摩塞尔十五世), a joint venture between the Austrian Moser Family and the pioneer wine estate Changyu. Having opened in August 2013, Chateau Changyu-Moser is part of Changyu, China's oldest and largest wine brand, founded in 1892 by Zhang Bishi. Today, the entry-level Cabernet Sauvignon is ubiquitous in the European market. In January 2020, the winery released the world's first and only Cabernet Sauvignon Blanc de Noir aged in French barriques.

In the past, rich people bought expensive French wines, but now rich people buy vineyards in France and other countries like the Napa Valley in California and the hinterlands of Australia.

Notably, famous actress Zhao Wei (赵薇) bought Chateau Monlot in Saint-Emilion in 2011 for USD 42 million. Due to her fame, it is prevalent in China. Her wines from Château Monlot, mainly the cheaper range under the Monlot label, often rank as the most popular wines on Alibaba's Tmall.com. The same year of Zhao's purchase, retired NBA star Yao Ming (姚明) announced the establishment of Yao Family Wines company. Two classic wines were produced: YAO MING Napa Valley Cabernet Sauvignon and YAO MING Napa Valley Family Reserve Cabernet Sauvignon. Further, billionaire and wine lover Jack Ma of Alibaba bought batches of vineyards in Bordeaux, including Château de Sours, Château Perenne and Chateau Guerry. According to Vineyards-Bordeaux, an investment advisory specialist, Chinese investors have bought about 175 Bordeaux wine estates since 2010.

I always ponder the question not of how but of why China could grow so fast and so well in the last 40 years. Favorable macro situations made it possible for the Chinese to do business, giving them the freedom to be capitalists. Still, one thing people always forget is the Chinese's ability or the Chinese's willingness to adapt to new lifestyles and tastes. For example, eating cheese. It was never something we ate when we were growing up. But how fast the Chinese learn to eat and love it! And wines! The Chinese wine market is deemed the world's second largest in terms of revenue after the United States. By all accounts, Chinese-made wines are improving in quality by the day, and many have finally received the world recognition they deserve.

Making Money Through The Chinese Stock Market

When I first visited China in the 1980s, there was no financial market. Chinese had no other means to make money beyond their standard paychecks. And then, in December of 1990, the first stock market in the country opened out of Shanghai. Seven months later, in July 1991, the Shenzhen Stock Exchange was launched under the helm of an erudite gentleman called Wang Boming (王波明). He was a journalist in New York in the eighties and then went on to co-found the Shenzhen stock exchange. He was one of the founding fathers of China's securities market.

On the first day of trading on the Shenzhen Stock Exchange, only one company was listed, while there were eight stocks on the Shanghai Stock Exchange (today, they are referred to as the "old eight stocks"). Like everything in China, even the stock exchanges have transformed dramatically. In the beginning, only a couple of hundred people traded stocks, but these days, roughly 200 million people in China trade stocks. There are over 4,000 stocks in the A-share market, making it the largest in Asia, with a USD 10 trillion market value. It is bigger than the market capitalization of Hong Kong (5.1 trillion) and Japan (5.66 trillion). But, America, at 35.5 trillion dollars, remains the behemoth.

For a long time, foreigners complained that the Chinese financial market was not open to them. However, the landscape has changed to accommodate. Starting on September 15, 2018, foreigners who worked on the Chinese mainland and their home countries or regions that have established regulatory cooperation mechanisms with the China Securities Regulatory Commission (CSRC) could apply to open security accounts to trade A-shares. The financial market broadened even more in 2020 when Daiwa Securities Group won regulatory approval to set up a majority-owned joint venture on the Chinese mainland. The Japanese brokerage and Investment Banker owns 51 percent of this new venture. AMEX became the first foreign firm to do bank card clearing in China, and Blackrock was approved to establish the first wholly foreign-owned mutual fund company.

Shanghai and Shenzhen Stock Exchanges sell A-shares using RMB to sell to primarily Chinese. B-shares are bought in U.S. dollars or Hong Kong dollars. To purchase stocks in China, like the United States, you must apply for an account before trading.

Since China is the fastest-growing economy in the world, it has some of the best and fastest-growing businesses on the planet. Companies like Baidu, Alibaba, and Tencent are the equivalent of major United States stocks FAANG. Others like JD.com, Meituan, PDD (Pinduoduo), and China Fortune Land Development all made a fortune on the stock market. Some, like Tencent, have made a 50,000 percent increase. And Alibaba Group Holding's market capitalization ballooned after its shares soared on the New York and Hong Kong markets in July 2020, helping it vault past Facebook to become the world's sixth-most valuable company, according to South China Morning Post. Tencent's founder, Pony Ma, is still the wealthiest person in China and 18th in the world, with an estimated wealth of USD 54.4 billion. Alibaba's co-founder, Jack Ma, ranks the second-richest person in China and the 19th richest worldwide.

Many billionaires are created through Shanghai, Shenzhen, Singapore, Hong Kong, or USA Stock Exchanges. Many Chinese citizens have made a lot of money, too. And this money is new.

Alibaba was founded in 1999 and went public for the first time in 2014, raising $21 billion, making it the largest IPO in U.S. history.

The Chinese stock market is overflowing with opportunities and challenges. In recent years, with the rapid development of the economy, more investors have flocked to the market, promoting the continuous expansion of the market size. With the transformation and upgrading of China's economy and the deepening of financial market reform, the A-share market is increasingly focusing on value and long-term investments. Secondly, with the advancement of technological innovation and the rise of emerging industries, the Chinese A-share market will have more investment opportunities, and more people will pay attention to high-quality enterprises in fields such as technology, the Pharmaceutical industry, and green energy.

The bankruptcy of Evergrande Group has had a significant impact on the Chinese stock market, relevant enterprises, and the entire financial system. It reminds enterprises to pay attention to risk management, blind expansion, and excessive reliance on bank credit for investment and operation activities. At the same time, at the regulatory level, it is necessary to strengthen institutional construction and adopt more targeted policy measures to prevent illegal operations and other issues.

However, the Chinese stock exchange – while successful – is still in its infancy and is indeed a space to watch.

Travel By Private Planes
In 1997, Zhang Yue (张跃), founder, chairman, and CEO of

Broad Air Conditioning (Yuanda), was the first Chinese to earn his pilot's license and buy a private plane – a Cessna citation "CJI". Yet this timid gentleman became an instant celebrity due to his novel purchase and company.

Today, Beijing possesses the largest number of private business jets, with a total of 34, and there are 29 in Yangtze cities and 25 in Hong Kong. There are now seven major players in the business jets market in China: Gulfstream (nearly 40 percent of the Greater China Market), Bombardier (30 percent), Dassault, Textron, Embraer S.A., Boeing and Airbus. The Chinese today make commercial and military aircraft but not private planes. Surprisingly, the coronavirus pandemic has improved the utilization rate of private planes due to safety for travelers. But the 22 percent taxes (5 percent import tariff and 17 percent value-added tax) imposed by the Chinese government on private jets has undoubtedly dampened the buying spree. At USD 65 million, a Gulfstream 6 is costly; you still need to wait a year to get your hands on it.

Owning a private plane in China is very complicated compared to the United States. There is strict control over landing rights for private planes, and the application needs to be more straightforward. Most private aircraft are put under the maintenance contract of big airline companies such as Air China and China Eastern Airlines. Owners find this protocol easier because the airlines can handle the aircraft's engineering, flight planning, and administration. Moreover, their licensed and very experienced pilots can be utilized to fly their planes. Most Chinese airline companies have a division where you can charter airplanes for personal trips. Next on the agenda are private clubs that can charter planes for you; however, as of this writing, I still have not seen fractional ownership like NetJets. But I have no doubt this will surface very soon.

And outside private airplane travel, the commercial sector is soaring – no pun intended. Aircraft giant Boeing is slated to deliver an additional 8,560 commercial jets to China from 2023 to 2042. China already comprises 20 percent of the global market for air travel, and by then, it will be the highest in the world.

Chinese are adventurous and, after decades steeped in such isolation, are eager to taste as much of the planet as they can.

Cats And Dogs As Pets

Do you recall that the Chinese used to eat dog and cat meats? They were expensive and only served on special occasions. The mayor of Pan Yu, my father's hometown, once invited me to lunch, and I remembered how excited everybody was when one specific dish called "fragrant meat" was brought out. What disappointed my host was that I could not eat it at all when I found out it was dog meat. It was supposed to be good to consume in the winter because it "warms" your body, yet all I felt was sickness and sadness spinning in my stomach at the thought.

Thankfully, even in this area, lifestyle has changed. The Chinese no longer eat dogs and cats. China boasts the world's largest pet population of 188 million, while there were almost none 40 years ago. These pets are just as spoiled as their Western counterparts. Chinese millennials are the driving force behind this booming market. Sales of pet health supplements have grown 50 percent year-on-year from 2017, and there are more than 13,000 pet hospitals nationwide. Almost every one of my friends owns a cat or a dog.

The 2020 Pet Fair Asia held in Shanghai, even without foreign visitors due to the pandemic, saw record attendance, and it was still the largest exhibition for pet supplies globally. Many attractive offerings included everything from pet dating apps to pet funeral services. By the end of 2021, the market of pet-related businesses in China reached US $36 billion and continues to grow exponentially.

Scan the QR code and travel from East to West with Yue-Sai Kan, an Emmy-winning television producer, best-selling author, entrepreneur and humanitarian.

My wedding to James McManus

James's family and my family

Vacationing in Aspen with James and his
children

In Zhong Nan Hai (The Chinese
Whitehouse) with my parents and
Chinese leaders, 1986

The interior look of my NY home

A gorgeous view from the garden of my NY home

My Shanghai home

With Bill and Hilary Clinton

2015 President Obama at a White House state dinner for Chinese President Xi Jin-Ping. With the Vice President Joe Biden

With King Charles III

I really like Prince Albert, and I am on the board of his philanthropy round table

With Michael Bloomberg and Ted Turner

With Queen Sirikit of Thailand and Dr. Kissinger, who I interviewed a few times

Hosted mass wedding for 100 couples in China twice

I was ordained the Dame of Malta; Received the
Ban Ki-moon Award presented by Ban Ki-moon,
Asia Initiatives

The Global ambassador for Sheba Medical
Center, Israel in 2009

Honored by Sri Chinmoy

Xinhua News Agency voted me one of the
20 most influential women in the world

People Magazine, May 17, 1987 issue

TIME Magazine,
Dec. 19, 1988 issue

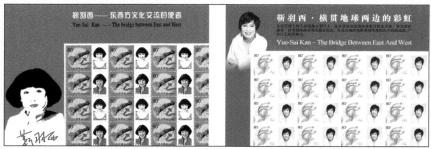

I am the only living American featured on a government-issued Chinese postage
stamp twice, in 2002 and 2005

I published 10 best-selling books in Chinese in China

MY RETURN TO
PARADISE

I teemed with anticipation of what I was about to see: a parcel of land up for auction on the northern tip of Oahu, about an hour from my Honolulu apartment. While the sales video promoting the plot online was overly polished and dramatic, I wasn't sure what the land would be like in person.

From the Kamehameha Highway, Oahu's round-the-island route, we turned off onto a two-track country road flanked by shrubs and tall ironwood trees. We passed a few small farmhouses and, on the left, an Oahu landmark, the abandoned Marconi Station. When the facility opened in 1914, it was briefly the most powerful of a string of radio stations around the globe bearing the name of the Italian inventor Guglielmo Marconi, who figured out, for the first time, how to send morse signals wirelessly over long distances. Local lore has it that this station alerted the mainland of Japan's attack on Pearl Harbor on December 7, 1941. The building, whose doors and windows were long gone, its paint eroded by the sea winds, stood crumbling, unable to tell its emotionally wrought history.

Past the station, edging toward the ocean, I saw it for the first time: the nearly five-acre plot for sale, right next to a 60-acre bird sanctuary and the 15th hole of the gorgeous golf course designed by champion Arnold Palmer for the Turtle Bay Resort. I witnessed no human imprint for miles, just birds and the occasional golfer in the distance. We drove deeper into the land and got out of the car on the little knoll at the far end of the property.

As we stood there, the blue-green waters of the majestic North Pacific rolled out before us. A kohola, a humpback whale, spouted then breached, soaring into the air before crashing into the water. Further down the untarnished sands, an elegant monk seal stretched along the beach. Albatrosses soared overhead. It was a scene out of a dream. And that air? Although salty, it was fresh and sweet, carrying the scent of gardenia and plumeria. It was love at first sight.

My bid won the auction, and once the small crowd departed, I stood alone as close as possible to the water's edge.

"This land is mine!" I thought, resisting the urge to pinch myself. "But what will I do here?"

It was hugely different from the bustle of Shanghai and New York City, but it was exactly what I needed for my next chapter of life. As I walked the flat, empty land, I imagined a farm like my father's farm in the New Territories of Hong Kong, a jewel wrapped inside the thinly populated countryside. There, I'd spent my joyful weekends home from school, picking lychees and bananas right off the trees. I would plan an orchard of all my favorite Hawaiian fruits – longan, calamansi, lemon, lilikoi, jackfruit, banana, mango, coconut, and papaya. I would plant flowers and flowering trees – ginger, gladiolus, hibiscus, and pikaki – to attract bees to produce the sweetest, most healing honey. I would build greenhouses to protect my more delicate plants from the salt air and intense winds, enabling me to grow orchids, herbs, and the vegetables I love to eat from bitter melon, bok choy, choy sum, and Kahuku sweet corn to celery, eggplant, lettuce, ong choy, and yams.

I imagined how wonderful it would feel to grow food to bring to my table and sell and donate some of the harvest to those in need in the nearby town of Kahuku. We would join in the efforts to protect the albatross that mate on my land and in the sanctuary next door.

I was home. I had completed a full circle return to the sweeping sanctuary farm space and open air that defined my Hong Kong childhood. The prospect of transforming the barren land into something useful excited me. Furthermore, I was not alone. My partner, Allan, and I would do it together.

After my divorce from James in 1996, I fell into a few relationships with some interesting men, but I didn't get seriously involved with any of them. Then, one dreary London day in 2014, while attending the 60th wedding anniversary of my dear friends Bea and Stanley Tollman, I met Allan Pollack – a lean, good-looking man with a captivating smile. Allan seemed very interested in me right from the moment our eyes connected across the room.

I had long been suspicious of younger men and, as a rule, didn't go out with them. But Allan seemed different. He was a gemologist and grew up as the only boy in a family of a mother and three sisters. He was used to being around women and taking care of them. After a two-year bicoastal relationship, he left Los Angeles and joined me in New York.

Allan hailed from Panama and was remarkably worldly, having lived in France, Italy, Spain, and Japan for years, and spoke five languages. Such skills make traveling with him around the world a pleasure. Today, he is studying Chinese diligently and getting more impressive daily. Allan's studiousness is quite a departure from James, who never attempted to learn any Chinese beyond saying Ni hao (你好), meaning "hello."

What I love about him now is that he is so different from any man I ever dated. I spent decades cavorting with high-powered, intensely ambitious types – often powerful, famous, or shining entrepreneurs. But Allan is none of that, and I mean that in the best of ways. He lives in the moment, embracing every unique experience that enters his lap. Despite his charming looks, Allan is probably someone I wouldn't have thought a second thought about going out with in my twenties or thirties, forties or even fifties.

But that is the beautiful gift of age – your eyes open to different people and different things, and you value the offering of tremendous company over so many other virtues that no longer feel important. Every decade of existence introduces varying needs and wants, and for love to work, one must really listen to and follow those burning desires within.

Allan and I have been together for almost a decade at this writing. He is gracious and remarkably close to my sisters, niece, and grandnephew. And it doesn't hurt that he is also really handy. In any of my residences – whether in New York, Honolulu, or Shanghai – if something breaks, Allan can fix it. He exercises daily, eats healthily, and sets an excellent example for me. Further, Allan is a great judge of character, and I always like to hear his opinion of the people we meet.

When I met him, he was 53, single, never married, had no lingering ex-girlfriends, and no children. As I never wanted children, my preference was also a man without children.

In our time together, Allan and I have wintered in Honolulu for three months each year to escape the New York cold. But by March 2020, when we were ready to leave Honolulu,

Hawaii had very few COVID-19 cases, and New York City was experiencing a spike of the scary new virus.

Hawaiian weather is amazingly mild all year round, has fantastic - often underrated - food and the most wonderful people on earth. We would wait it out in Paradise, we thought. I never imagined that we would stay in Oahu for 18 months. While the Hawaiian Islands are in the middle of the Pacific Ocean, I could do almost everything I wished to do face-to-face, thanks to Zoom, invented by my fellow Chinese American the brilliant Eric Yuan (袁征). Via Zoom from Honolulu, I was able to pull together and chair a successful fashion gala to benefit the non-profit China Institute in New York, where I am co-chair, raising almost as much money as we did when we held the same event in person at the Plaza Hotel. The best part was that the event was accessible to participants worldwide – a first and definite step forward in spreading the China Institute's message of peaceful cultural exchange.

As the pandemic lockdowns took hold, many psychologists and health professionals emphasized that COVID-19 could make or break a relationship. Allan and I became instantly closer. The isolation and shuttering of life as we knew it made us assess our life on the island and decide that we should try to find a home with direct access to the ocean. We inspected more than 20 homes all over Oahu without success.

"My baby," Allan said one day, addressing me as he always does, despite his being more than a few years my junior, "You know what?"

"What, Baobei (宝贝)?" I replied, naturally calling him "treasured baby" in Mandarin, as I often do.

"There is a piece of land next to the ocean on the North Shore being auctioned off in three days," he continued. "Would you like to see it?"

And that is how we ended up in Kahuku, bringing me full circle, back to a plot of land merely 15 minutes' drive from Brigham Young University Hawaii, in Laie, my first United States home.

Working with a persistent wind from the East and primarily hard coral soil, Hoku William Swartman – an expert on Hawaiian plants – and Ben Lessary, a local Hawaiian Mormon farmer, began to dig up the firm surface, making hundreds of holes, putting down good soil and mulch to amend the land and plant a windbreak to shield our plot. Slowly, they prepared it for the farming I yearned to do.

In my enthusiasm, I informed my friends on social media that I was going into farming, drawing hundreds of queries and a few jokes from my friends worldwide. When some people enter later years, they give up their motivation to do new things. Yet I still feel as though I am just beginning, and so much more awaits.

IT'S EASY TO FEEL AT HOME IN HAWAII

You won't find a more Asian part of America than Hawaii. Of course, pockets of big cities on both coasts of the mainland feature Chinatowns, but there is nowhere in America as culturally Asian as Hawaii. 38 percent of Hawaii's residents are of purely Asian ancestry, more than any other state in the U.S., and another 24 percent are multiracial – including a considerable number who are at least partly Asian.

We feel very safe in Hawaii. In the summer of 2020, Black Lives Matter demonstrations on the island were peaceful and did not result in looting and clashes with the police as in many mainland cities. Further, anti-Asian hate crime in Hawaii is low. Hawaiians overall are compassionate, law-abiding, and focused on family – not just their immediate family but family as a concept. The traditional Hawaiian concept of "Ohana" extends family well beyond parents, siblings, grandparents, uncles, aunties, and cousins. Ohana is the connection with all other humans we meet, treating each of them as we would a member of our own blood family.

Hawaiians' generosity of spirit toward their fellow humans stems from a deeper understanding of the traditional concept of "Ha," which means "breath" and the sharing of breath. Hawaiians embody the life-giving breath and generosity each human must practice with the earth. Our planet gives itself to every one of us every day, with every sunrise and every sunset. Suppose we humans are the beneficiaries of life on this miraculous earth. In that case, each of us, individually and collectively, is duty-bound to give back to the planet to act as its steward. We must be caretakers of the earth itself and all the creatures that walk its surface, fly its skies, and swim in its waters.

Treading lightly on our planet is a core principle for Hawaiians, especially upon this paradise comprised of water and fire, the closest parcel of heaven on earth. Once, Allan and I approached a lone fisherman on the beach near our property and asked the man holding a net trying to catch fish if we could pay him to acquire a few for our table. He gently declined, saying he would reel in only as many as his family could eat.

BLESSING THE LAND

In my newfound role as a steward of a small plot of Hawaii's land, I wanted to anoint the land and honor those who lived before me. I recognized that the terrain was powerful, had been here for thousands of years, and would last long after I was gone. In harmony with the universe, I pledged to nurture this gift of mother nature.

On a beautiful morning in November 2021, I invited Kordell Kekoa, a well-known local Kahu, or priest, to preside over a blessing ceremony to which I gathered a few special friends as witnesses. This included one such friend, David Kawananakoa, a member of the Royal House of Kawananakoa who the closest living blood relative to Her Majesty Queen Lili'uokalani is, the last monarch of Hawaii, imprisoned in her own palace on a trumped-up charge of treason in 1893 when the military of the United States forcefully absorbed Hawaii as a territory. If Hawaii were still a Kingdom, David would be its King. I was very touched that David and his wife, Maria, gave me the most precious gifts from the royal garden – an ohi'a lihua with red flowers and a kukui, or "candlenut" tree, revered by ancient Hawaiians for the oil its nuts produce, used for light, both literally and spiritually.

Standing on the ocean bluff in the small circle of shade provided by a lone wizened heliotrope, a tree native to Southern China, Kahu Kordell, dressed in his simple priest's robe, commenced the ceremony by explaining to my gathered guests how his instruments – a bundle of tea leaves, a pouch of Hawaiian salt and a small coconut shell bowl of blessed water – would remind us of the guiding principle of Ha, which teaches that we, and all the living things around us, all share the same breath and must, as a result, treat every living creature with the respect with which we would wish to be treated ourselves.

"Many people think that Hawaii is disconnected from the rest of the world because of the ocean," Kahu Kordell emphasized. "But our Hawaiian way of thinking is that we are connected because of the ocean and are so very fortunate."

With the trade wind blowing, Kahu Kordell's quiet, focused Hawaiian chants enhanced our awareness of our presence in, and connection to, the landscape and its history. Towards the end of the ceremony, Kahu Kordell asked all of our friends to clasp their hands over my hands and Allan's. He then poured the blessed water over our hands, allowing its coolness to splash off us and onto the land around the heliotrope's trunk and roots, the land we were blessing. This ceremony was very simple, yet it evoked a deep sense of interconnectedness and meaning.

To anybody who has known me in my hectic Shanghai life or my high-society New York existence who protests, "Won't you be lonely out in the middle of the ocean?" I reply with the serene confidence of Ha: "I am never lonely. I am always connected."

A month after the blessing, I brought my sisters Brenda and Vickie – visiting from Rome and New York, respectively – along with friends from China and California out to visit the land. By then, I'd officially named and registered my property "Da Farm by Da Sea." Another friend who joined us on that December 2021 day was Cecilia He (贺俐), a talented young woman from Shanghai who I met over a decade ago.

IN THE WORDS OF CECILIA HE

My Yue-Sai story starts at an event about doing business in China posted by the business school at Xiamen University (厦门大学) in Fujian (福建), where I had studied. I saw that Yue-Sai was a panelist. I'd known of her since high school when she sold Yue-Sai Cosmetics to L'Oreal. That was a big deal. I don't know why, but I remember that. I wasn't allowed to use cosmetics in high school.

I started a business in university, so that's where my business acumen started. I met Yue-Sai in person at the event. I was very curious about her. She was talking about everything and was so inspiring. How come, I wondered, this woman has so many wonderful stories and experiences and still has such a big heart?

I chatted with her, and she said she needed help putting on Miss Universe China. This was 2011-12. So, we worked together on a charity gala with hundreds of auction items.

Yue-Sai raised so much money. I saw her work so hard. She replied to every single email. I couldn't understand how she could do this. She remembers everyone's name. That was very encouraging for me to see.

And after the gala, I went to New York, I went to Cornell, to study for my MBA. I had a student loan. A portion of the tuition and school expenses were covered by myself and sponsored by my parents, and I had another portion that meant I needed a student loan. I chatted with Yue-Sai about that, and she said she would be my co-signer. So, I leveraged her credit to get a super-low interest rate.

The moment she offered that to me, I was shocked. I was a stranger to her. Why would she want to bank with me? If I don't pay, she'd have to pay. So I thought, 'Wow, this is a life-changing experience. How can you do this for me? I'm nobody.'

So, she did that for me, and I went to Cornell with this low-interest student loan. It really changed my life. Yue-Sai's always a person who can tell you what she wants and what she can do for you. I learned that from her. I became the first international student to deliver the commencement speech at Cornell University. That was a big moment for me in 2014. When I think back, that speech on my graduation day was possible because Yue-Sai inspired me to serve the community.

What I learned from Yue-Sai became a part of my daily work: reply to every email and be nice to everybody. Sometimes it's the little things that add up to make a big difference.

Sherry, my long-time loyal advisor and friend, also joined

us on the North Shore in the waning days of 2021. She has seen me through thick and thin, and I was so delighted to have her and her husband, the equally amazing Sam, visiting us from their home in San Francisco.

A true friend like Sherry is never jealous. She has been nothing but supportive of my vision since we first met. This doesn't mean that she and I always agree. In fact, it is quite the opposite. Without Sherry as a friendly critic and sounding board, I would have made far more mistakes than I did as we grew Yue-Sai Cosmetics.

In Hawaii, days before Christmas and enveloped by the season of gratitude, the conversation turned to the November virtual summit between U.S. President Joe Biden and Chinese President Xi Jinping (习近平). Fear, exacerbated by disgraced former President Trump's thoughtlessness, had governed relations between our two countries for some time. By this point, relations between the U.S. and China had reached a new low over the lack of scientific exchange and transparency around COVID-19, a lingering trade war, disputes over issues of sovereignty, self-governance and non-interference, and the issue of respect for universal human rights, including freedom of expression.

Sherry reminded me and others listening in over lunch at the nearby Turtle Bay Resort that, on multiple occasions before, I had risen to the challenge of serving U.S.-China relations. First, in 1984, my eye-opening TV series "One World" on CCTV helped China prepare its citizens to meet the rest of the world. in 1989, Just as most apprehensive foreign businesses left China, taking their capital with them and causing no small hardship for the country, I launched Yue-Sai Cosmetics in 1992. Ever since, Sherry has loved to call me a "ni xing zhe" (逆行者), a woman doing things no one dared to do, things no one considered doable at the time. I take this as a compliment and agree with her, adding that I did what I always did to improve relations between the U.S. and China. It is a luxury to be able to do as much philanthropic work as I do, and I do not intend to waste a moment.

IN THE WORDS OF ALLAN POLLOCK _____

In 2017, Yue-Sai got her hip replaced by her friend, Dr. Edwin Su, at the Hospital for Special Surgery in New York. After the surgery, she's in the recovery room and going in and out because of the sedation. The head nurse of HSS comes into the room and says, "Ms. Kan, we don't know each other, but I saw your name, so I had to come and visit you. Twenty-five years ago, you sponsored me to learn English at Hunter College. I just want to thank you because I never got a chance to do so."

Wow. Yue-Sai will never admit it, but they both started crying. And this is just one of the few women she helped we happen to have learned about. She has done so much for so many. Do you know how much she's doing for the China Institute and the Fashion Institute of Technology?

Even here in Oahu, Yue-Sai sponsors projects and people you will never hear about. She loved Hawaii when she came here for school. That's why when we returned and visited the

North Shore, she fell in love with it again. It also reminded her of her childhood farm with her dad, picking fruits off trees. The farm Yue-Sai will build will remind her of her dad and keep them connected emotionally.

She's pretty healthy now. I would like my dearest love to be a little healthier. Swimming is good for Yue-Sai, but she did not know how to swim at the beginning of Covid. We'd be in the pool, which was only up to her waist, but if she slipped, she would scream because she was so scared. Now, Yue-Sai swims out to the buoys at the edge of the coral in the ocean. I am enormously proud of her. I think it's another way she reconnects with her dad, a champion swimmer in his youth.

Though Yue-Sai doesn't ever have to work for money again, she's always busy, mostly doing things for others. She is always giving herself a challenge. These days in Honolulu, Yue-Sai doesn't have a driver. She wants to be more independent. She decided to learn to drive. Like learning to swim, she is still scared but improving gradually.

Every day, Yue-Sai studies Spanish for at least half an hour. I don't think she knows what she wants to do with it, but she is determined to speak fluently one day. She thinks it's great that she will speak Chinese, English and Spanish, three of the most spoken languages in the world. That is what Yue-Sai is: someone who always strives to improve herself.

Our return to the North Shore reminded her of when she was 16 when she first moved here and had nothing. Reflecting on how far she's come, it's absolutely amazing.

When I was crowned Narcissus Princess in 1968, I never

imagined that decades later, a young woman from the North China coastal city of Qinhuangdao (秦皇岛) who not only read one of my books but followed in my footsteps by studying in Hawaii and competing for the Narcissus Princess title like I did, would track me down and befriend me. That is precisely what Yuan Dan (苑丹) did.

IN THE WORDS OF YUAN DAN ⸻

In 2011, I traveled with Honolulu Mayor Peter Carlisle to the Shanghai International Film Festival, where Yue-Sai was the ambassador in charge of inviting all the famous international movie stars.

She was sitting backstage, and I thought, "Oh my God, this is the person who inspired me." I wanted to introduce her to Carlisle, and since I really grew up in Hawaii, I had learned Ohana, the Hawaiian word for extended family, which can include anybody. I went directly to Yue-Sai and said, "Hi, Yuxi Laoshi (羽西老师), my name is Dan-Dan (丹丹), I'm from Hawaii. Do you mind if I introduce you to the Mayor of Honolulu?"

She didn't know me but left her friends and followed me. They talked, and I sent her the picture they took together that night. The following fall, I was helping the Mayor's office write China talking points when I heard Yue-Sai was coming to town.

"You know Yue-Sai is coming to receive her Lifetime Achievement Award at the Hawaii International Film Festival," I told Carlisle. "Do you have time to meet her?"

"You can arrange that for me," he said.

So, I asked Yue-Sai's assistant about her schedule and learned her birthday was October 6. An idea crossed my mind.

"Would it be possible to make an Official Proclamation when Yue-Sai visits on October 4?" I asked.

"Yeah," Carlisle responded. "But you know a Proclamation takes a month."

I was a student. My English was not good enough to write the Proclamation on behalf of the Mayor. So, I asked a local friend to work with me over three nights on the difficult task of condensing Yue-Sai's accomplishments onto one page. Eventually, I gave it to the Mayor, and he signed it. When Yue-Sai was in Hawaii, I got to see them meet. Mayor Carlisle was so funny. He treated Yue-Sai like an old friend, showing her around the office, even the bathroom. They had a great conversation, and when Yue-Sai saw that they were approaching the end of the tour, only then did the Mayor get serious and sit down at his desk and, listing all her accomplishments off the Proclamation that, right at the end, said that henceforward, October 6, her birthday, would be known as 'Yue-Sai Kan Day" in Hawaii.

She was so moved, so happy.

I came in 2001, at the age of 21, to study English at Hawaii Pacific University. In my suitcase, I had only one book: Yue-Sai's "The Complete Chinese Woman (中国淑女)." The book taught me to be more ladylike, how to talk, and how to think about Western education. It also mentioned a few tips about relationships with men and how to throw parties. I had read the book many times and wanted to know more about Yue-Sai.

Not so much now, but 20 years ago, many Chinese women

still needed to be coached and trained in proper etiquette. Yue-Sai brought lipstick to China and carried on her legacy as a teacher, one of the few Chinese women as influential as men. She taught us to act appropriately and be more than a woman.

Today, when we're not meeting in person that often, Yue-Sai inspires me to be a better version of myself, even with small things. I know she's busy with many things, but occasionally, I receive a message or WeChat or email, "How are you, Dan-Dan?"

I don't want to bother her, but I tell her I've been thinking of her, and she says, "Just do it. Reach out!"

I've always wondered how she manages all her friendships all over the world. The great thing about her is she's sincere with people. She notices a lot of detail and small things and keeps them in mind.

A NEW LEAF, MORE LEARNING

Imagine: Honolulu now has an official "Yue-Sai Kan Day." This is so far from where I started here in Hawaii as a student, back when my parents sent me care packages filled with shrimp noodles and dried chicken gizzards from Hong Kong, that I know they are looking down on me, smiling with approval.

I am reviving sweet memories of a time of discovery and growth in Hawaii and now enjoying reaping the benefits of a life's work. I can now share this place's magical experience with my friends and family. In my experience, sharing is the quickest way to feel joy.

In all my life, I had never owned a piece of land nor built a house from scratch. But what an incredible learning process – filled with hurdles, surprises, fun and excitement. Hawaii is known to be somewhat slow and bureaucratic, and I now fully understand what that means. I am learning all about building a prefab house from China, shipping its parts and clearing customs, building a green home powered by solar panels, and all the problems one encounters with septic tanks. FEMA rules specify that our barn and house must be eight feet above ground! Who knew?

I am also learning what kind of greenhouse we will build for what plants and what trees and fruits will survive on my land. All this learning excites me as it helps me arrive at the belief that farming ought to be considered by everyone. Imagine growing organic, non-genetically modified produce that goes straight from farm to table. Going forward, people should try their best to live green and take on the responsibility of becoming self-sustaining.

At my age, I am fortunate to be in such a position. Circumstances may not allow each person on earth to own an actual plot of land. If that's not possible, growing hydroponically at home is a fine option. The goal is to be sure we leave the world a better place for the next generation.

LEARNING CONSERVATION FROM THE YOUNGEST IN MY FAMILY

I do have a favorite person in the world. He is the youngest in our family, my grandnephew in Kuala Lumpur, Malaysia. Being half French and half Chinese, Adrien is a most beautiful boy. When he visits, my heart is full. At the time of this writing, he is nine years old and a confident genius of a child whose knowledge about animals and birds seems to know no bounds. Adrien says he wants to be a conservationist one day and always excitedly wants to help me with my new farm. He has already sent me pictures he found online of a modern chicken coop – that his research found were not smelly – in addition to information about where to buy the peacocks I told him I would like to raise on my farm. Adrien warned me not to get more than one male peacock. If there are two, they will fight over the peahen, he instructed.

Perhaps coming to the farm is coming home for all of us.

While thousands of miles separate Adrien and me for most of the year, we can chat face-to-face on Zoom anytime we wish with the touch of a button. I am also so pleased that Adrein's mother, Jaimie, my sister Brenda's daughter, won't allow him to play video games. I have never played a single video game in my life because I don't think it will benefit me, and I don't believe they are helpful to a child's development.

It makes me proud that the current Chinese leadership has moved to limit kids to three hours of gaming a week. Such a policy is wise beyond words.

HOME AGAIN

Our future dwelling will have a whole wall of windows facing the sea – it remains a work in progress. We will be able to sit on the deck and peer out at our neighbors, the monk seals and humpback whales, who swim past us between November and April, coming from the international dateline 1,300 miles away.

My perspective on the world has changed since I started this renovation farm project. In time, I began to appreciate the shape of a tree, the beauty of a flower, and the purpose of my life. After returning to Hawaii, my perception of the world has changed.

Over the last decade, the bird sanctuary next to my plot has become home to the Laysan Albatross, a seafaring avian giant with a wingspan of up to 10 feet and a lifespan of 50 years. They usually arrive and begin breeding and nesting in November. July and August cap their nine-month breeding season.

Chinese people believe it is good luck when birds build their nests on your land. Thus, I was excited when, one day in December 2021, I spotted an albatross just outside my property line, sitting on its mud and thatch nest atop an egg. Our contractor built a sturdy little windscreen to protect the bird and its single egg for three months. During incubation, the longest of any bird, downy feathers form in the egg.

Our albatross was doing well for about two months until one morning; she was gone, her egg stolen and eaten by a mongoose. Corporate pineapple growers brought in that nasty animal to kill the rats threatening their crop. However, it proved a failed experiment since rats are nocturnal and mongooses hunt during the day. Oahu is now bristling with mongooses, and I was heartbroken that one killed my beloved albatross chick.

Not long after I bought the land at Kahuku, I met devoted conservationists like Karen Turner, who are fervent in their efforts to help the albatross population grow. Equally enthusiastic and knowledgeable are Adam Borello, head of the North Shore Community Land Trust, and Dr. Sheldon Plentovich, coordinator of the Islands Coastal Program. According to Dr. Plentovich, we are among the lucky few on all of Oahu whose land will be paid regular visits by the Hawaiian Green Sea Turtle and the endangered yellowface bees, Hawaii's only native bees. These bees are important pollinators and vital to the survival of many native plant species. We consider our location's remoteness and attractiveness to these species a happy coincidence and its stewardship a great privilege and honor.

To assist in all the recommended conservation efforts, we will devote ourselves to clearing any and all plastic and fishing debris from our shoreline and promise to use only amber bulbs for lighting, shielding our electric lights and turning them off when they're not needed, especially during the sea turtle hatching season in July.

Occasionally, I take a quiet moment to reflect on how far I've come from birth, from the time when my parents put a feather – "Yu (羽)" – in my name, Yu-Xi (羽西) and tied me forever with "Xi" (西 /West) to my birthplace, Guangxi Province (广西省). I hold dear that my new chapter commences near the nests of albatross hatchlings, whose downy feathers will first feel the salty winds of the North Pacific, halfway between China and America. The distance from Honolulu to New York is 4,957 miles. The distance from Honolulu to Shanghai is 4,936 miles.

And if I can impart any lasting words of wisdom, it would be – if you still have the chance – to have your parents write letters of your life, your childhood, your growth and what you brought to their lives. I safeguard nothing more critical than those handwritten notes, overstuffed with love and memories my parents wrote about me before their passing.

As you grow old, you will begin to more and more miss those who you have loved and lost in your life. If you still have the chance now, spend as much time as possible with your parents. While writing this book, I realized there are large chunks of my life that I know little about. Namely, how my parents escaped from mainland China to reach the shores of Hong Kong. The honest answer is that I never thought to ask them, and now that they are gone, I will never know. Those older than us have so much wisdom to share, whether they realize this or not. With time comes experience, which is incredibly valuable to a young mind.

Also, try to keep a diary. A few minutes a day documenting worthwhile happenings is a beautiful record for one day when you want to do your own memoir. Memoirs need not be for the public but for family, children, and grandchildren. Your descendants will inevitably treasure this. My dedication to journal writing over the years has been invaluable in reminding me of the things I did, the places I stepped foot in, and the feelings that accompanied the many verses of my existence. Writing this memoir, I was forced to go inside the recesses of my memory and wade through the thick, dust-collecting diaries that I kept on and off through the passage of time. I am so grateful I kept them. As I fell into every page, I jotted down the things I needed to record. After that, I discarded the pages since I now know I never need to see them again. It was an eerie sensation – listening to that vaunted rip and watching the remains float into the wastepaper basket like snow flurries melting before they hit the ground, disintegrating into nothing. How easy it was to discard my entire life. So now, what is life all about?

Traditionally, the best Chinese wish for someone older is "to live a long life" (长命百岁). For me, simply living long is not so desirable. It's only covetable, as my mother said, "if you are healthy, financially comfortable and surrounded by people who love you and you love." But here I add: if you can still contribute to improving this world. Hopefully, the sunset phase of your epoch on earth is still a colorful, enriching time of giving to yourself and others.

And in this time of division between peoples over political systems and belief or disbelief in science, I will live my next chapter as a witness to continued connection. Change does not happen instantly but instead transpires through steady, moral victories. From here, I will stay connected to China and America and continue to do all the bountiful projects I love to bring more understanding between the two nations. Like an albatross, we will travel between the countries over the ocean, reminding us that we are all connected.

From Hawaii, right in the middle of the Pacific, I am confident in the reminder that the ocean does not separate us. The ocean connects us. We are – for the better – one.

I especially urge young people to practice gratitude daily and never take life's dealings for granted. Appreciate your parents, recognize the sacrifices they have made along the way, and take time to understand – truly understand – that you can achieve anything you desire in this world, but only because of those who came before you and paved the winding road. I often find myself in quiet moments, entangled in thoughts of Chinese history and the magnificent role the last generation of Chinese people and leaders have undertaken to turn a decaying country into a gigantic and prosperous nation in a mere forty years. Each person made sacrifices and took daunting chances, venturing into the open and the unknown in the hopes of a better tomorrow.

As you continue on your expedition of life, remain mindful of the past, hold on to the present – which can only be felt in the moment – and keep striving for the future. Keep both a strong and tenuous hold on your life. Every moment is a chance to be strong, just as every moment is not guaranteed. Say thank you from the deepest indentations of your heart as often as you can because without your predecessors, you are nowhere, and you are nobody.

This book has no end. Because my life has not ended, and the memories and lessons continue to materialize each and every day. See you in another episode of my life!

Mahalo.

Mayor Carlyle proclaimed Oct 6, my birthday, the "Yue-Sai Kan Day" in Hawaii

With the Governor of Hawaii Josh Green

Mayor Rick Blangiardi and wife Karen, and wonderful neighbors Sushil and Lorene Garg

Gorgeous Hawaiian sunset with good friends

My surprise birthday party with some of my favorite people in the world!

Land blessing ceremony on Da Farm

My beach, my farm, and my visitors, the beautiful albatross

Gloria Wang and former Hawaii First Lady Jean Ariyoshi; with Allan Pollack

What a happy return to my Alma Mater BYU Hawaii!

A birthday party for Rusty Komori

My Chinese friends in Honolulu

My Hula dance group with Kumu Peter Espiritu, and Hawaiian Singer Raiatea

At the Honolulu Chinese New Year Parade

Chinese New Year Party with Lion Dancers

Friends in Honolulu

Visiting the studio of Ji Jian Jie, with Mr.& Mrs. Zhang YaQin, Lynn Lin, artist Ji Jian Jie, Lucy Xie. Tai Chi Master Yang Dezhan came to Hawaii to teach us Tai Chi

EPILOGUE

ON BEING AMERICAN AND CHINESE

Many decades have passed since I arrived in Hawaii from Hong Kong. But just as I was embarking on a new path, the country of my birth was turning a fresh page, too. At the end of 1978, at the 11th National Congress of the CCP, the Chinese government set about new policies building a new platform for what became the miracle economic reformation of all the years since. These parallels of fate were to guide my life and career for almost the next five decades. It is easy to recall the powerful, emotional experience of becoming a naturalized U.S. citizen today. Although today's America has changed drastically since I swore that Pledge of Allegiance decades ago, and not always for the better, it is still the country I'm overjoyed to call home.

The first Chinese immigrants arrived in America in the mid-19th century. Since then, we have faced and overcome many challenges to achieve our American dream, contributing significantly to the betterment of the U.S. along the way, all while overcoming stereotypes that plagued our every step and persist today. The first Chinese in America worked the goldfields in California and later built the Transcontinental Railroad. Roughly 15,000 Chinese laborers participated in constructing the transportation lifeline that connected America's coasts and propelled the nation's economic growth for decades. Many Chinese railroad workers died on this dangerous job. However, in a photograph taken in 1869 of the final spike being driven into the railbed, completing this incredible feat of engineering, all the faces belonged to white men. Sadly, the photograph did not include a single Chinese person.

Instead, when the railroad was completed, Chinese Americans were slapped with the Chinese Exclusion Act of 1882, preventing hardworking Chinese men from bringing wives over from China to start families in the America they'd just helped to enrich. The Act remains the only American law ever passed banning the immigration of a specific ethnic group. Chinese suffered racial discrimination at every level of society. Employers were eager for cheap labor, but the public was stirred into anger by racist politicians and media and fought against the so-called "Yellow Peril."

The Chinese Exclusion Act was at last repealed 61 years later, in 1943, when 105 Chinese were allowed to enter the U.S. It wasn't until 2012 that Congress expressed its regret for the racist law, and not until 2014 that California formally recognized the many great accomplishments of its American Chinese community. In America, there is a tendency to punish immigrants of color and their first-generation American descendants for problems stemming from their ancestral homelands. After Japan bombed Pearl Harbor, 120,000 Americans of Japanese descent, most of them American citizens born in the United States, were hurled into concentration camps in desolate parts of the country. At the same time, American Germans and American Italians remained free through the course of World War II. During and after the Iran hostage crisis of late 1979, many Persian refugees who'd settled in America were attacked. After the terrorist bombings in New York and Washington on September 11, 2001, Americans from majority-Muslim countries, and many Americans mistaken for being Muslim, were terribly abused.

In recent years, as the general attitude towards China has turned negative in many parts of the world, anti-Asian crime has risen. In the U.S., where former President Trump described COVID-19 as the "kung flu" and blamed China exclusively for a natural, if tragic, pandemic, American Chinese have withstood the worst of racism and hate.

When I was growing up in the 1950s and 60s in British Colonial Hong Kong, we paid little attention to what was happening on the Chinese Mainland. My parents, both from land-owning families, had escaped as refugees. The British allowed them and millions of others to stay. My parents had witnessed so much political turmoil that they did not want to discuss politics or China.

Growing up, China was totally closed off, and very few people were allowed to visit. Millions of Chinese died in the land reform movement in the early 1950s, followed by millions more during the famines caused by the Great Leap Forward later in the decade. I remember my mother trying to send boxes of supplies to her relatives in mainland China only to have them returned because they were scared that others would find out that they had politically incorrect "foreign connections."

We young Hong Kong Chinese felt as if nothing, but dreadful news was coming out of this mysterious land our parents used to call home. Living in a British colony, we were taught that English was the most important language, and the Chinese language was secondary, matching our status as second-class citizens of Hong Kong. In those years, being Chinese was not a point of pride.

When I first arrived in New York City, I did not feel it was possible to be proud to be an American Chinese. We were so few in number, and even the most successful of our kin ran restaurants and laundries. No one paid any attention to us. China was never part of the conversation.

However, the nature began to change after 1971 when the Republic of China's UN seat was removed and replaced with a seat for the People's Republic of China. Soon after, an American table tennis team was invited to visit China. Images of those matches of ping-pong diplomacy captured the American imagination, representing the first positive pictures coming from behind what was then called the Bamboo Curtain. Then, when President Richard Nixon went to China in 1972 and started normalizing a relationship that was anything but ordinary, American Chinese watched events unfold in disbelief. There were mixed feelings for some, but for most of us, it was beautiful that the land of our ancestors was becoming a friend of our chosen home country.

On January 1, 1979, Beijing and Washington established formal diplomatic ties and a few weeks later, Congress passed the Taiwan Relations Act, which says that the United States "will make available to Taiwan such defense articles and defense services in such quantity as may be necessary to enable Taiwan to maintain sufficient self-defense capabilities."

Nevertheless, China soon put that strategically ambiguous language to one side and sent Premier Deng Xiaoping to visit

America. He wore a cowboy hat to a rodeo in Texas. Pandas were loaned to U.S. zoos. Relations between the U.S. and China were blooming. In the mid-1980s, President Ronald Reagan walked hand-in-hand in the rain with Premier Zhao Ziyang, an image symbolizing the height of the new Sino-U.S. love fest.

After the opening up, China became a significant exporter, and its entry into the World Trade Organization in 2001 allowed it to become the "factory of the world." At the heart of everything China has done since – the infrastructure, the development, the growth – was the profit earned from being granted access to the world to trade.

There are considerable advantages to strong central control, as we saw during the start of the COVID-19 pandemic when the Chinese government forced a lockdown that kept the virus spread in China to a minimum. China's centrally controlled economy makes it challenging for foreign companies to compete, except in consumer products like cosmetics. But the rapid growth of China's economy has been a blessing for most Chinese people.

China became the second-largest economy in the world in 2010, and today, it is a powerful player in all markets around the world. Not only did China's fast economic growth of the early 1980s, middle-to-late 1990s and all the 2000s, right up through the Beijing Olympics in 2008, pull hundreds of millions of people out of poverty, today the profits of that growth are financing the construction of infrastructure in many parts of the developing world.

For American Chinese, citizens of the United States whose century-long dominance is most threatened by China, the

2010s were challenging. The rise of harsh rhetoric between Beijing and Washington made us feel wedged in the middle and highly uncomfortable. Today, I feel as if the progress in our nations' friendship built over the last 40 years has almost vanished. It feels like we will have to rebuild trust from the bottom up.

Not all is lost; leading by example with compassion and empathy is the only way forward. In February 2022, The Department of Justice of the United States stopped an initiative started under former President Trump that targeted scientists of Chinese descent working in America, prosecuting them for alleged treasonous behavior. None of the claims were substantiated. The lesson is that if all Americans care for American Chinese, America as a whole may grow a respect for China, too.

Respect and trust are fundamental. Jerry Yang, founder of American Internet giant Yahoo, has pointed out that America owes much of its global economic and geopolitical leadership in recent decades to American Chinese scientists and innovators. American Chinese scientists have played an integral role in U.S. history, from the Manhattan Project to the space race to the ongoing digital and green tech revolutions.

"Yet the perception of Chinese Americans as perpetual foreigners whose loyalties to America are always suspect continues to limit their positive impact," Yang noted. "This bias must end if America seeks to sustain and reinforce its science, technology, and innovation competitiveness. We have seen throughout history that progress is born out of diversity, of talent, of minds and opinions."

American Chinese such as Andrew Yang (no relation to Jerry), whose run for the 2020 Democratic presidential nomination I supported with multiple fundraisers in my New York home, are American through and through. It's impressive that Andrew was brave enough to run and did well. We Chinese don't have the culture of being in politics. That's not American Chinese culture or even Chinese culture. We don't run for things. That's not what we were taught to do. Yet Yang pushed for civil rights for all, an essential component of American democracy and did so, even more importantly, while representing an inherent level of respect for Chinese culture and for China lacking elsewhere in American politics. Andrew Yang is at the vanguard of a new wave of American Chinese politicians.

This new wave of American Chinese beginning to run for office had the groundwork laid for them by Gary Locke, the former Governor of Washington who went on to become U.S. Ambassador to China and U.S. Secretary of Commerce, and by Hiram Fong, the only Republican Senator Hawaii's ever known, who ran in the Presidential primary in 1964. But Locke and Fong, whose ancestors came from Mainland China, were exceptions to the rule.

Nowadays, American Chinese and other Americans of Asian descent are running for office in increasing numbers. I support as many as I can with donations. I didn't know much about Michelle Wu, the new mayor of Boston, but my American Chinese friends in Boston who came to support Andrew Yang when I hosted him at my New York home supported Wu's campaign, so I did, too. It's a reciprocal thing. Americans of

Asian descent are beginning to support their own. There's a wave. It's becoming something.

I donated money to Grace Meng, the Democratic Congresswoman from Queens who has been extremely helpful in the predominantly Chinese Flushing district. She hasn't gone national yet, but Grace co-sponsored the COVID-19 Hate Crimes Act that made it easier to prosecute anti-Asian crimes related to the pandemic. Grace was also a highlight of my Women Who Dared charity in the fall of 2021, honoring ten remarkable American Chinese women from different fields. We raised $400,000 to support women artists.

I also gave money to California Democratic Congressman Ted Lieu and to Andy Kim, an American Korean Democratic Congressman from New Jersey. Most of my contributions have gone to Democrats, but I feel less aligned with any party these days.

Emboldened by these brave Americans of Asian descent working in public service in America and yet still mindful of helping China, I was moved when COVID-19 hit China to join the American Chinese community to scour the globe for masks, surgical gowns, and medical supplies to boost China's depleted inventories of these crucial supplies. Then, as the invisible enemy ravaged Europe and later the United States, we shifted gears.

Every American Chinese organization and business leader I know supported American frontline workers by sourcing medical supplies, donating masks to police officers and emergency medical workers, and providing free meals to doctors and nurses.

To get around city and state bureaucracy, I donated money through American Chinese WeChat groups and, living as I do in Honolulu, I drove to Straub Medical Center, the biggest hospital in Hawaii, and to the office of Honolulu Mayor Kirk Caldwell to drop off dozens of boxes of anti-viral masks. I also personally delivered more masks to lifeguards on Oahu's beaches and sent thousands of masks to police and firefighters across New York through the offices of my New York Congresswoman, Carolyn Maloney, and then Acting Queens Borough President Sharon Lee, an American Korean politician to watch.

In short, I joined with many of my concerned American Chinese friends and business leaders to support American communities by protecting those fighting the battle against COVID-19. Thanks to the enormous outpouring of American Chinese support for our country during this dark period, I have never been so proud of my heritage. But at the same time, I have never been so alarmed by the sharp increase in hostility and overt prejudice toward the American Chinese community.

We all should contribute to our communities. We all should step up to do the right thing in times of crisis because humanity knows no national borders and no divisions of race or ethnicity.

Confucius said, "Don't do unto others what you would not wish them to do to you." The Bible expresses the same Golden Rule in reverse in Matthew 7:12: "Do unto others as you would have them do unto you."

I call upon my fellow Americans of Asian descent, all

Americans and everyone around the world to continue to pay attention to the truth that we are all one, and we must forever battle against bigotry and prejudice.

Our work is never over. This story might end, but together, we are only just beginning.

APPENDIX: AMERICAN CHINESE CONTRIBUTORS

Business:

Jerry Yang, co-founder of Yahoo; Eric Yuan, founder of Zoom, without which the COVID lockdown would have been unbearable; the late Charles Wong, founder of Computer Associates; Anla Cheng, founder of SupChina; Andrew Cherng, founder of Panda Express; Ge Li, founder of Wuxi PharmaTech; Ming Hsieh who founded fingerprint recognition firm Cogent; Min Kao, co-founder of Garmin, the world's leading manufacturer of GPS systems; Howard Li, founder of Waitex Group; Dominic Ng, Chairman of East West Bank; Patrick Soon-Shiong, transplant surgeon, bioscientist, billionaire businessman and owner of The Los Angeles Times. Jensen Huang, founder of Nvidia, a gigantic multinational technology company; Jerry Guo, founder of Casa Systems, leading provider of telecommunication equipment and solutions; Jenson Huang, President of Nvidia; Lisa Su, CEO of AMD; Eric Yuan, Founder and CEO of Zoom.

Architects and Interior Designers:

The late incomparable I. M. Pei, one of the best architects in the world; architect and sculptor Maya Lin; Chien Chung Pei, founding partner of PEI Architects; interior designer Tony Chi.

Space:

Astronaut Leroy Chiao

Athletes:

Figure skaters Michelle Kwan, Nathan Chen, Tiffany Chin; Skier Eileen Gu; Basketball player Jeremy Lin; Tennis player Michael Chang

Musicians:

Cellist Yo-Yo Ma; Opera Singer Tian Haojiang; Oscar-winning composer Tan Dun

Movie Makers:

Producers Janet Yang, Chris Lee

Actors:

Joan Chen, Lucy Liu, Lisa Lu, Awkwafina, Constance Wu; Liu Yifei, Daniel Wu, Justin Lin, Russell Wong, and the late, great Bruce Lee

Directors:

Ang Lee, Alice Wu

Comedians:

Ronny Chieng, Joe Wong, Bowen Yang, Sheng Wang

Playwrights:

David Henry Hwang

Ballet:

Tan Yuanyuan

Writers:

"Joy Luck Club" author Amy Tan; "Tiger Mom" author Amy Chua; "Crazy Rich Asians" author Kevin Kwan; "The Woman Warrior" author Maxine Hong Kingston; New Yorker writer Hua Hsu

Amusement Parks:

Disney Legend and former Imagineer: Wing T. Chao

Fashion Designers:

Vera Wang, Phillip Lim, Jason Wu, Anna Sui, Derek Lam, Alexander Wang, David Chu.

Scientists:

David Ho, renowned for his contribution to AIDS research; Peter Tsai who invented the N95 mask.

Nobel Laureates:

Samuel C.C.Ting, Tsung-Dao Lee, Steven Chu, Yuan T. Lee, Daniel C. Tsui, Roger Y. Tsien and Charles K. Kao.

Government:

Hiram Fong, Gary Locke, Andrew Yang, Michelle Wu, Grace Meng, Ted Lieu, Lily Chen, Judy Chu

Philanthropists:

Lulu Wang, Ronnie Chan, Oscar L. Tang

FRIENDS FROM ALL OVER THE WORLD

YOU ARE THE RAINBOW IN MY LIFE!

Garden Party for my very illustrious friends in NYC

A girls' night out in NYC with Angela Chen, Sun Wei Christianson, Carolyn Maloney, Irene Chu, HE Amna Almuhairy

My buddies in crime

A memorable gathering in my New York house

Besties Paula Begoun and Mary Ma

Besties Grace Pen and Rachel Zhu

Besties Alia Tudor and Lulu Wang

Friends I can't do without, Christy Ferer and Elizabeth Segerstrom

My oldest friends in Honolulu, Mr. and Mrs. Warren Luke, Judge Wilson Loo, Mrs. Loo, Annette Pang

My best Filipino friend Mayenne Carmona with Mrs. Sharon Bush and Kimberly Guilfoyle. My dear friends Yaz and Valentine Hernandez

Angels in my life, Mr. Ge Wen Yao, Mr. and Mrs. Xu Chuang

Pakistani President Asif Zakaria in my NYC home. He is now the President again

Dear friends I can't do without: Shirley Wang, Barbara Tober, Trish Blake and Carrie Lee

With Jean Doumanian and Jaqui Safra, Linda Wang, Mr. & Mrs. Nasser Kaseminy, and Dr. Oz

With Jim Issler, Tina Sheff, Dr. Angela Pratt, Ellie Ventura-Honda

Great friends Xu Ting, Rose Chen, James Xu, Dr. Dexter Sun, Mei Sun, Jennifer Yu, Dr. Chen Bin, Liu Haiyan, Yang Ying

A visit to my garden by guests from
Guangxi Province

Fun night in New York home

So long ago in NY home with Ivanka
Trump and friends

With good friends in NYC home

On Broadway with Bette Midler and
Hawaiian friends

In New York City, with Tan Dun, Silas
Chou, Martha Liao, Pan Shiyi, Jane
Huang, Celia Chou, Zhang Xin

In New York, we worked hard to try to
make Andrew Yang our first Chinese
President of the USA!

David Weinreb, John Rossant, Christian
Louboutin, and Guru Deepak Chopra

Celebrating Miky Lee, who won the Oscar for her movie "Parasite." Miky Lee, Fiona Cibani, Elizabeth Segerstrom, Quincy, Grace Pen, and me

At the Segerstrom Center with Leszek Barwinski, Gina Alice Redlinger, and Lang Lang

With Prince Victorio Aliata and Princess Dialta Montereale, Sybil Robson Orr, and Matthew Orr. In Paris with friends Patricia Della-Giovampaola and Jean-Paul Enthoven

I was the Grand Marshall in the 125 Golden Dragon Parade with Kevin Chen, President of the Chinese Chamber of Commerce

In LA with Elizabeth Segerstrom, Princess Padmaja, Ritsuko Roche, Robert Roche, Ian Kelly, Vamsi Mootha, Kush Pamar, D.A. Wallach

Dinner in LA with amazing friends Les Moonves, Julie Chen, Allan Pollack, Karen and Paul Ottosson, Luo Yan, Anne Kopelson, David and Linda Shaheen, Mel and Sue Geliebter

In Silicon Valley with David and Diana Wei family, Eric Yuan, founder of Zoom, and great interior designer Luke Van Duyn

In LA with Joyce Rey, Janie fong and Michelle Wong from Hong Kong. Vicky Cayetano and former Hawaii Governor Ben Cayetano

In LA with Adrien Brody, Dustin Hoffman, and Lionel Richie

Study in China Alumni Association celebrating 2024 Chinese New Year

With Cherie and Michelle Liem, Dominic Ng, Gorretti Lo Lui, Lisa Lu, and Janet Yang

Sally Shi, Maya Rogers, Bai Haptian, Rebecca Li, my publisher Sequoia, Chanel Miller, and Anne Shih

San Francisco with friends from Guangxi Province

Peter Liu's lunch for me in San Francisco

In France with my great friends at Bal de Versailles

In Paris, Amer Lodhi, He Yi, Cora Tang (Ehang). With Ravichak Norodom, grandson of King Sihanouk and Hans Dorville

Paris with great friends

Rome. Jerry Whitlock, Claudia, Lizzette de Ponce, Constantino Pozzi

London with friends

In Singapore with brilliant friends in the stunning home of Mr. and Mrs. Elijah Widjaja

Singapore close family friends

In Bangkok with old friends

Kuala Lumpur, Kim beck Stuart Beck and ambassador Mrs. Axel Cruau with my family. With Lady Linda Davies and Sultana

In Australia's Great Barrier Reef with Sarina Russo and family

MEIHODO Intl Youth Visual Media Festival in Fukuoka. In Tokyo for the MAMA award with superstars from Japan and Korea

In Japan with dear friends Mr. Kazumi Arikawa and Shigemitsu Takami

With Quincy in Singapore. He calls our group "Asian Mafia!"

Director Lee Daniels, Miss Universe Olivia Culpo, model/trainer Lu Sierra, Oliver Stone, and Keiko Bang at my Birthday party

Karlie Kloss, Jeanne Lawrenc, Guo Pei, Carmen Dell' Orefice, Cathleen and Nicole Ihasz

Melvin Chua and great photographer Patrick Demarchelier. Dr. David Ho Joseph Zheng. Berlin with Liz Mohn

2022 Princess Reema hosted our visit to Saudi Arabia - One of the most memorable trips I have taken

In Qatar during World Cup, with my host Prince Ahmed Al Thani and the Chinese Ambassador to Qatar Zhou Jian; With Dr. Dexter Sun and princess Al Mayassa

Hosting a dinner for the King of Udaipur Arvind Singh Mewar at my home in Beijing

In Shanghai. Some of my favorite people in China are in this group

Book signing events in Chengdu and Wuhan in 2023

With Kai and Grace. With Badr Jafar

Book signing in my hometown Guilin, Guangxi Province

With great friends in Beijing

In Shanghai with great friends from all over the world

Hangzhou Bronze Master Zhu Binren and Zhu Yanhong. Taiwan Shining Sung and friends

In Shanghai with Eddie and Shelly Lim's family, Harry Hui, Dong Lei, and children

Legend Charles Aznavour travelled to Shanghai to sing at my charity. Charles Heung, birthday girl Lu Yu, Jacky Heung, Chen Lan

In Shanghai with friends

In Hong Kong with Pansy Ho, and Amy Chen; In Fujian with Mr. Cao De Wang

With brilliant friends in Hong Kong

Gathering with my Honolulu friends

My dear neighbors and friends in Hawaii

Joan Tang, Peggy Cherng, Andrew Cherng, Kirk tang, Pat Lee, Dr Lee, Linda Wang, Dita Holifield

In Lao Ge's home, men do the work!

Dr. James Lin, Moon Shi, Ming Hsieh, and Stella Li

My favorite family in my garden, Ambassador of UAE Mohamed Abushahab, Consul General Amna Almuhairy, and their lovely children

With Adrian Chang, famous writer Kevin Kwan of "Crazy Rich Asians," and great supporters Angela Bi, Jun Wei, Lisa Ye

Clint Eastwood, Michelle Yeoh, Michael Douglas, Lee Byung-hun, Denzel Washington, and Awkwafina

Mike Tyson, Robert Di Niro, Kenny G, Victoria Beckham, Paris Hilton, Susan Sarandon

Stevie Wonder, Rihanna, Janet Jackson, Gayle King, Patricia Hearst, Ne Yo, Justin Bieber

Sylvester Stallone, Jennifer Lawrence, Sameul Jackson, Jude Law, Liv Tylor, John Travolta

ABOUT THE PUBLISHER

Di Angelo Publications was founded in 2008 by Sequoia Schmidt—at the age of seventeen. The modernized publishing firm's creative headquarters is in Los Angeles, California. In 2020, Di Angelo Publications made a conscious decision to move all printing and production for domestic distribution of its books to the United States. The firm is comprised of eleven imprints, and the featured imprint, Aspire, was inspired by Sequoia's great passion for business and business leaders. It is the entrepreneurial spirit and the leadership and principles displayed by Yue-Sai Kan that allow small businesses to thrive.

YUE-SAI KAN

Official Website
www.yuesaikan.com

Biography Video
https://youtu.be/Na3HrRjLvZQ

Instagram
@yuesaikan

Sina Weibo
靳羽西

WeChat
Jinyuxi

Little Red Book (xiaohongshu)
靳羽西

One World Foundation
http://www.yuesaikanoneworldfoundation.org